# *Life's* WORK

*How Tara VanDerveer and Stanford Women's Basketball Changed the Sport Forever*

Michelle Smith

Library of Congress Cataloging-in-Publication Data available upon request.

This book is available in quantity at special discounts for your group or organization. For further information, contact:

**Triumph Books LLC**
814 North Franklin Street
Chicago, Illinois 60610
(312) 337-0747
www.triumphbooks.com

Printed in USA
Design by Patricia Frey
ISBN: 978-1-63727-867-3

*To Jerry, Annie, and Matthew—*
*my life's work*

# Contents

# Foreword

**GETTING A RECRUITING LETTER** from Stanford when I was in high school was definitely real.

Growing up in Houston, the opportunity to play basketball while getting a college education was something I knew I wanted to do. Then, when the letters from colleges started coming in, it became, "Oh, I can go where I want to go." It was a whirlwind, and it was really fun to celebrate that with my family.

But getting a letter from Stanford—that's when I started to more clearly see my future. I thought, *That diploma is the one I want.* Stanford is a school so many dream of attending. To know Tara VanDerveer, then the women's head basketball coach at Stanford, thought I could be that kind of student-athlete cultivated a special kind of confidence in me.

Back when I was being recruited, in the mid-2000s, there were more restrictions on recruiting and less use of social media. I would hear from Tara via texts, emails, and letters—mostly letters—and we would have periodic phone calls, talking so I could get to know the program and get to know her. But I spoke to many at Stanford too—Tara did a really good job of making sure I spoke to everyone on the staff. She wanted me to get to know everyone, which was different from other schools that were trying to recruit me. I got the feeling that there was an aspect of family and team at Stanford—a collaborative culture they established early on.

I was raised Nigerian American, and we believe the individual is never greater than the community. From the moment I landed for my visit at Stanford, I felt it. I thought, *This is where I'm going to go.*

In addition to the family atmosphere, what really drew me to Stanford was the discipline of it all. There was an expectation that we would be team players and students, and that we would uphold a certain standard without it having to be directly communicated to us all the time. We just knew, and that was because of the culture of excellence Tara fostered in the women's basketball program.

It was apparent in how everyone connected to Stanford was walking the walk, and how that commitment to consistency was similar to how I was raised. One of the first things I learned at Stanford was that I didn't need to box myself into anything. There were things I discovered on my own, and in being part of the program, that taught me not to limit myself to what other people thought I could do. This was not always easy for me. Despite the confidence I project, I struggled with a lot of impostor syndrome. I remember watching Stanford as a high schooler at the Tampa Final Four and thinking, *Oh my gosh, look how they are hooping.* When I joined the team, it became key to figure out what my role was and to make sure I was at the right place at the right time.

Expectations were high. At Stanford, it was Final Four or bust. The standard of excellence was non-negotiable, something I had already learned from my family. I was able to use my discipline and hard work to play outside the box. That was true on the court and in the classroom.

Tara had a specific way of doing everything. We had three hours of practice, and there was something happening every minute of those three hours. Practices were harder than the games, and that's the way she wanted it.

There is something they call "swimming duck syndrome" at Stanford. Everybody appears like they are just cruising along, but they are fighting for their lives under the water. We had Richard Sherman when I was there, and Andrew Luck. We had all of these different collegiate sports stars, but it never felt that way because the students were stars too. The next big app was coming out of these dorm rooms, people such as Issa Rae were there doing their thing—it was an impressive group, and there was this overall notion that excellence was the norm. That was the environment. It was hard to ask for help.

My sophomore year I was struggling with my classes. I thought I had to be perfect on the floor and that my grades had to be perfect. Tara brought me into her office and told me she knew I was struggling. She asked me what I could do to find better balance. She helped me figure out something that suited me more so I could be successful athletically *and* academically. She told me it was important to ask for help and that people would step in to help me. She said asking for help was a sign of strength. I never forgot that; I carry it to this day.

Being coached by Tara made me a student of the game. The things we did every day—we call them "daily vitamins" on my WNBA team now—were the daily sustenance we needed to function, the things that kept us sharp, the building blocks of continuing to expand as players and people. That was how Tara did things. You worked to get better every day.

Being a part of the Stanford women's basketball program also gave me a way to find my voice, and it gave me the foundational components of being able to bring people together and celebrate our collective success.

Playing for Tara at Stanford gave me a special insight into how identity and a sense of belonging are intertwined with achievement. The way she operated, with purpose and discipline and a relentless work ethic, helped us feel connected to the present and part of the future, and it also gave us reverence and appreciation for the history of the program and the people who had helped to make it what it was.

I remember Tara telling me one day how alike we were. My first reaction was, "Really?" I didn't see it. Side by side, we couldn't have appeared to be more different. But as Tara pointed out, we are both eldest daughters from large families. Our parents are educators. Those commonalities helped us understand each other. It wasn't until after I graduated that I fully realized how really alike we are. As a result, our relationship is even stronger now than it was when I played.

I respect the way Tara lives by example. We are not people of too many words, though I think we have both gotten better at opening up. We like to gather information and feel things out before we do them. We know when we've done the work. Being prepared is vital, and that is something that deeply connects us.

As unglamorous as it may be, it's the decades of consistency that make the legacy of Stanford women's basketball. The team has always been in the mix for championships and NCAA tournament appearances. It has always comprised a consistent group of high-level, high-standard people and achievers who go about doing things with integrity. Winning, and winning the right way, was woven into the fabric of Tara's teams.

Tara's impact lies in the roots and just about every branch of women's basketball. Her relationships with her players have created a web of influence in playing, coaching, and the business of the game. At the center of it all is empowerment. She doesn't always say it explicitly, but she lives it, and it's something I am very grateful to have experienced firsthand.

Thanks in no small part to that modeling, I matured a lot at Stanford. I became more confident in myself. Much of my success is a credit to the amazing Stanford coaching staff. I would not be the player, person or professional I am today without the experiences they helped see me through.

I don't remember a lot about my first day in a Stanford uniform, but I remember the last one. We lost to Baylor in the Final Four. I remember that we prepared all week. We were ready. I remember playing as hard as I could to win that game. Our whole team wanted to win it so badly. When it was over, after we lost, I don't remember feeling sad. I remember feeling *proud*. I was at peace knowing I had left everything I could on the court that night.

Looking back, I realize it more now than ever. Tara and I are a lot alike. I could never compare myself to her legacy. But because of Tara, I am who I am.

—Nneka Ogwumike

# Foreword

**WHAT IS STANFORD WOMEN'S BASKETBALL?** What started as an outrageously ambitious dream—to turn a basketball program at one of the world's top academic institutions into a national power—became an amazing reality. The dream was to excel both in the classroom and on the basketball court. With administrative support, hardworking coaches, tireless recruiting, resourceful staff and, of course, talented and unselfish players, our program developed into a women's basketball powerhouse. Stanford women's basketball is distinguished by its consistency of excellence, a long and earnest pursuit of victory on the court combined with achievement and leadership in the classroom and beyond. It is a legacy that includes many joyful wins and a few painful losses, talented teams, players with game and players with heart, and committed and dedicated coaches. For 38 years, it was my privilege to helm the program, and it is my story as well.

I hope this book will reveal the magic of the Stanford sisterhood, which more than anything else defines our program. It is less about X's and O's and more about personal journeys of some of the most elite student-athletes in our country as they passed through a world-class educational experience as Cardinal. The banners painted on the walls at Maples Pavilion bear testimony to the sum of these narratives: 27 Pac-10/12 championships, 15 Pac-10/12 tournament titles, 15 Final Fours, and 3 national championships.

In the 38 years I coached at Stanford, I rarely gave thought to the whole picture; instead I tended to focus on the next scout, the next practice, the next game or tournament. Our story played out one day at a time. All the practices, games, championship runs, and seasons blurred together and connected to one another, and before I realized it there was a legacy. That legacy consists of hundreds of exciting plays and games, scores of great players, and countless incredible memories.

Of all that we accomplished together, I am most proud of our Stanford sisterhood—the lifelong friendships and deep relationships we have built over the years. I am also deeply proud of what our players have gone on to do in their careers and communities. Another source of pride is our consistency. My Stanford teams perennially achieved and overachieved by surpassing the sum of any one player's individual potential. We did it together. Through a system of teaching, mentoring, and strategic planning, our teams improved and competed at the highest level. We finished as one of the top three teams in the Pac-10/12 for 37 consecutive years.

When I reflect on my coaching career at Stanford, I cannot help comparing the early days to the exciting state of the game today. I am frequently drawn back to my childhood experiences. I grew up in the 1960s, when girls playing basketball was neither accepted nor supported. There were no teams for girls in junior or senior high school. There were no girls' basketball camps, travel teams, scholarships, or professional opportunities. I was very active as a child, playing every sport. I have no idea why I was so crazy about basketball, but it had a hold on me. I played with neighborhood boys (only because I had the best ball, and if they wanted to play with my ball,

I got to be in the game), I watched all the boys' teams practice after school, and tuned in to any professional game on television, usually the Boston Celtics.

In college, I took Coach Bobby Knight's basketball coaching class and got an A! He allowed anyone in his class to attend his closed practices. I attended virtually every day. Through observation and meticulous note-taking, I was preparing for an opportunity that at the time did not exist. One of my favorite people, and a former Olympics assistant, the late Nancy Darsch, liked to say, "Tara, timing is everything," and as bad as my timing was for playing basketball, my timing was impeccable for coaching. In 1972 Title IX passed. This legislation opened the door for my career in coaching.

Michelle Smith has written a book that highlights the memories of the players and coaches that comprise Stanford women's basketball. My own memories are filled with satisfying moments of joy. As Peter Ogwumike, Nneka and Chiney's dad, says, "Every disappointment is a blessing," and there were plenty of blessings. Coaching is like riding a roller coaster—with lots of ups and downs, tremendous highs, wild corners, thrills, and times when you want to throw up. Still, I cannot imagine a more exciting, fun, or rewarding life's work!

Like every worthwhile accomplishment, coaching takes hard work and continual reinvention to grow as the game changes. Throughout the journey, the one thing that never changed is that I loved coming to the gym. The gym is where the magic happens. This is where the ingredients for success come together with drills, scrimmages, whistles, corrections, sweat, elbows, cheers, and tears. I admit I enjoyed planning and going to practice more than games. I loved the process. The gym was our palette, and we were able to create masterpieces.

Game time at Maples was special. Our faithful fans generated an electric atmosphere. I was driven by hating to lose more than enjoying winning. When I was younger, I would get so upset if we lost. I learned through the years to use each game, a W or L, as an opportunity for our team to improve and grow. I learned to be more in the moment and appreciate our success and share in the excitement and enthusiasm of a game well-done.

My own growth through the years is largely thanks to what I have learned from our Stanford players. I have met and maintained lifelong friendships with the most amazing women I have coached. Their impact on me—their sisterhood, kindness, resilience, leadership, and competitiveness—all motivated me. I wanted to be poised, fearless, competitive, and prepared to give them the best chance of being successful. They inspired me to be the best version of myself. I wanted to take our team to a place they couldn't reach by themselves.

The thrill of cutting down the net or having a Gatorade bucket dumped over my head was the best reward. Players, coaches, and staff hugging and dancing after big wins or championships was the ultimate high.

For me, there is no better job than being a coach, and through the game I have lived a charmed life. I have traveled the world, met presidents, won gold at the Olympics, been honored by several Halls of Fame, and humbly accepted awards. The best part is the people I have met and the friendships I have established.

I could not imagine I would ever retire. Now that I have, it feels so right. I am able to do many things that coaching didn't allow time for. I have never felt that I was defined by being just a basketball player or coach. I have always had a variety of interests and passions. Now I will go to operas and symphonies, play bridge, ski the powder slopes and glassy water, travel, take longer dog walks and swims, and cheer for Stanford and UC–San Diego, where my sister Heidi is the head coach. I am ready to have fun and be a fan.

It is thrilling to see the support for women's basketball. I have always thought that the more people see the game, the more they will enjoy the game and become dedicated fans. We are just scratching the surface of how good and exciting women's basketball can be.

I admit that I still regret not having the playing opportunities that girls and women have now. When I was a young girl, I was out in the driveway shooting by myself visualizing playing on a team, with a uniform, in front of a crowd. I pretended to be at the foul line with the pressure on me to win a championship. What is happening now doesn't surprise me—the explosion of a game many of us have always loved and valued. I could see this very clearly as a 10-year-old. Now as a 72-year-old, I get to attend games, and I pinch myself. This isn't a dream; it is wonderfully real.

Thank you to Michelle Smith for working so hard and long to capture the essence of Stanford women's basketball and my life's work. I appreciate her dedication to writing about our great teams, players, and program. Thank you to our fans, administration, coaches, staff, and players. I am so fortunate to have had the opportunity to get to know each of you. *Go Card!*

—Tara VanDerveer

# Introduction

**AS A GAME WAS BORN,** the women of Stanford University were there.

On April 4, 1896, in the first intercollegiate women's basketball game ever played, Stanford beat the University of California 2-1 at San Francisco's Page Street Armory, a building that would eventually be destroyed in the 1906 earthquake that leveled much of what locals call "The City."

Historical records say there were 700 people in attendance that day—all women. Only women reporters were allowed to cover the game. Men weren't allowed in the gym for modesty's sake, though some climbed onto the roof to peer through the windows.

James Naismith had invented the game of basketball on the other side of the country in Springfield, Massachusetts, just four years earlier. And three and a half years after that first game, Stanford would ban all women's athletics "for the good of students' health."

But the games went on. The rebellious women of Stanford formed a basketball team without using their school's name, calling themselves the Palo Alto Club, and went on to play in facilities at Cal in Berkeley and Mills College in Oakland. A Stanford-Cal women's basketball rivalry continued for years through the early part of the 20th century at Hearst Hall on the Berkeley campus.

The game they played bears little resemblance to today's fast-paced, dynamic game that showcases players' athleticism, size, and physicality. But in fact, it would look very much the same for the next 70 years, the court divided into thirds, with three players assigned to each zone. Eventually, the court was split in half, with offensive and defensive sides. Three forwards and three guards (six players total) played on each side, unable to cross the center line, each allowed only two dribbles, with three to five seconds to pass. Only "home (offensive) players" were allowed to shoot the ball. The idea was that women were too fragile to play a full-court game.

The 1974–75 season was Stanford's first as a collegiate women's basketball program, as part of the Northern California Intercollegiate Athletic Conference (NCIAC). There was no postseason tournament. Gay Coburn, an unpaid graduate assistant, coached the team.

Despite the 1972 passage of Title IX—the landmark federal law barring discrimination based on sex at institutions receiving federal funds—the women's team at Stanford did not receive the same treatment or resources as the men's team. According to Mariah Burton Nelson, who had chosen Stanford over Cornell in 1976 in order to play basketball and get a Stanford education, the women's team wore white T-shirts draped with red pinnies (essentially a scrimmage vest made of mesh) and red shorts. For warm-ups, they wore hooded red Stanford sweatshirts they bought with their own money at the bookstore. They bought their own shoes and taped their own ankles. They played in Roble Gym, with enough seating for only about 20 people on a single bench between the sideline and the wall. Burton Nelson and two of her teammates went to athletic director Dick DiBiaso's office to demand equal treatment and to remind him that Title IX had passed in 1972.

By the time Burton Nelson, who would go on to author *The Stronger Women Get, the More Men Love Football* and five other books about women and sports, graduated in 1976, the Stanford women's team was playing games in Maples Pavilion and had received uniforms, a trainer, and access to the weight room. Postseason opportunities came that season as well. Stanford played its first game under the auspices of the Association for Intercollegiate Athletics for Women (AIAW), which administered the women's collegiate national championship until 1982.

Under Dotty McCrea, the program's first full-time head coach, hired in 1977, Stanford reached the AIAW regional tournament three years in a row, from 1979 to 1981. McCrea had been Cathy Rush's assistant at Immaculata College, the three-time national AIAW champion. McCrae's assistant coach, Susan Rojcewicz, played with the 1976 Olympic team that had won a silver medal.

McCrea and Rojcewicz hit the recruiting trail and offered the first scholarship in program history to Kathy Murphy. The NCAA women's tournament began in 1982, and Stanford, coming off a 19–8 season, reached the first round.

Playing in an NCAA tournament at all was a hard-fought opportunity for the Cardinal women. In the 10 years after president Richard Nixon signed Title IX and kicked the door open to high school and collegiate female athlete participation, opponents of the law worked to undo it, protesting the smallest measures of equality offered to female athletes. Women had to build their own spaces in college sports.

The woman-led AIAW governed women's collegiate sports following the enactment of Title IX in 1971, while the NCAA focused on men's sports and the revenue those sports could generate. Within a decade, the AIAW grew to 280 member schools, offering 41 championships in three different divisions of women's collegiate sports.

Eventually, the NCAA began to view women's sports as an opportunity to grow the organization's financial footprint and suddenly took an interest in running women's championships, including the first women's NCAA Tournament in 1981—in direct competition with the AIAW. Within a year, the AIAW was dissolved and the NCAA was running all championships for women's college sports on their terms.

For Stanford, despite the first-round loss in 1982, an NCAA berth was an emphatic sign of a program on the rise. McCrea coached the Cardinal to a 129–125 record over nine seasons before Stanford athletic director Andy Geiger recruited in an up-and-coming head coach named Tara VanDerveer from Ohio State in 1985, determined to turn the program into a national power.

VanDerveer came to The Farm, the campus nickname that originated from the fact that the university was founded on the site of the Stanford family's stock farm, to build a program at one of the most elite and competitive academic environments in the world.

Stanford alumni include: author John Steinbeck; former president Herbert Hoover; Google founder Larry Page; PayPal cofounder Peter Thiel; justice Sandra Day O'Connor, the first woman justice on the US Supreme Court; Instagram founder Kevin Systrom; Nike founder Phil Knight; US senator Cory Booker, who played football at Stanford; golfer Tiger Woods; British prime minister Rishi Sunak; and Olympic swimming legend Katie Ledecky; among others.

It was an environment equal parts stimulating and challenging, particularly for a coach trying to put together great basketball teams in a recruiting pool limited to the nation's best students. "At other schools, you stand out as an athlete, especially if you are a part of a successful team," said former Stanford player Vanessa Nygaard. "But here, at Stanford, you'd be in class, and it was like, over here is a concert pianist, and on the other side is this kid who is great at physics, and over there it's Tiger Woods. You don't feel like being exceptional is different." It was an atmosphere in which VanDerveer would not only thrive but prove herself to be singular even among the exceptional.

Nearly 130 years have passed since that first women's basketball game in San Francisco. Stanford's legacy has become ever more intertwined with the history of the women's game itself. In the history of the game, Stanford ranks only behind Tennessee and Connecticut with 1,240 wins (through the 2024 season) and fourth all time in winning percentage among Division I women's programs at .779 (through 2024). The Cardinal have won three national titles and 26 conference championships, and made 36 consecutive appearances in the NCAA tournament.

To say the world has changed since 1896 is a profound understatement. But the role Stanford women's basketball has played in the history of the game cannot be understated. The Cardinal and VanDerveer were among the first programs to embrace the three-point shot, one now redefined by Caitlin Clark's launches from the logo. VanDerveer's willingness to step away from her program in 1996 to coach the US women's basketball team to a gold medal in the Atlanta Olympics led to the rebirth of professional women's basketball in the United States, a legacy that lives on as the WNBA prepares for its 30th season in 2026. And the record-breaking success of the Golden State Valkyries' WNBA franchise is directly attributable to the passion and interest created around the women's team playing down the 101 Freeway in Palo Alto. Stanford, as former All-American Chiney Ogwumike would say "is a certified cornerstone in the house of hoops."

## CHAPTER 1

# The End of an Era

**AS A PACKED HOUSE** at Maples Pavilion rhythmically chanted her name—"Ta-ra! Ta-ra!"—Tara VanDerveer laid claim to her piece of history.

The Hall of Fame Stanford women's basketball coach moved to the head of a very exclusive line, stepping in front of the likes of Duke's Mike Krzyzewski, Syracuse's Jim Boeheim, and North Carolina's Dean Smith. Most bittersweet to VanDerveer, she had already surpassed the late Pat Summitt of Tennessee, whom VanDerveer would happily have stayed behind forever if it meant Summitt, her dear friend who had died of early-onset Alzheimer's in 2016, were still there.

Stanford's theme for the celebration marking VanDerveer's 1,203th coaching win—making her the winningest coach in the history of college basketball—was #onlyher. And those who filled the stands created a full house of love and admiration for VanDerveer, who admitted to being overwhelmed with the attention. "I am really very humbled," VanDerveer said to the crowd. "I'm not usually at a loss for words."

When VanDerveer won the 900th game of her coaching career back in 2017, Stanford was participating in a Thanksgiving tournament in Mexico. The game wasn't televised. The celebration was confined mainly to the team and the family members who made the trip on the holiday weekend.

When she became *women's* college basketball's winningest coach in 2020, moving past Summitt, it was during the height of the COVID-19 pandemic. The game was played in an empty gymnasium at the University of the Pacific in Stockton, California, but this time in front of a national television audience. The team marked the occasion with a masked closed-door celebration in the visitor's locker room.

But this celebration of VanDerveer's greatness, her consistency, and her excellence at Maples was finally for everyone—for the fans, for her current and former players and staff, and for the legendary head coach herself.

Former Stanford guard-turned-broadcaster Ros Gold-Onwude spoke to the more than 7,000 people who stuck around to participate in the postgame tribute. Stanford's university president and provost were in the building. Former NFL quarterback Andrew Luck, who played college football at Stanford, sat along the baseline, eschewing media interview requests because he wanted to get back to watching history with his young daughter, who was sitting on his lap to get a better view of history. The Pac-12 Network stayed on the air for an extra hour to capture the postgame ceremony for fans and admirers across the country. VanDerveer indeed belonged to them all: current and former players; staff members; longtime season ticket holders; the university community, where she is a towering figure; and even the Stanford band members, whom she would greet personally before every game to thank them for being in the gym to support her team.

A representative from Nike flew across the country to present VanDerveer with a leather-sleeved bomber jacket adorned with tally marks for all of her 1,203 wins. Some of the tally marks were stitched into the lining, with a few extra patches in the pockets so VanDerveer could add more into the future. Red-light bracelets—1,203 of them—were handed out to members of the crowd to become a visual representation of her accomplishment.

Billie Jean King, Lisa Leslie, Dawn Staley, former secretary of state Condoleezza Rice and Coach Krzyzewski himself, who had held the record since 2019, appeared in a congratulatory video tribute. Krzyzewski called VanDerveer "a guardian of the sport."

Alumni stars such as Gold-Onwude, Jennifer Azzi, and Chiney Ogwumike told their best Tara stories to the crowd, while the current players sat together on the bench next to VanDerveer, knowing they had finished a job that needed to be done: winning. It was a job VanDerveer had prepared them to do, while simultaneously preparing them for all that was next in their lives.

As the tributes flowed, VanDerveer's four assistant coaches sat on the bench next to the Stanford players. This quartet of women—Kate Paye, Katy Steding, Erica McCall, and Jeanette Pohlen—represented the different eras of VanDerveer's coaching career at Stanford.

Steding was one of VanDerveer's first recruits when she arrived at Stanford back in 1985—one of the 161 players challenged and changed by VanDerveer in her 38 years on the Farm. "As incredible as it is, this feels like it's a fairly predictable outcome," Steding said of the historic moment. "She's the architect that built this program into the powerhouse that everyone expects to see. And she's still here, cranking it out, adapting with what's going on in the world of basketball, and leading as well, which is incredible. It's just a relentless pursuit of excellence."

At the end of the ceremony, with the floor of Maples Pavilion blanketed in gold confetti, VanDerveer's current and former players encircled her in a huge group photo, while their children made confetti angels in the glittery paper covering the floor in the background.

And as VanDerveer stood alone in a spotlight at the center of the stage, erected at the center of the court she had defined and redefined, she looked around reflectively at what she had built, nurtured, and maintained for nearly 40 years. The championship banners, the people, the game itself. "I've had such an incredible life. I don't want for anything," VanDerveer said. "What I have is right here."

Six months earlier, Tara VanDerveer sat in her cabin in northern Minnesota, the place that had served as her respite from a nonstop coaching life, looking out at a shimmering lake. Every summer VanDerveer loaded up her dogs, Enzo and Piper, for the journey east to stay in Minnesota for a few weeks. She dusted off her water skis and recharged in a small lakeside home, originally built in 1938 and remodeled—it had no bedroom or shower when she bought it—after she led the US Olympic team to the gold medal in Atlanta in 1996.

She grew up next to the water; spending summers in a lakeside cabin was a VanDerveer family tradition. First, it was Schroon Lake, then Saranac Lake, both in Upstate New York. Her family eventually bought a home on Lake Chautauqua in western New York that they turned into a bed-and-breakfast.

VanDerveer's cabin in Minnesota has been her joy and her refuge. While there, she skis nearly every day. She hosts family and friends. She cooks salmon and rides her mountain bike. There isn't a restaurant within 20 miles, but there is a boat slip, storage for her speedboat, and a view of the water in every direction. It is the place where she has been able to breathe deeply, think clearly, and rest.

But even the lake wasn't much solace on the morning of August 4, 2023, as she woke up, checked her phone, and absorbed the unfathomable: the Pac-12 Conference, the league she led and loved, would be gone as she knew it in less than a year. The conference's leadership couldn't find a way to a media-rights deal that member schools found financially palatable. The league had already lost the Los Angeles market in 2022 when USC and UCLA decided they would move to the Big Ten for the big-time football television payday.

At the time, watching USC and UCLA depart had deeply concerned VanDerveer. Speculation about the future of the conference without the Southern California schools was already picking up steam. "Without UCLA and USC, we weren't going to have what we'd always had," VanDerveer said. "I was a little bit singularly focused on basketball, so I didn't try to figure it out or plan it out or talk about it a whole lot, but that's what people would tell me—'Next year you'll be in the Big Ten'—and I was thinking, *Okay, whatever.*"

*Whatever* quickly turned to more legitimate worry as the summer of 2023 began without a clear path forward for the conference as media-rights negotiations stalled. VanDerveer watched anxiously from a distance as the ground began to crumble underneath the 108-year-old conference, despite the calls for optimism from the conference office.

On July 27, 2023, the University of Colorado announced it was leaving the Pac-12 to return to the Big 12. That left the Pac-12 with nine teams and a now-desperate fight for survival.

On August 4, the conference was prepared to hold an early morning meeting, Pac-12 leadership was feeling confident they had a plan to keep the league intact. But minutes before the meeting began, Oregon and Washington called Commissioner George Kliavkoff to inform him they were leaving for the Big Ten to join UCLA and USC.

And that was it. The wheels, as VanDerveer put it, had come off the cart. "You invest 40 years into something, and to watch it unravel in 40 minutes, it's sad," VanDerveer said. "And you have to process who you are angry with, you know?"

Pac-12 women's basketball always "made sense" to VanDerveer: like-minded, high-profile academic institutions competing against one another on the West Coast. It was a group of schools that never received the same kind of attention as athletic programs on the East Coast or in the South, particularly in sports such as women's basketball. There was a deep bond forged among Pac-12 coaches by that perpetual underappreciation, not to mention the excellence of their female athletes.

The women's basketball coaches of the Pac-12 were always more collegial than most around the country in large part because VanDerveer made sure of it. They worked as a collective on improving the scheduling of Pac-12 teams to boost the league's ratings percentage index (RPI) in order to get more teams into the NCAA tournament. They legitimately rooted for one another's success.

The decisions made that determined the fate of the Pac-12 in the summer of 2023 didn't have anything to do with them; this was about football and money. But the impacts on sports such as women's basketball (and others such as baseball, softball, and volleyball) would be seismic, from recruiting to travel schedules to the dissolution of regional rivalries.

VanDerveer wondered whether television executives who had driven this realignment had daughters who might attend UCLA or Stanford or Oregon someday, and whether they would want their own children to do what they would be asking future student-athletes to do—to constantly travel cross-country while trying to balance their sleep schedules, their mental health, and their academic lives. "There are all kinds of situations in our world, where instead of standing up and saying 'This isn't right,' we live with it," VanDerveer said. "I don't see this as being good for us. It is not just about the travel but the breakdown of a great league, and the implosion of our league's very rich history."

She tried to compartmentalize her frustration and separate it from her deep sense of loss. "I've been part of the Pac-12 journey the whole time," VanDerveer said. "And I've loved it, so it's a death. It is a grieving process."

The remaining Pac-12 schools were suddenly looking for lifeboats. Arizona, Arizona State, and Utah quickly joined Colorado in the Big 12. Stanford and Cal's lifeboat moment came on September 1, 2023, when the two schools announced they would be moving to the Atlantic Coast Conference (ACC), which includes schools such as North Carolina, Duke, Louisville, and Notre Dame. It was more than a new conference; it was a whole new world, three time zones away.

In the first couple of weeks after the move was announced, none of the ACC coaches called or texted VanDerveer to welcome the Cardinal. That was already different from what she was used to. She immediately held a Zoom meeting with her players, who had not yet returned to campus for the fall semester. She asked if they had questions. She heard them tell her they were happy to be in a competitive power conference.

It was time to prepare for the coming season. Because heading into the 2023–24 season, there was work to do on multiple fronts with her current team.

Gone were veterans Haley Jones, Fran Belibi, and Ashten Prechtel to graduation—players who had helped lead Stanford to a national title in 2021. And more surprisingly, three players had chosen to transfer, including the nation's top recruit in 2022, post player Lauren Betts. Betts, who landed at UCLA, was joined in the transfer portal by guards Agnes Emma-Nnopu (to TCU) and Indya Nivar (to North Carolina). All three had been bench players the previous season but would likely have been counted on for bigger roles in the coming season. To see three Stanford players in the transfer portal in one season was a sign of the changing landscape of the game.

Traditionally, the Cardinal program has not been one many players choose to leave. The value of playing for VanDerveer and earning a Stanford degree was compelling enough to stay, even for those who did not get the playing time they wanted.

But the game—and college sports in general—was changing in a big way. The ability for players to transfer without having to sit out a season, thanks to a change in NCAA rules, was drastically increasing player mobility across college sports. The capacity for student-athletes to earn money through Name, Image, and Likeness (NIL) deals was also becoming a more important decision point for many.

The 2022–23 season had been a disappointing one for women's basketball at Stanford, despite the team's 29–6 record. A second-round NCAA loss at Maples Pavilion to Mississippi was the culmination of a team that struggled with cohesion with one another and the coaching staff. VanDerveer's culture of "sisterhood" had frayed in ways that needed to be addressed. So she addressed it. She made changes in the coaching staff, bringing back former assistant coach Tempie Brown and sports information director John Cantalupi, both sources of stability in important positions.

She enlisted the counsel of a leadership coach from the Stanford business school, something she would later say she wished she had done long before. "As coaches, all we know is what we know," VanDerveeer said. "Maybe having a [leadership] coach sooner would have helped me avoid some of the challenges I've had with players through the years, or would have helped me to be a better leader and a better coach for my players. I don't pretend to be anywhere near perfect, and there are so many things I could have done better."

A big dose of good news came when Hannah Jump, one of the best three-point shooters in program history, made the decision to return for a fifth season provided by the eligibility waiver the NCAA granted to players who had played during the COVID-19 pandemic. All-American center Cameron Brink anchored the team along with Jump and sophomore point guard Talana Lepolo. And VanDerveer had high hopes for junior forward Kiki Iriafen, who had shown flashes of elite-level play the previous season. Stanford was picked in the preseason coaches' poll to finish third in the final Pac-12 Conference race.

As the conference's teams gathered in Las Vegas in October 2023 for the league's annual preseason media day, the Pac-12 elephant in the room was huge. As 12 coaches and the players representing their programs came into the press room at the Park MGM Grand, they all talked as teams talk at the beginning of the season—about growth and expectations and excitement for a season that was only a handful of weeks away. National preseason polls came out, and teams discussed their need to prove themselves, to test themselves, and to measure themselves against their own standards. The usual stuff, in a most unusual set of circumstances.

VanDerveer was the one, unsurprisingly, to address the impending breakup of the conference head-on, calling it "heartbreaking." "This has been my whole life. I woke up when I heard about it, and I said, 'I'm in a bad dream. This is a nightmare,'" VanDerveer said to the press that day. "But we are committed to this year being a great year. Our team's theme is 'Best year ever,' and I think that's kind of what everyone wants."

And so it began for the Cardinal, which started the season ranked 15th in the country in the preseason Associated Press poll, their lowest preseason ranking since 2015. It was a sign that the outside world was uncertain about what Stanford was capable of.

The Cardinal quickly showed themselves to be an elite team. They jumped out to an 8–0 start, including nationally televised wins over No. 9 Indiana and Duke, both at Maples Pavilion. Stanford went to Las Vegas for a tournament over the Thanksgiving break and earned with another confidence-boosting win over No. 13 Florida State. By Week 4 of the season, Stanford had ascended to the No. 3 ranking in the country.

But the first stumble of the season came at Gonzaga on December 3, a game the Cardinal schedules almost every season against one of the top mid-major programs in the country. The Cardinal's 96–78 defeat was the program's most lopsided loss since 2020, notable because Brink played just 12 minutes, missing the entire second half due to illness.

Iriafen, however, was showing signs of being the standout player VanDerveer hoped she would be. She had scored at least 20 points in four of Stanford's first six games, including a 30-point, 17-rebound game against Florida State. There was plenty of reason for optimism.

As the final Pac-12 schedule began in January, Iriafen, the Los Angeles native, asserted herself as one of the nation's breakout players. The biggest day of her career was still to come on the biggest stage of the regular season.

On Saturday, January 21, 2024, the day before VanDerveer became the winningest coach in college basketball history, a group of approximately two dozen former players gathered in the Stanford athletics commissary, known as Jimmy V's, to have lunch with their coach. It was part of the scheduled alumni weekend festivities, and was well-timed for the celebration the Cardinal and athletics department staff members had been building toward for weeks.

VanDerveer was in a position to overtake Krzyzewski as college basketball's all-time-winningest coach with a win over Oregon State. That is, *if* her players could handle the pressure of a nearly sold-out Maples Pavilion, the absence of Brink to injury, and a surging and talented Beavers team intent on spoiling the party.

The former Stanford players who showed up for lunch that day didn't come alone. Quite a few of them brought their children—a chance to introduce their beloved head coach to their own beloveds, to show VanDerveer what became of the foundation she had laid for their lives. VanDerveer took pictures with the kids, which promptly were posted on social media. Former All-American center Jayne Jayne Appel Marinelli labeled the kids VanDerveer's "grandplayers" on her Instagram post. Afterward, VanDerveer went home to finish preparing for a game in her career that would be like no other.

Many of those same Stanford alums—some traveling from as far as Maine and New York—and quite a few more gathered in Maples Pavilion the following day to show their respect and their love, and to pay homage. Appel Marinelli brought her four young children, all donned in Stanford gear. Bethany Donaphin took a weekend away from her duties as the WNBA's head of league operations to come west with her daughter. Lindy La Rocque, the head coach at UNLV, arrived hours after her own team won a conference road game in New Mexico.

For all the program history in the gym, the focus was on the current team and their ability to win a pressure-packed game in front of a crowd primed to celebrate. The Cardinal players ultimately got the job done behind the transcendent Iriafen, who would finish with a career-high 36 points and 12 rebounds. By the time Stanford shook off the butterflies of a slow start and Brink's absence and the final seconds ticked down on a 65–56 win, the crowd was chanting VanDerveer's name.

VanDerveer's celebration and the attention of her milestone lasted for days and included many national television appearances in her new Nike jacket, a few radio shows, and a photo in a Palo Alto restaurant with San Francisco 49ers star (and Stanford alum) Christian McCaffrey. But there was still half a season to be played. The hardest half.

The Pac-12 season, always a grind, was grindier than usual in 2024, with multiple teams ranked among the top 10 nationally throughout the season. Conference teams notched a handful of high-profile wins, including Colorado upsetting defending champion LSU on opening day in November, USC knocking off Ohio State behind star freshman JuJu Watkins, and UCLA beating Connecticut.

Watkins and USC came to Maples Pavilion on February 2 and pulled off a stunner against the Cardinal, with Watkins scoring 51 points and No. 15 USC coming away with a 67–58 win. It was the Trojans' first win on Stanford's home floor since 2001, before Watkins—or any of her teammates, for that matter—were born. The Maples crowd oohed and aahed at every basket from the game's newest prodigy. "She's an incredibly talented player," VanDerveer said of Watkins after the game. "We tried a lot of different people guarding her, we tried some different things against her . . . . We didn't do the job we needed to do."

Stanford rebounded with four straight wins before another gut check, a 68–61 loss to an unranked Arizona team, another game in which Brink was unable to play, this time due to the flu. A troubling trend had developed, the way Stanford struggled when Brink, one of the nation's top interior players, was not on the floor. Her absence was particularly difficult for the guards. Jump, one of the nation's best long-distance shooters, was more easily bottled up without Brink earning defensive attention, and Stanford's young guards shot the ball inconsistently from the perimeter.

But one game later, with Brink back at what she described as "60 percent" of her normal self, Stanford defeated Arizona State to wrap up at least a share of its 27th Pac-12 title. No other program in the conference had more than five. "If you look right up [in Maples Pavilion], at the banner where it says 'conference championships,' there is a spot waiting for 2024," VanDerveer told the crowd after the game. "And we are not done."

With wins at Oregon State and Oregon, the Cardinal captured the outright regular-season title and the No. 1 seed in the final conference tournament in Las Vegas. But it would be upstart USC and Watkins who would take the last Pac-12 tournament title with a win over Stanford in the championship game. Stanford had created a new defensive scheme to deal with Watkins, one that Trojans coach Lindsay Gottlieb said she had never seen from the Cardinal. "Tara Tara-ed," Gottlieb said. "I've long learned I shouldn't try to outsmart Tara or outthink her. She was going to do something."

While Watkins was successfully bottled up with nine points on 2-of-15 shooting, fifth-year senior McKenzie Forbes scored 26 points and USC outrebounded Stanford by 20. With the loss, Stanford's time in the Pac-12 was officially over. "All season, it felt like you knew the train was leaving the station and you didn't really want to get off," assistant coach Katy Steding said. "Tara spent her life building up the Pac-12. It was sad for her and it was sad for me, because my freshman year was the first year of the Pac-10. A lot of the season was about trying not to think about it. But there were a lot of mixed emotions, frustration about what had happened and excitement about the end of the season."

The loss to USC cost the Cardinal a No. 1 seed in the NCAA tournament in an eventful week in which Brink announced she would be leaving after four seasons to enter the WNBA Draft, where she was projected as a top-three pick. Brink was eligible for a fifth season due to the COVID rules, but with her place as one of the best posts ever to play at Stanford secured, she chose to begin her professional career.

When the NCAA tournament brackets were revealed on Selection Sunday at Maples Pavilion, the team sitting in front of the big screen that hangs over the court—Brink, Iriafen, and junior Brooke Demetre—bristled that Stanford had a No. 2 before its name.

VanDerveer had long been adamant that she didn't care about seeding. If the notorious Harvard game back in 1998—when the Cardinal became the first No. 1 seed in the history of the NCAA tournament to lose to a No. 16 seed—taught her anything, it was that having a healthy, well-prepared team counted most when it came to postseason success. "The seed is not what's important. The team is in a good place, working hard, healthy. . . . I know there was a lot of talk that we would be a No. 1 seed. In our minds we are the same team," VanDerveer said. "We know what we need to do: run offense, play defense, rebound, and enjoy playing with each other."

As a record-tying seven Pac-12 teams headed into the NCAA tournament and three others continued playing into the postseason in the WNIT Tournament, VanDerveer sent a group text to all of the coaches in the conference. "I said, 'As we end our Pac-12 family, just want to wish everyone the best of luck in the tournament. Going our separate ways, we've had a great and special thing,'" VanDerveer said. "If anything it was, 'Best wishes, but remember how special it has been.'"

UCLA coach Cori Close thought the group text showed just how far things had come for a collection of schools about to scatter to other conferences. At least half the conference's teams had earned NCAA berths in the previous seven years. Going back to 2012–2013, six different Pac-12 teams had made nine Final Four appearances. "I just thought, you know, it used to be 'Stanford and the 11 dwarfs,' and now look at it, and who is the first person to champion that balance? Tara," Close said. "I just think it really has been a very special experience. We've built this together. Taking off our institutional hats and choosing to grow the game and grow the conference was more important, and that was a really big honor to be a part of."

Heading into the win-or-go-home postseason, Stanford's "best season ever" vibe was working. Team chemistry among the players and the coaches was in a good place; the group was tightly knit. And in their first NCAA game at Maples Pavilion against 15th-seeded Norfolk State, it showed, with the Cardinal winning 79–50. But a second-round matchup against Iowa State was a significantly tougher challenge. The seventh-seeded Cyclones were balanced with inside-outside play, youth and experience, and great coaching from longtime head coach Bill Fennelly. And after the previous season's second-round ouster on their home floor, Stanford had a mental hurdle to overcome as well.

Iowa State got a star-making performance from freshman Audi Crooks in its own first-round win, Crooks going 18 of 20 from the floor with 40 points to defeat Maryland. Fennelly said it reminded him of the night when Stanford's Appel scored 46 points against his team back in 2009.

VanDerveer and the Cardinal were ready for Crooks. Yet it was still a battle to the finish. Though Stanford held Crooks to 10 points on 3-of-21 shooting and she fouled out late in the game, the Cardinal had their own foul issues. Brink fouled out in her final home game at Stanford with 2:11 to go in regulation, and it was again Iriafen who led the way, with a career-high 41 points. Brooke Demetre's three-pointer with 18 seconds to go in overtime was the icing on the cake as the Cardinal won 87–81 and moved on to the Sweet 16.

The brutal battles of the Pac-12 season had prepared Stanford for this moment. The Cardinal were headed to Portland, Oregon, Brink's hometown, for the regional semifinals, just two wins away from the Final Four.

After the Iowa State game, VanDerveer called Iriafen an "absolute warrior." The players celebrated their ability to pick each other up in tough moments, and said they were ready for more. But nobody knew what was going through VanDerveer's mind as she walked off the floor. "Knowing we couldn't play another game in Maples, I just said, 'If this is my last game, damn, this was fun.'"

Two days later, Stanford landed in Oregon to face North Carolina State—a future ACC opponent—in the regional semifinals. The Cardinal were confident as the game began and built a 10-point halftime lead. But the Wolfpack went on a 13–2 run to open the third quarter and assumed the lead. Stanford's effort to play catch-up was failing. Brink once again struggled with fouls, limiting her time on the floor to less than 24 minutes. She fouled out for the second straight game, the final two games of her decorated college career.

Iriafen's 26 points and 10 rebounds were not enough this time against a Wolfpack team whose guards had grabbed the momentum and held on, building a 15-point fourth-quarter lead. Jump contributed 13 points, but outside of Iriafen, Brink, and Jump, the rest of the Stanford lineup contributed only 15 points.

The disappointment was palpable, but emotions were in check. VanDerveer paid tribute to Brink and Jump at the end of their careers, and had effusive words for Iriafen's improvement over the course of the season. Iriafen would be primed to be one of the best players in the country as a senior. "I think we have a lot of young players that will learn a lot from this experience," VanDerveer said. "I don't think anyone on our staff or our team has to hang their head. We've had a great year."

The ending of this season of change had arrived. The ending of Stanford's history-making, standard-setting run through the Pac-12 had arrived. The endings, it turned out, were just beginning.

## Chapter 2

# The GOAT

**"BASKETBALL"—DUNBAR VANDERVEER** told his daughter Tara as she spent another night shooting hoops in the driveway—"is never going to take you anywhere."

Yet again, Tara was being summoned from playing in the dark, the sound of the bouncing ball reverberating across the neighborhood. Her algebra homework was waiting for her. Young Tara rolled her eyes. "Algebra is never going to take me anywhere," she muttered under her breath. Years later, Tara VanDerveer would get her chance at rebuttal, sending her parents, Dunbar and Rita, postcards from China, Australia, Brazil, Italy, Lithuania, and Russia.

Basketball had indeed taken her everywhere she wanted to go...and beyond. A passion that ignited in her as a school girl helped her navigate multiple family relocations and kept her chasing opportunities, first to play and then to coach. Basketball became her compass.

Rita and Dunbar VanDerveer met as graduate students at Springfield College in Massachusetts, in the same community that now houses the Naismith Memorial Basketball Hall of Fame, where their eldest daughter is enshrined. Both happened to be in a school office when a local photographer came in looking for students to be part of a photo shoot the school had commissioned to boost its enrollment. He asked if they wanted to participate. Both agreed. They stood together, smiling for the camera, books in their arms, and then went their separate ways until Dunbar came across Rita in the library one day soon after. He asked how she thought the photos had turned out. By the end of the conversation, they had scheduled their first date.

Dunbar was the first male teacher in the elementary school in Melrose, Massachusetts, where Tara was born; he eventually became a school administrator. Rita was a speech pathologist. The VanDerveers initially settled in Schenectady, New York.

At home in Schenectady, the VanDerveer kids—Tara, Beth, Marie, Nick, and Heidi—were active, largely due to their parents' influence. "My parents' idea of a great Friday night was going to the YMCA, so we could jump on a trampoline and go swimming," Tara VanDerveer said.

The oldest of the five children, Tara—named for the setting of *Gone with the Wind*—was curious, adventurous, and a little bossy. She swam, sailed, skied (both water and snow), hiked, performed in the town's annual opera, and played the flute. The flute was her passion as a young girl; her parents spent $1,000 on a brand-new instrument when she was 10 years old. She played for years and trained under one of the top flutists in the world who happened to live in the area. But her passion for playing the flute was eventually supplanted by the passion that was first seeded several years earlier on a fateful day in third grade PE class.

Tara's physical education teacher ran the class through a basketball drill called a three-player weave, in which participants pass to one another without letting the ball touch the floor, curling around teammates as they make their way down the court. The final player in the "weave" completes a layup, and the drill goes the other way. VanDerveer participated with both enthusiasm and fascination. It was, as she put it, "the coolest thing ever."

"I liked the teamwork of it—the passing, the moving, the screening," VanDerveer said. "I liked that you had to play both offense and defense. You had to be good at both things."

She later joked that if she hadn't discovered basketball that day, she might have played hockey like many of the other kids who grew up in Western New York. As in basketball, the movement of hockey appealed to her, but playing outside in the cold, on the ice, did not.

She joined every neighborhood basketball game that would have her. When the boys wouldn't let her play day after day, she decided to change her tactics. She saved her allowance and went out and bought a brand-new basketball. Then she showed up at the playground with the ball wedged under her elbow—if they wanted to use her ball, they would have to let her in the game. It worked.

As a seventh grader, Tara found a recreational women's league to play in for a brief time. She was the youngest player on the floor by at least 10 years.

Tara would ride with her father to Milne School, a campus lab school affiliated with the University of Albany (SUNY Albany), where Dunbar was working on his PhD in education. After school, Tara would watch the boys' basketball team practice while she did her homework in the bleachers. On other days, while she waited for her father to finish his afternoon classes, she scoured the shelves in the school library for books on basketball. The librarian eventually pulled her father aside, saying, "I'm really worried. Tara has read every book about basketball."

At home, Tara's obsession with basketball continued to blossom. She watched Boston Celtics games on television with her father, diagramming plays, discussing game plans, and filling out shot charts as they watched together.

There was no girls' basketball team at Milne School, only "play days" where small teams would travel to another school three or four times a year to play recreationally. But there was no practice and no gym time for the girls. So Tara had to settle for watching the boys' team play. Figuring her parents would have no choice but to take her to games if she had a role to play, Tara volunteered to be the mascot, a bear. The costume was hot, and she couldn't see out of the eyeholes. She was quickly relieved of her mascot duties because she spent more time with the bear head tucked under her arm watching the game than she did leading cheers. As VanDerveer put it, "I was encouraged to find other ways to show my school spirit."

Dunbar VanDerveer never discouraged his daughter's love of the game; he just didn't see where it would lead. To be fair, neither did Tara. "Coaching wasn't something I ever thought about. It wasn't an option," VanDerveer said.

Tara was happy in school. With no girls' basketball team to play on, she focused on academics, working out her competitive spirit in the classroom. The flute, meanwhile, had become a chore. Her teacher—a "great teacher" VanDerveer will say to this day—was demanding and wanted her to practice "all the time." VanDerveer said, "No matter what I did, I never practiced enough, and I was becoming physically ill at lessons from the stress." So she quit the flute at 15. "My response to the flute taught me two things," VanDerveer wrote in her 1997 book, *Shooting from the Outside*. "One, it showed me that I'm an all-or-nothing person. . . . Two, I learned how crucial a teacher can be in nurturing or ruining a student's passion."

In the middle of Tara's sophomore year, her family moved to Niagara Falls, where her father had been promoted into a new job. She was not happy to leave her school or her friends. For Christmas, at their new house, her father bought her a basketball hoop, hoping to cheer her up. For months Tara refused to use it, declaring herself "too old for basketball." VanDerveer said, "I would dribble around on the side of it, work on my ball-handling, but I wouldn't use it. For a while I had a love-hate relationship with that hoop." Studious Tara had turned into miserable Tara.

Eventually, Tara found herself back in the driveway, shooting at her hoop in the dark, the ball noisily banging against the pavement and the wooden backboard. Her youngest sister, Heidi, rebounded for her until the call came from inside the house to return for dinner or homework. The dinner bell usually rang several times before Tara would come in.

"Basketball, for me, was playing in the park, it was playing in the driveway," VanDerveer said. "It was going to an open gym and playing with old guys. It was being ready on the sideline when they had an odd number and being able to play when they had an even number."

All through her young life, Tara had waited impatiently, even resentfully, for the neighborhood boys to ask her to join their game. While she waited, she dribbled the ball around her feet, through her legs, and behind her back, switching hands. She was becoming a better player. But to what end? The neighborhood boys were not particularly happy as her skill set improved. They didn't want her in their games. They still didn't want to get beat by a girl. As Tara got older, the inequities of the situation "really started to chafe." She found it extremely painful not to be able to play competitively. The game was not available to her in the way it was to the boys.

In her high school yearbook, the gym teacher wrote, "To the best basketball player, boy or girl, in the school." And the best male basketball player on the school team wrote, "You will go to the

Olympics someday." Those were nice notes, sure, but they didn't feel like compliments. They were frustrating—infuriating, even.

At the start of Tara's junior year in high school, her parents moved her again, this time to Buffalo Seminary High School, an all-girls prep school. The school offered multiple sports, including field hockey, tennis, and basketball; and she had friends who competed on ski teams. The change in scenery was transformative. "That worked for me," VanDerveer said. "Looking back on it, I had been acting like a spoiled brat. But I was happy at Buffalo Seminary."

VanDerveer listened to nearby Niagara University basketball games on the radio, and attended as many as she could so she could watch guard Calvin Murphy, who would go on to play in the NBA.

The opportunity to play at Buffalo Seminary was exactly what Tara had been hoping for. While the team only played a few scheduled games, she had the opportunity to *play* in competitive games. For a girl craving not only the competitive outlet but the structure and discipline of being coached and playing with teammates, it was life-changing. "Trying to learn the game without a coach or a team is like being handed a stack of books at the beginning of the school year and being left alone to learn what you could," Tara said. "Buffalo Seminary made basketball OK for me again." It also compelled her to choose a college where she could play.

Upon graduation, Tara wanted to play at Mount Holyoke College, but finances were an issue and she ended up playing her freshman year at SUNY-Albany. She led the team in scoring, rebounding, assists, and blocked shots. But calling it "varsity" basketball was kind. The uniforms were gym suits used for PE class, and players had to buy (and replace) their own shoes. The level of competition didn't feel like enough.

That spring, after her first collegiate season, VanDerveer convinced a group of friends to drive 14 hours with her from Albany to Normal, Illinois, to the Association for Intercollegiate Athletics for Women (AIAW) Division I tournament. "I was there to find my next team," VanDerveer said. She was the only one who brought a notebook and watched every game intently, from morning to night, falling in love with the Indiana University Hoosiers. She was struck by the joy with which they played, and by how well they played together as a team. It was then and there that Tara decided she would transfer to Indiana. There was no tryout, or official process for joining the team.

"I wasn't recruited. I watched them play in the AIAW Tournament and decided to transfer," VanDerveer said. "It was different back then."

VanDerveer stepped on to the Indiana campus in the fall of 1972—the same year Title IX became the law of the land, and the beginning of a time that would set the course of her life. At the time, Indiana's women's program was just getting started, having become a varsity sport in 1971. The team wore red shorts and white tops that doubled as uniforms for the School of Physical Education. The numbers were embroidered on.

VanDerveer was the equivalent of a walk-on for the Hoosiers, playing without any scholarship assistance. In her first season in Bloomington, VanDerveer lived in a dorm next to the gym. Her sophomore year, she moved into a different dorm, and convinced her dormmates to come to the women's games to watch her play. As a junior, VanDerveer would move into an apartment with three teammates.

She played under head coach Bea Gorton. The team finished the season with a record of 17–3, won the state and regional titles, and ultimately lost to Queens College at the AIAW Final Four (the same tournament in which Tara had watched them play from the stands the previous year) in New York. It was the first time the team had ever traveled to a game by airplane.

Gorton was just six years older than VanDerveer at the time. But to VanDerveer she seemed much older. "She had that coach's respect and boundary," VanDerveer said. "She was not a hanger-outer in any way." Gorton's example would soon become a valuable one for VanDerveer. In three seasons at Indiana, VanDerveer was a starting guard.

Indiana went 7–1 in the 1973–74 regular season and were facing elimination in the district tournament against Indiana State. With the season on the line, Gorton benched all of her starters—including VanDerveer—for the next game. The coach wasn't happy with her players' effort and she wanted to send them a message. It was VanDerveer's senior season, and the reality was, it could have been her last game. "The message was: 'Play hard or you're not going to play,'" VanDerveer said. "That stuck with me as a coach, and I've told our teams that story about what happened to me and how it got my attention."

VanDerveer jokes that she never could have played for herself, that she was never as skilled a player as the young women she has been able to coach. "I would have driven myself crazy. I'm slow, I can't shoot, I hardly play any defense. I was always interested in the strategy of the game," VanDerveer said. "I was never in shape. But I could pass and screen, and I loved to play. I played all the time." She would play pickup in the gym with the boys for three or four hours at a time. Playing with shooters was her favorite, because she loved to pass. She loved getting the ball inside down low to the post players as well. Facilitating other people's success was already in her blood.

VanDerveer recalled a game in which she finished with more than 10 turnovers. She went to Coach Gorton after the game with her take on the proceedings. "I read where John Wooden said turnovers are OK," she said to Gorton, quoting the legendary UCLA men's basketball coach and trying to plead her case. "It just means you're trying to make things happen." Gorton replied, "Try to make a little less happen."

When VanDerveer wasn't headed to the gym to play for hours every day, she was devouring books by Wooden, and she took a coaching class taught by Bobby Knight, the mercurial head men's basketball coach at Indiana, who would go on to his own Hall of Fame career. Coach Knight invited the students to come observe a practice, which were normally closed to outsiders. VanDerveer took that invitation and ran with it. Rather than watching "a practice," she watched every practice, scribbling plays, drills, and key words in her notebook. She made note of the team's pace, its purpose and intensity, and the focus on defense.

The volatile Coach Knight, famous for being a stern disciplinarian who barely let his own players speak during practice, would occasionally acknowledge her with a look or a nod. She sat a few rows up so as not to catch his line of sight when he unleashed on his team. "I know he was wondering what in the world I was doing there every day," VanDerveer said.

As a player, she earned invitations to tryout camps to represent USA Basketball at the World Games in 1972 and on the Olympic team in 1974. She did not make either roster.

VanDerveer graduated from Indiana in 1975 with her degree in sociology. Her plan for the future was to go to law school. "Though, I imagine somewhere in the recesses of my mind lived the unlikely notion that I might be a coach," VanDerveer wrote in *Shooting from the Outside*. "Why else would I retrieve from a trash can a brochure about a coaching clinic with Bobby Knight and Abe Lemons?"

After graduation, VanDerveer planned to travel around the country for a year. She visited friends, crewed on a sailboat in South Carolina, and refereed volleyball matches in Florida. But her money ran out just before Christmas break. She returned to her parents' home in New York without a plan. So much for a year. Her parents watched her play chess with her brother Nick, hang around in the basement, and sleep. "I never really worried about her, because she always seemed to be in control of what she wanted to do," her mom, Rita, said. "She didn't seem unhappy."

Tara's father felt differently. By the middle of January 1976, Dunbar VanDerveer was compelled to help his daughter fill her calendar. He asked her to coach her sister Marie's high school junior varsity team at Niagara Falls High School. "Dad, they just lost 99–11 last night," Tara pointed out. That's precisely why she was going down to help, Dunbar said.

It wasn't the first time she'd served in a coaching role. As a teenager she taught swimming and sailing at a summer camp in western New York. She had a group of "polliwogs" (beginner children as young as six years old), and she had planned out the entire lesson. She walked around the pool deck telling kids what to do. When she was done, she asked a fellow swim teacher named Beth, "How did I do?" Beth responded, "You'll never be a good teacher unless you get into the water with them." It was a lesson that would stick with Tara throughout her career.

Coaching Marie's team was her first chance to coach basketball. Truth be told, the team wasn't very good, and players kept missing practices for dates or hair appointments. Still, Tara quickly grew to love it—the strategy, the preparation, the opportunity to make the team better. Tara cemented her life plan then and there: she wanted to be a coach.

By spring, VanDerveer's law school plan was dead. She began sending letters out, writing to programs across the country looking for a coaching job as an unpaid graduate assistant. She heard back from two schools, University of Southern California and Ohio State University. Ohio State was in the same conference as Indiana—a more familiar place than a school way out in California. The athletic director remembered Tara's playing career at Indiana.

VanDerveer chose to go to Ohio State in 1976 and coach the JV team as a volunteer coach. She needed to get ready for her new job. So she grabbed her younger sister Heidi, who was also developing an interest in basketball, and they made their way in her yellow Volkswagen Bug to the Cathy Rush Basketball Camp in the Pocono Mountains. It was run by Rush, the coach who had led Immaculata—a team known as the Mighty Macs—to three consecutive AIAW national titles from 1972 to 1974. VanDerveer knew of Rush because her Indiana team had played Immaculata, in the 1972 season. Hearing that Rush was running a camp, VanDerveer called and asked if she could help out as a counselor. Rush said yes. Heidi signed up as a camper.

"It was like basketball on steroids all summer. I was teaching, and I was watching and talking basketball all the time," VanDerveer said. "We would coach during the day and play pickup games at night. It was work, but I loved it."

The camp was staffed by East Coast players. VanDerveer didn't know anyone when she arrived, but that changed quickly. There she met Debbie Ryan (who would go on to coach at the University of Virginia), Marianne Stanley (future coach at Old Dominion, Penn, USC, and others), Phil Martelli (later the coach of the St. Joseph's men's team), Rene Muth Portland (who would coach at Penn State), and Theresa Grentz (later the coach of Rutgers and the University of Illinois). From that group, Ryan, Stanley, Grentz and VanDerveer would ultimately end up in the Women's Basketball Hall of Fame. "We were all 21 to maybe 24 years old," VanDerveer said. "There were no real jobs out there for people. We were all just starting out." VanDerveer would return to the Rush camp several summers in a row.

Upon her arrival at Ohio State, where she was studying for a master's degree while she coached, VanDerveer realized she needed to make ends meet outside of her volunteer job. She took a paying job at the student rec center on campus, working the 6:00 AM to 2:00 PM shift, wrapping herself in a sleeping bag during the winter to keep warm. She lived for free for a year in a friend's trailer. "I was on food stamps, and my car was totally rusted out. The heat usually didn't work. The brakes needed replacing, but I didn't have the money. I think the car cost $300, and it wasn't even worth that. But I was happy," VanDerveer said.

She drove the team van to games in the middle of Midwest winters. She watched all the film she could. And her notebook containing plays and drills and nuggets of coaching advice was filling up. That notebook was a compilation of what she had gleaned by watching practices, having conversations with coaches, and viewing televised games. Her team went 8–0 that season.

After that first season, VanDerveer received her first paid coaching offer from fellow Rush camp counselor and friend Marianne Stanley to be an assistant coach at Old Dominion. Stanley had been a player on the groundbreaking Mighty Macs in the mid-1970s. VanDerveer turned Stanley down, wanting to finish her master's degree at Ohio State.

After a year at Ohio State, VanDerveer interviewed for three West Coast coaching jobs—at the University of Colorado, the University of Montana, and the University of Idaho. At Colorado, they told her they wanted to win a national championship in two years. VanDerveer didn't think that was realistic. At Montana, the players who interviewed her asked her "What is your philosophy?" Tara responded, "Work." They seemed confused and asked her to elaborate. "Hard work," she replied. "I didn't get that job," VanDerveer said.

VanDerveer was offered her first head coaching job at the University of Idaho. Her salary: $13,000. At 25 years old, she was just two years older than the oldest players on her roster. The program had existed for only five years, and the team had gone 2–18 the previous season.

To be sure, it was a bare-bones operation. The new coach had to arrive early at the gym to pull out the bleachers to get the facility ready to host the game. Only 20 people showed up at the team's first exhibition game. At one point, the men's team's radio broadcaster pulled VanDerveer aside and told her that the men's game needed to start on time at 7:30 and that if her team's game went into overtime, it would need to be decided by a sudden-death basket to move things along. Tara responded, "And I said, 'If anyone comes on the court, there will be sudden death. But I will be killing them.'"

Her first career win came in her head coaching debut on December 1, 1978, when Idaho slipped by Northern Montana 70–68. The game came down to the final seconds. "There was a timeout, and I remember telling our team, 'All right, just play great defense; don't foul.' And of course, we fouled. The game went into overtime. I said to myself, 'This is going to be harder than it looks.'" Still, Idaho hung on for the win. It was one of Tara's great lessons as a head coach: Don't tell your players what *not* to do. Tell them what to do. That's the thing that sticks.

VanDerveer was intense and detailed. She conditioned her team into better shape than most of the teams they played, into better shape than any of the players had ever been in. She wanted them ready to win in the final five minutes of the game. She looked young enough to be mistaken for one of the players when the team went on road trips. But she was very much in charge, the bossy big sister returning to form.

The men's coach at Idaho was Don Monson, and Tara's relationship with him started off on the wrong foot. "I got into a fight with him the first day I was there, because he wanted to run the girls' basketball camp. I'm like, '*I'm* running the girls' camp.'"

It got worse from there. Stretching her tiny salary, VanDerveer economized by not buying snow tires—in Idaho. She recounted, "So I'm driving to school one day, I lose control of the car, and I run into the car in front of me. It's Don Monson."

But the relationship blossomed as VanDerveer showed up at Monson's practices to watch and then stopped by his office the next day to debrief. When opposing teams came to play the men's program, she would ask if she could watch. She and Monson eventually became close friends. She invited him to come to Colorado Springs to help her with the Olympic team preparations before the 1996 gold medal run in Atlanta. "We had fun; I really liked him a lot. Years later he helped me teach the matchup zone with our Olympic team, and it came in handy against Australia in the semifinals," VanDerveer said.

Tara always made sure her players had what they needed. "We never felt slighted," said Willette White, a former point guard who transferred to play at Idaho after VanDerveer's first season and later became a graduate assistant under VanDerveer at Ohio State. "We felt like we were kind of given the things that we deserved at that point with where athletics were. . . . I know [Tara] had a lot of behind-the-scenes fights with facilities and practice times and all of these things that we never felt. But I don't think we ever realized how much she was fighting."

In Tara's two seasons at Idaho, the Vandals went 42–14. Attendance had jumped to nearly 2,000 per game. In her second season, they reached the NCAA tournament. Suddenly VanDerveer had options. She was offered the head coaching job at Ohio State, the place where she had begun her coaching career as a graduate assistant. She was 26 years old at the time she took the job.

She recruited the Buckeyes' home state hard, putting thousands of miles on her car driving from one end of Ohio to the other. She employed the same punishing conditioning regimens she had established in Idaho: Three-and-a-half-hour practices in which every moment was mapped out. No dribbling unless you were going in for a layup. The ball must keep moving. And a relentless quest to be the most well-conditioned team on the floor. "We never finished a game more tired than the other team. Never," said former Ohio State guard Kristin Watt, who was part of VanDerveer's first recruiting class at OSU.

As it had at Idaho, VanDerveer's hard work paid off. In her second season in Columbus, VanDerveer had the Buckeyes in the NCAA tournament. Over five seasons from 1980 to 1985, she compiled a 110–37 record with four 20-win seasons. She won four Big Ten titles and reached the NCAA tournament three times.

In what would be her final season at Ohio State in 1985, she led the Buckeyes to a 28–3 record and an NCAA Elite Eight appearance. That season included a 79–47 win over Stanford in Columbus. She had built a program that could compete for a national championship. But there were days when it felt all-consuming, like there wasn't room in her life for anything other than basketball. She craved something she didn't feel she had in Columbus, an environment that didn't just challenge her, but stimulated her.

And indeed there were big things on the horizon. The Buckeyes had a huge Big Ten conference win over Iowa in that 1985 season, played in front of more than 22,000 fans at Iowa's Carver-Hawkeye Arena. It was this huge upset which would catch the attention of Stanford athletic director Andy Geiger—who was looking for a new head coach to build the Cardinal program into a West Coast power to compete with USC—and would change VanDerveer's life.

Chapter 3

# The Start

**EMILY WAGNER'S ROLE** in the history of Stanford women's basketball is probably underestimated. She never set a record, won a title, or earned a postseason award. Her basketball career with the Cardinal, in fact, was brief—cut short by injury. But her impact may be immeasurable.

The 5'9" guard from Pleasant Ridge, Michigan, was being recruited by Tara VanDerveer at Ohio State. She was also being recruited by Stanford. Wagner called VanDerveer one afternoon in February 1985. The coach answered the phone with a raspy voice and a fuzzy head courtesy of a flu she'd caught midseason.

Wagner had come to the Stanford–Ohio State game in Columbus, Ohio, and seen VanDerveer's Buckeyes demolish the Cardinal. She was unfailingly polite as she told the ailing VanDerveer that despite what she had seen on the floor, she had decided to go to Stanford. VanDerveer didn't have the strength to do anything but wish her well. "I said to her, 'Emily, that's a great decision,'" VanDerveer said. "To myself, I was thinking, *You are going to get your head beat in, but you are going to get a great education.*"

Wagner went on to tell VanDerveer that she wanted to get a degree from a place where, if she got hurt at some point during her playing career, she'd have a chance to get a great degree. VanDerveer couldn't argue with that logic, and she wished Wagner the best of luck.

During Wagner's recruitment at Stanford, she had the opportunity to meet with athletic director Andy Geiger, who was thinking about hiring a new head coach for the women's basketball team. Wagner brought up how much she would have liked to have played for VanDerveer. A seed was planted.

Meanwhile, in Columbus, VanDerveer was starting to feel unsupported. A new athletic director had arrived at Ohio State, and VanDerveer was informed that her program was significantly over budget—a budget she'd never seen. She asked to order new basketballs as teams across the college game transitioned to a smaller ball for women's basketball. She was turned down. And she was refused again when she asked to order running shoes for her players for team workouts. As much success as she'd built at Ohio State, she was starting to question whether her program had the support from the university that she needed. So she took a few interviews—at the University of Arizona, the University of Washington, and Stanford University.

Wagner, already committed to Stanford, watched and waited. VanDerveer was Geiger's first choice. The first time Geiger offered VanDerveer the head coaching job of the women's basketball program at Stanford in the spring of 1985, Tara traveled to the Palo Alto campus, toured the facilities with Geiger, and then returned back to Columbus to consider the offer.

There was a lot to weigh for an up-and-coming coach. She was building a nationally elite program at Ohio State, and had a great class of recruits coming in. Stanford was a leap, and not just geographically. The team had gone 14–42 in the previous two seasons. The high academic standards, among the most selective in the nation outside of the Ivy League, would limit her pool of potential recruits. Trusting that Geiger was willing to invest the way he said he was would be an exercise in faith. VanDerveer's family and friends seemed similarly skeptical, including her father, who didn't hesitate to share his opinion with his daughter. "He told me [Stanford] was a coach's graveyard," Tara VanDerveer said.

"You're crazy," Dunbar VanDerveer said. "You'll be home in three months, because you can't win at Stanford." Her friends reminded her of the great job she already had, one with plenty of room to grow and succeed. She wasn't convinced that going to Stanford was anything but "crazy." So she turned it down.

Geiger didn't take that *no* for an answer. "Why won't you take the job?" he asked VanDerveer.

"I don't feel like I know enough about it," she replied.

"Well, then," he responded, "come back."

Wagner called VanDerveer again, as polite as ever. "I'd really like you to come to Stanford and be my coach," Wagner said.

"Emily, it sounds like *you* are recruiting *me*," VanDerveer said.

But VanDerveer was intrigued enough by Geiger and Wagner's persistence to board a plane west for a second time. It was on that second trip that VanDerveer saw Stanford in a way she hadn't the first time. She saw possibilities and potential. She saw a place that would challenge her intellectually outside of basketball. And she believed Geiger wanted what she wanted—to build a championship program. "That demands a lot of support, it takes a lot of energy, and you have to have the right pieces in place," VanDerveer said. "I thought I knew what it would take. And I wanted to make sure that, in fact, we were going to have those resources and that support."

Geiger had already given her reason to be hopeful, organizing a booster club to fundraise for women's sports called the Cardinal Club, which had raised $1 million for the women's athletics programs with a large-scale fundraising effort.

Stanford track coach Brooks Johnson, who would become one of VanDerveer's closest friends on campus, was dispatched by Geiger to seal the deal. Geiger told Johnson to keep VanDerveer walking around campus until she said yes. Tara wondered why it took them so long to head back to the office that day. Johnson was selling her hard. He promised to help her recruit, and agreed to run VanDerveer's conditioning program, which he would end up doing for eight years. He also assisted with recruiting and designed drills to improve players' vertical jumps and speed.

VanDerveer was enticed by the California weather, and the opportunities she would have to do things she loved, such as skiing. Tara came to see Stanford as the ultimate challenge. And she believed she was up for it.

The second time Geiger asked, VanDerveer said yes.

One of the first events VanDerveer attended as the new Stanford head coach was an end-of-season banquet that lauded the accomplishments of all of the Stanford athletics teams, many of which were NCAA champions. Multiple coaches reeled off the names of their All-Americans. "With each one, I sank lower in my chair until I was nearly on the ground," VanDerveer said. "I wondered if we would ever have players that good or have that much success [on the women's basketball team]."

VanDerveer's ability to find success at Stanford would depend on her ability to recruit more skilled and competitive players than they currently had on the roster. She would need to hit the recruiting trail hard. And she would need to build relationships with the players who were already there.

Guard Charli Turner (now Charli Turner Thorne) was one of those players. Her parents were both professors at UCLA, but Stanford had always been her dream school. When the interview process for the new Stanford coach began, she was a student-athlete representative on the interview panel. Truth be told, VanDerveer wasn't her first choice.

Turner Thorne's first sit-down with VanDerveer after she was hired was a little intimidating. It's not easy to be part of the group of players left over after a coaching change, even one that the Stanford players had embraced and advocated for. "She sat down and said to me, 'You better come back in the best shape of your life,'" Turner Thorne said. "And I did."

As a sophomore in VanDerveer's first season at Stanford, Turner Thorne built relationships with assistant coaches Amy Tucker, Julie Plank, and June (Brewer) Daugherty—young coaches, all of whom had played at Ohio State. VanDerveer intended to set high standards and establish a culture of excellence. And she had assembled a strong staff to help get there. Plank worked with the guards, Daugherty with the posts. Tucker worked with the wing players and was VanDerveer's strategic go-to. Tucker had an eye for talent and recruiting and built strong relationships with the players.

VanDerveer was no-nonsense, Turner Thorne said, but with a dry wit that would surprise people who didn't see it coming. And it was apparent to Turner Thorne that VanDerveer knew she needed to improve her team through recruiting new players.

VanDerveer watched her team play its first pickup game, and the drop-off in talent from her team at Ohio State was startling. For starters, she didn't have enough size. And she needed more skilled players in the backcourt. "She got the most out of people," Turner Thorne said. "But we were not as talented as we needed to be."

Virginia Sourlis was a senior when VanDerveer arrived. The program's identity before, she said, was more about "playing and having fun." The new head coach intended to win championships, and she was going to do what it took to get there.

VanDerveer rolled out a 10-page book of plays, which her players devoured as the diligent students they were. And she created goal sheets, a version of which Turner Thorne said she used with her own Arizona State teams, where she later coached for 25 years.

That first season under VanDerveer, Stanford finished with a 13–15 record, the only losing record of VanDerveer's coaching career. The Cardinal went 1–7 in conference play, had a nine-game losing streak in the middle of the season, and lost 11 games by at least 10 points. There were so few fans in the gym they rarely had to pull out the bleachers.

There were moments, VanDerveer later admitted, when she wondered why she had left such a talented team in Ohio State. At the same time, she was optimistic about her ability to build at Stanford. "There were no better people than those players on my first Stanford team," VanDerveer said. "They wanted to be successful, they wanted to be a better team, and I think we had fun. It was hard, and I think they liked that."

But VanDerveer saw a brighter future for the program. She told her father that they just needed to land three or four of the best players from around the country, knowing full well that was easy to say and would be much harder to do. Then as now, recruiting athletes to Stanford required both identifying talent and helping them to prepare themselves for the academic rigor required to be admitted. The Stanford Admissions Department made no exception for student-athletes, who were held to the same admissions standards as every other student who applied. And those standards were exceedingly high, demanding outstanding grades, test scores, and advanced coursework.

VanDerveer was already carving out her own recruiting lane for Stanford. She was not recruiting against the Ivy League schools, because they didn't offer scholarships to their athletes. She would compete for athletes with schools such as Duke and Vanderbilt, but convincing student-athletes from the East Coast to come to Stanford would take work and the ability to show them her vision for the program.

Meanwhile, in her own conference, UCLA and USC were strong academic schools, but didn't face the same admissions standards VanDerveer had to navigate. "I remember going to a tournament, and Linda Sharp from USC waved her hand and said, 'Tara, you can [only] look at those players over there,'" VanDerveer said, referring to a small pool of players to illustrate her limited choices for the country's best talent.

VanDerveer estimated she did more than 30 home visits in her first recruiting season, trying to convince athletes to come to Stanford. And she talked daily with the admissions office. Finding players who could both play at the highest levels and meet the school's academic requirements became a challenge VanDerveer and her staff relished.

Tucker would go to a tournament and see a player that piqued her interest, and VanDerveer's first question would be, "Does she have the grades?" If the players were younger, Tucker would advise them on the types of classes they would need to take and the grades they would likely need to achieve in order to apply. In other words, get A's.

One of VanDerveer's first targets was Katy Steding of Lake Oswego, Oregon. Steding was a 6'2" forward, the best player in the state, who had set the Oregon state high school rebounding record, and she was already being recruited by Cal and Washington. VanDerveer saw Steding at the End of the Trail Tournament in

Oregon City, one of the biggest girls' summer tournaments on the West Coast.

Steding was "sold on" the idea of Stanford even before VanDerveer arrived. "I remember seeing pictures of the campus in my high school counselor's office. They had sent me a letter, and I couldn't believe they thought I was good enough to go there," Steding said. "I was smitten with everything about it—about the academics, about the athletics. I didn't know about another school that combined things in that way. It was my dream school." When VanDerveer got the job, she quickly reached out to Steding. Coming to Stanford was an easy sell, and Steding committed.

But Steding admitted she wasn't necessarily thinking about winning championships. In fact, when VanDerveer told her newly gathered team in one of their first meetings that they were going to play for a national title by the time they were seniors, Steding said she chuckled to herself and thought, *This chick is high*.

VanDerveer saw more in Steding than she thought Steding saw in herself. VanDerveer's demands proved to be something of a culture shock for Steding. She likened the experience to summiting a mountain—just getting to a college program—and then realizing there were more mountains to climb. "I think I thought once I got there, that would be kind of it. And then I quickly realized, no, there are a lot of people here who are better than you," Steding said.

Such as an incoming freshman guard from Tennessee named Jennifer Azzi. Azzi first caught Tucker's eye at a tournament. Tucker quickly called VanDerveer to tell her she had found a great high school point guard who was smart and skilled, perfect for what they were building at Stanford.

"There's one problem," Tucker said on the phone.

"What's the problem?" VanDerveer asked.

"She's from Tennessee."

"Oh," VanDerveer said. "That is a problem."

Azzi was from Oak Ridge, Tennessee, 40 miles from Knoxville, where Pat Summitt had built the University of Tennessee women's program into a powerhouse. VanDerveer assumed Summitt would compete for the homegrown talent. But to VanDerveer's surprise, the Lady Vols passed on Azzi, though Vanderbilt and Ohio State were both in the recruiting mix.

Azzi's parents, Jim and Donna, were excited about the prospect of their daughter getting a Stanford education. "I didn't even know where Stanford was," Azzi said. "I didn't know anything about them because they weren't good at basketball."

Azzi had stacks of recruiting letters at home. She had divided them into three piles: *yes, no,* and *maybe.* She put Stanford into the *no* pile. Her father convinced her to move it to *maybe.* He told his daughter, "Let's keep it alive."

VanDerveer showed up at Azzi's home for an official visit. Jennifer's first impression was not great. She found VanDerveer cerebral and serious, but she wasn't sure it was a good fit. Her parents, however, thought VanDerveer was "brilliant" and that it was worth an official visit out West. "They kept Stanford in the mix, where I would have probably been done with it," Azzi said.

Again it was her father who sold her on the idea of a Stanford education. "He's very blue-collar, if you will. We didn't have money growing up," Azzi said. "My dad just said, 'Listen, the network you are going to make out there, the relationships you're going to make, will set you up for life.'"

Like Steding, Azzi also admitted she wasn't necessarily thinking about national titles when she picked Stanford. But she wanted to play good basketball. She had gone 86–11 in her high school career. VanDerveer had some convincing to do to get Azzi to both understand the reality of a rebuilding program and to embrace it.

Azzi's initial weeks on campus were a struggle. She was homesick in California, paired with a roommate who didn't know much about basketball, and her brand-new bike was stolen in front of a restaurant after the team's first workout in the summer of 1986. Not to mention she was playing on a team with a .500 record in an empty gym. "About midway through my freshman year, I was like 'What in the world am I doing?' We lost more games that season than in my whole life of any sports put together," Azzi said. "But hearing [Tara] over and over say that we were going to win a national championship and we were going to sell out the arena . . . it's what I wanted too deep down, and that was what I came there to do. And I've always loved doing things that have never been done before."

Azzi, with her relentless conditioning and after-hours shooting sessions, was an intimidating presence for the other players, including her classmate Steding. "My first impression of Jen was, 'Oh my god, she's so fast. I'll never be able to run like that,'" Steding said. Azzi, meanwhile, was cajoling VanDerveer to make the team run even more.

Steding's struggles with conditioning and confidence weren't entirely a surprise to VanDerveer. She'd had a successful high school career, but the top programs weren't necessarily beating down the door to recruit her. One of Steding's scouting reports characterized her as "weak and slow." Years later, when Steding had won an NCAA title and an Olympic gold medal, VanDerveer joked, "Not bad for weak and slow."

But getting Steding to buy in to VanDerveer's vision in those early days was only one challenge facing the new head coach trying to lay a winning foundation. VanDerveer did what she had always done, accounting for every detail, burying herself in video and game-planning, and picking the brain of every coach she could find. And she found a good one in Pete Newell, the former Cal and

US Olympic team coach, regarded as the best centers coach in the history of the game. Newell held his famous Big Man Camps at Stanford before VanDerveer's first season, and VanDerveer—as she had done so many times before—showed up to soak it all in.

She watched Newell work with players preparing to begin their pro careers. She was struck by his patience. "He had one player repeating his left-handed layup, I'm gonna say 16 times. Just working and working on it," VanDerveer said. "The basketball culture at the time was able to help people get better, and he was the epitome of that."

VanDerveer waited until everyone else had cleared out when the day was over and she was the only one left to talk to Newell. "Let's go get Chinese food," Newell said. The two spent hours talking, with VanDerveer taking copious notes. There were many lunches after that, at that same Chinese restaurant, and many notebooks full of Newell's advice. He would bring a legal pad and diagram plays. He would talk about his own experiences as a basketball coach. When he scouted for the Los Angeles Lakers and he would come to town, he would invite VanDerveer to sit with him courtside.

With Steding and Azzi leading the way, Stanford went 14–14 in their freshman season. On paper, it was only one win better than VanDerveer's first season at Stanford, but the Cardinal were miles ahead of where they had been a year before, with Steding and Azzi gaining important experience and with two more significant recruits—guard Sonja Henning from Wisconsin and forward Trisha Stevens from Oregon on the way to the Farm. And VanDerveer had a recruit from Delaware on her radar—the kind of "big body" she knew the program needed; her name was Val Whiting. Building the Cardinal into a contender was beginning to pick up steam.

## Chapter 4

# The Titles

**RITA VANDERVEER BOUGHT A BOOK** for her daughter before the start of the 1989–90 season: the classic *The Art of War,* by Sun Tzu. "Opportunities multiply as they are seized," the ancient Chinese strategist wrote.

Opportunity had indeed arrived at Stanford at the start of that season, the women's basketball program's slow build gaining considerable momentum based on the previous two seasons. The Cardinal had talent, experience, and a winning culture that had taken hold in three seasons under Tara VanDerveer's vision.

In the 1987–88 season, with Jennifer Azzi and Katy Steding leading the way in a starting lineup that included one junior (Jill Yanke), two sophomores (Azzi and Steding), and two freshmen (Sonja Henning and Trisha Stevens), Stanford set a program record for victories with a 27–5 season (including a 14–0 start) and its first-ever win in the first round of the NCAA tournament over the University of Montana.

The following season, in 1988–89, the Cardinal won its first Pac-10 regular-season title with a 28–3 record overall, an 18–0 record in conference play, and another trip to the NCAA tournament, where they were knocked out in the Elite Eight by Louisiana Tech.

So by the time the 1989–90 season rolled around, expectations were sky–high around Stanford, which had by then firmly established itself as one of the nation's elite programs. The calculus had changed inside the locker room as well. No longer an upstart program, the Cardinal were primed for something bigger.

VanDerveer invited Stanford swim coach Richard Quick to come and speak to her team. Quick had led the Texas women's swim team to five NCAA titles before coming to Stanford in 1988 and leading the Cardinal to one in 1989. He told the Stanford players that in order to win a title, they first had to get comfortable with the idea that they *could* win one. VanDerveer latched on to that advice.

VanDerveer announced at a preseason press conference that she thought her team had the makeup to "go all the way" to the NCAA title. She went so far as to print a sign that read, *Get comfortable with it. 1990 National Champs,* and posted it on the locker room door. Players put their own signs in their lockers. "Not winning never entered our minds," Azzi said.

The Cardinal were defining a West Coast style for women's basketball—one with fluidity, tempo, ball movement, and the utilization of the three-point shot. The NCAA had adopted the three-point line for men's and women's basketball in 1986–87 as an experiment in specific conferences—including the Pac-10—and implemented it universally across the college game in the 1987–88 season.

VanDerveer was an early adopter, thanks to a game the team played in China in the summer of 1987. One opposing player made 10 three-pointers against the Cardinal. "That's when I said to myself, 'We can use this,'" VanDerveer said.

She knew of other coaches who would pull their players out of a game for attempting a three-pointer. She went a different way. In the summer of 1987, following that trip, Stanford players holed up in the practice gym, shooting hundreds of three-pointers each day. "I thought the three-point line was our equalizer, because we didn't have the big, physical bodies some of the other elite programs had," VanDerveer said. "They played a different style than we did, and they won with it, but the three-point line gave us an edge. And we embraced it."

Azzi never considered herself a good shooter. She ultimately became one of the best in the country, alongside Steding and Henning. "We lived in the gym," Azzi said. "Not many other teams had long-range shooters like that."

In 1987–88 Stanford shot 278 three-pointers at a 36 percent clip, more than double the NCAA average that season. In 1989–90 that number jumped to 306 with a 44.1 percent success rate. Skip far ahead to the 2019 season, when Stanford shot a program-record 920 three-pointers, making 320 of them. "We were the Steph Curry era before Steph Curry," Azzi said. "We expanded the game. I don't think people realized that [VanDerveer] is really the one to take credit for that revolution."

In addition to the three-point shot, VanDerveer was remaking the game in the film room. She was a film junkie, even when technology was practically primitive compared to today's ubiquitous editing, viewing, and playback options. In high school, she used an 8mm camera to interview her high school classmates for a school project, doing a set of interviews with her classmates and teachers to capture the highlights of her senior year of high school. "I'm a very visual person, and I feel like when I can see things, I can figure them out," she said.

She used video of opposing teams to guide her practices, using her reserve players to mimic the plays of other teams and beginning Stanford's reputation of running some of the best scouting report defense in the women's game. She paid students to sit in the stands and film Cardinal games. She logged clips, watched film from her stationary bike, and made video work with her team an embedded part of their routine. She earned the moniker Video VanDerveer from her fellow coaches.

The benefits of her innovation were starting to show on the floor as the 1989–90 season began. The Cardinal were dominating opponents with an inside-out game that included a regular barrage of three-point shots, spreading defenses and creating space for Stanford to succeed inside. But this was not merely a "system" program, where a team succeeds based on *how* they play as much as *who* is playing. The players themselves were regarded as some of the best in the country.

Azzi was honored as Stanford's first All-American, the award given to the top players in the country, in her junior season, and she was a two-time All-Conference player. She was the only returning All-American in the nation to start her senior season. The up-tempo offense that Azzi was driving was causing opponents problems. "She was a give-me-the-ball-and-go-to-hell kind of player," VanDerveer said. "She was just like, 'Boom, let's go.'"

Azzi had a relentlessness that even wore out her relentless coach from time to time. She was the one who wanted to scrimmage longer, to run more. She called VanDerveer one evening, and VanDerveer answered meekly, in the middle of a midseason stomach bug. Azzi wanted her to come down to the gym and rebound. "I'm throwing up sick and it's a Sunday, but I [went]," VanDerveer said. "I thought she would never be done."

Meanwhile, Steding was finding her way as an upperclassman. In her first two seasons, she had been asked twice by VanDerveer to change positions, to move from her more natural position at power forward (the 4) to small forward (the 3) to make room for Trisha Stevens and Val Whiting in the post. VanDerveer wanted to take advantage of Steding's perimeter shooting ability and create size mismatches for the opponents trying to guard a bigger, stronger player on the wing. It was not an easy adjustment for Steding, nor one she really wanted to make. She had finally become comfortable at power forward after coming to college and shifting from the center position she had played in high school. She wasn't thrilled about yet *another* transition, particularly one that would push her skill set that much. "She told me that I needed to learn to handle the ball," Steding said. "I had already gone from a center in high school to a power forward in college, and now in two years' time I am playing small forward. I was like 'What am I doing?' Tara told me that this was what I needed to do to be the best player I could be."

While Steding would eventually realize VanDerveer was pushing her to reach her potential, she was still resisting. "[VanDerveer was trying to] set the table for me," Steding said. "But it was up to me to do the work. And it was not easy."

In fact, her relationship with the head coach was becoming downright tense. The two had a heated discussion on a plane ride back from Los Angeles at the end of Steding's sophomore year that left Steding questioning whether she wanted to be coached by VanDerveer anymore. VanDerveer had taken her out of the starting lineup in a game against USC. Steding fumed. "I was immature, and I wanted her off my back," Steding said. "And she wasn't about to relent to me. I needed to grow up."

On that flight, VanDerveer was typically direct. She wanted to know that she was getting Steding's best. Steding wanted to know that the coach believed in her. Both of them ultimately got what they were looking for by the time the wheels touched down: a new understanding and a way to move forward. "I think I knew at that moment that she really cared about me as a person," Steding said.

With Azzi and Steding as cornerstones, the rest of the roster was stacked. Stacy Parson was a senior guard out of Sylmar, California, who was a player VanDerveer said "knew her role was a backup point guard, and she was going to star in that role." Parson, who played in 116 games in her Stanford career, was experienced and dependable, respected by her teammates. She never averaged more than 2.8 points per game, but her head coach considered her contributions invaluable. "A player like Stacy—you win titles because of people like that," VanDerveer said.

Sonja Henning was running the point as a heady, steady floor leader, excelling on her own merits while playing in Azzi's shadow when it came to accolades and national attention. "Jennifer might be the heart of this team, but Sonja is the soul," said assistant coach Amy Tucker of Henning. "She makes us go. Without her we are an above-average team, but with her we are a great team. It kills me that she doesn't get the credit she deserves, but it doesn't hurt her."

Henning, from Racine, Wisconsin, was a straight-A student who considered basketball her ticket to a Stanford degree with dreams of law school that she had harbored since middle school. To everyone in Wisconsin, she was viewed as the best player ever to come out of the state; she was the hardest-working player they knew. Which made her a perfect fit for VanDerveer.

Trisha Stevens, an Oregon native like Steding, was dominating under the basket. VanDerveer saw Stevens, a multisport high school athlete who won the Oregon state high school title in the high jump, at the same summer tournament where she first spotted Steding, making that a particularly fruitful recruiting trip.

Val Whiting was the big body inside that Stanford had been waiting for. VanDerveer had been watching her since she was a 15-year-old—Whiting was regarded as one of the best freshmen in the country, having led her high school team to four Delaware state championships.

Sophomore Julie Zeilstra was one of the best shooters in the country, while freshmen Chris MacMurdo and Molly Goodenbour looked primed to contribute immediately.

Guard Angela Taylor came into Stanford in 1989 as a walk-on from Mountain Home, Idaho. Her older brother Gary played football at Stanford. He would drop videotapes of his younger sister off at the women's basketball office as Angela hoped to get noticed. Taylor was being recruited by Oregon State, USC, Cal, and Boise State, but she chose to take her chances as a non-scholarship player at Stanford after a conversation with VanDerveer. VanDerveer was candid with Taylor that she was interested but did not have a scholarship spot open for her. Taylor wasn't sure her family could afford it, but once she was accepted to Stanford, the Taylors made a decision to make it work. Taylor arrived on campus to compete in a tryout with three other players, and she was the only one of the group to be offered a spot on the roster.

In December of 1989, right before Christmas break, VanDerveer offered Taylor a scholarship. "It was incredible," Taylor said. "My plan had always been to put my head down and work. When I was able to call my parents and let them know . . . it was life-changing. They weren't going to have to figure out how to scrape some nickels together to make sure I could go to the school of my dreams."

Goodenbour, another heady guard, came to Stanford from Waterloo, Iowa. "It was a place where I could excel," Goodenbour said. "I thought I'd have an opportunity to play, I thought that we would have an opportunity to be a highly successful basketball team and we'd be able to compete for a championship. When I got there, that's exactly what happened. Jennifer and Katy and Trisha, they were probably one of the most committed groups of individuals. They wanted to elevate the program, and we were kind of indoctrinated into that when we came in."

The Cardinal had the pieces they needed for a long NCAA tournament run and possibly a title, opening the 1989–90 season ranked No. 3 in the country. Stanford reeled off 20 straight wins to start the season by an average margin of 26.5 points per game. An 85–72 win over Tennessee at home was a promising measuring stick. The only team to close the margin to single digits against the Cardinal was Boston College, a road game that the Cardinal won 81–74.

In one of the biggest games of the 1989–90 Pac-10 season, Stanford defeated seventh-ranked Washington at home by 40 points. By the time Stanford traveled to Seattle for the rematch, they were 20–0.

Washington coach Chris Gobrecht arrived in Seattle the same season as VanDerveer started at Stanford, and established the Huskies as an early power program during that time. Gobrecht won the Pac-8 conference title in her first season, and the first Pac-10 conference title in 1988. Stanford was threatening their dominance. "Our early rivalry with Stanford was a driving force in getting our fan base fired up," Gobrecht said.

And the rivalry wasn't particularly friendly. The two teams were competing for recruits and titles, trying to build a home base on the West Coast for women's basketball. The pair of up-and-coming coaches traded barbs. "There are so many things I'm sure Tara and I perceived about one another," Gobrecht said. "I'm sure there were all kinds of things we perceived about the other one's actions that weren't true. I swore she was coming into the Northwest to go after kids just so we couldn't have them. Head-to-head, she got more of them than I did, but I was sort of like, 'What are you doing in my territory?'"

Charli Turner Thorne, who had played at Stanford under VanDerveer, was an assistant coach at Washington, along with Willette White, who had played for VanDerveer at Idaho.

Getting beaten by 40 at Stanford's Maples Pavilion was a tough pill to swallow for the Huskies. When the Cardinal arrived in Seattle weeks later as national title contenders, Washington's Hec Edmundson Pavilion was packed to its rafters for the matchup; the fire marshal had to ask people not to sit in the aisles. And the crowd was rowdy, chanting insults at Stanford players.

Stanford was on the back end of a difficult trip to Washington State that had included spending the night in a high school gymnasium off the two-lane highway between Spokane and Pullman, Washington, when a blizzard forced the bus to stop. The players and coaches slept on wrestling mats and blankets from the Whitman County Jail.

Washington won the rematch in dramatic fashion, 81–78—which would be the only blemish on Stanford's record for the season. (And just to rub it in a little, after the season was over, Turner had an idea to mail the Cardinal coaches a T-shirt that read "31–1." The *31* was small, and the *1* was large. "I don't think they thought it was as funny as we did," Gobrecht said.)

Stanford did not lose again before the NCAA tournament, winning seven straight games, none closer than 28 points. The Cardinal entered the NCAA tournament with an impressive 28–1 record, the new powerhouse knocking on the door of a title. They had not been ranked No. 1 during the entire season to that point. And only nine different teams had ever advanced to the NCAA Final Four, which began in 1982, before Stanford got there in 1990.

The Cardinal played their first three NCAA Tournament games at home, soundly defeating Hawaii in the second round (top teams earned first-round byes at that time) and sliding past Mississippi 78–65 with a performance VanDerveer called "horrible." "I was furious," VanDerveer said. "I had kind of a meltdown. I told the team that we could just go on vacation now if that's how we were going to play." VanDerveer had no patience for a lack of execution from a veteran team. "It makes me feel good when our team comes out and does what we are supposed to do, and when we don't it makes me mad. . . . It would be a crime to have all the talent and all of the hard things we've worked on all year go down the tubes because we aren't making the effort."

But the Cardinal had survived, and they would face a strong Arkansas team at Maples Pavilion for a chance to go to the Final Four. The coaching staff was anxious after the previous game. VanDerveer drove to Maples, running through scenarios in her head. None of them were particularly comforting. "Your mind does strange things," VanDerveer said. "I remember thinking about what would happen if someone crashed their bike on the way to the arena, or what if someone got food poisoning." When VanDerveer arrived at the arena, one of the Stanford security guards handed her a yellow scrap of paper. It was from Azzi, and it read: "Tara, relax. This one's for you."

It was Azzi, Steding, and Parson's last game at Maples. It was the game that would take Stanford to the proverbial promised land. Azzi came to Stanford on a leap of faith, believing VanDerveer told her that an empty gym would be filled and they would be competing for championships by the time Azzi graduated. Azzi believed her. It was VanDerveer's turn to believe Azzi.

Stanford went on to win 114–87 against the Razorbacks in front of the first sellout crowd in program history, in the highest-scoring game in program history. The echoes of once empty seats were replaced by building-rattling cheers. The Cardinal were headed to the Final Four in Knoxville, Tennessee, a 25-mile ride from Azzi's hometown. VanDerveer sat on the bus as it pulled up to Thompson-Boling Arena in Knoxville for the team's first practice. She thought, *You may never be back here. So you may as well win it.*

The team had been greeted in Tennessee by the news that the University of Oklahoma was dropping its women's basketball program, an announcement made on the eve of the biggest weekend in the sport. Oklahoma claimed that it was losing $250,000 a year on the program, and the team had just gone 7–22. Attendance at home games was averaging 65 people. Every coach who went to the podium at the press conferences before the Final Four—VanDerveer, Virginia's Debbie Ryan, Tennessee's Pat Summitt, and Auburn's Joe Ciampi—was asked about it. All four donned red ribbons on their lapels in solidarity with the Sooners. VanDerveer called it a "major slap in the face and a major step backward." The backlash to Oklahoma's decision was swift. There was an Oklahoma campus rally to support the women's program, and a lawsuit against the university was being considered. The Oklahoma state senate condemned the decision with a resolution. The outpouring did its job. Within a week, Oklahoma backtracked and reinstated the program, a reaction to the building national interest in the women's game.

At the Final Four for the first time, Stanford would not be distracted. The Tournament had been defined by upsets. Every team the Cardinal had faced in the first three rounds of the NCAA tournament had been the upset winner over a more highly seeded team, and the same would be true for their first Final Four matchup, a semifinal against the University of Virginia. Virginia—led by a dynamic point guard named Dawn Staley—had pulled off an Elite Eight stunner over powerhouse Tennessee to get to the Final Four, leaving Knoxville in shock that their Lady Vols wouldn't be participating.

Stanford played the first game that day, defeating Virginia to punch their ticket to the title game. Before the next game, VanDerveer sat in the stands to scout the game between Louisiana Tech and Auburn. She overheard two men talking about how this would be the "varsity" matchup. The team from the West Coast was definitely under the radar in this field. And then Auburn upset Louisiana Tech.

Regardless of the upsets or the opponent, the Cardinal women had already decided they weren't merely happy to be there. Azzi said her teammates never felt the desperation of the "last chance," even as seniors. "It never crossed our mind that we weren't winning it. It wasn't like 'Oh, we better do it.' There was just no question about it."

Auburn was a team making its third straight appearance in the national championship game. Stanford got off to something of a shaky start in the game, trailing Auburn 41–32 with less than two minutes to go in the first half. But the Cardinal, led by their building blocks—Azzi, Steding, Henning, and Stevens—blitzed the Tigers in the second half to win 88–81 and claim the NCAA title. Henning finished with 21 points and 9 rebounds. Steding set an NCAA record with 6 three-pointers and 18 points. Azzi finished with 17 points and 4 three-pointers, and Stevens finished with a double-double of 16 points and 10 rebounds.

In just five seasons, VanDerveer's vision of winning a national championship at Stanford had become a reality. "If I had died on that court at that moment, I would have no regrets," VanDerveer said. "Nothing in my life had come close to the pure joy I felt. . . . Nothing in my life, not even winning the Olympics, would replicate that feeling."

Azzi won multiple national Player of the Year awards. VanDerveer was named the National Coach of the Year. And the Cardinal got their first invitation to the White House along with the UNLV men's basketball team. President George H. W. Bush extended an invitation to the head coaches to visit the Oval Office. VanDerveer walked down the hall with UNLV men's coach Jerry Tarkanian, who put his arm around VanDerveer and said, "This is the big time." It was indeed.

As the 1990–91 season began, the Cardinal were facing life without Azzi and Steding, coupled with the pressure of being the defending national champion. Henning and Stevens were the new marquee players, with Goodenbour, Zeilstra, and Whiting playing critical roles.

The transition taking place was immediately apparent as Stanford opened the season with two losses in its first four games, more than it had lost in the entirety of the previous year. The Cardinal quickly found their footing. They went on to win the Pac-10 title for the third straight season, positioning themselves for NCAA title defense. But the attempt at a repeat was marred by injuries. Stevens, who at that point was the second-leading scorer in program history, sustained a ruptured knee tendon in the Sweet 16 game against Washington that required surgery, ending her season. Zeilstra, battling a sore Achilles tendon late in the season, had 17 points and 12 rebounds in a tough win over Georgia in the Elite Eight but was injured in pregame warm-ups before the next game, pulling a calf muscle just moments before tipoff of the national semifinals against Tennessee. Stevens and Zeilstra sat together on the bench before Stanford's semifinal game against Tennessee—Stevens in a full leg cast, Zeilstra with her lower leg cased in ice packs.

Even without their injured starters, the Cardinal led the semifinal game at halftime 28–21 and were up 54–50 with six minutes left in the game. But the injuries to Stevens and Zeilstra, and the subsequent damage to Stanford's depth late in the game, were too much to overcome for the Cardinal, who fell 68–60 to eventual champion Tennessee.

As the 1991–92 season began, the Cardinal were a team again moving on from the graduation of stars in Henning and Stevens, with one senior in Ann Adkins, All-American candidates in Whiting and Goodenbour, and five incoming freshmen—the nation's No. 2 recruiting class.

Practices did not start out well. The team looked ragged and inexperienced playing together. Goodenbour's passes were missing their targets. "At one point, I was standing on the sideline and the ball sailed over my head," VanDerveer said. "She was throwing the ball all over the gym."

On that particular day, VanDerveer went back to her office to call her sister Heidi, who asked how things were going.

"It was OK," Tara VanDerveer replied.

"How can you guys do this year?" Heidi responded.

"I think we can win it," VanDerveer said, unconvincingly.

"Let me talk to Amy," Heidi replied.

Heidi posed the same question about practice to associate head coach Amy Tucker.

Tucker replied, "It was horrible."

"Tara thinks you can win it," Heidi said.

"Win what?" Amy replied, incredulously. "Tara is on drugs."

Tucker estimated the Cardinal would be "lucky" to be a .500 team.

"Over my dead body," VanDerveer replied dryly.

But the head coach knew she had her work cut out for her. Goodenbour was filling Henning's big shoes as the team's leader and needed some molding. Whiting, with her size and physical play, had lived up to all expectations and was ready to build on her success. But with junior Angela Taylor injured early and out until conference play began, there were a lot of relatively untested players getting major minutes, such as freshman post Rachel Hemmer and freshman guards Christy Hedgpeth and walk-on Kate Paye.

Whiting, for one, did not buy in to the idea of a "rebuilding season." She said the team relied on the work ethic they had learned from players such as Azzi and Henning. "Your best players are also your hardest workers," Whiting said.

As the season progressed, the coaches and the team steadily gained their confidence, a process that sped up considerably when they knocked off top-ranked Tennessee 96–95 in overtime at Maples Pavilion.

The Cardinal won a fourth straight conference title in 1992 and knocked out Pac-10 foe USC in the regional final in Seattle, and then went to the Final Four in Los Angeles, beating Virginia 66–65 in a thrilling semifinal game. Tara's earlier, if unconvincing declaration to her sister Heidi that her team could win a title proved prescient when Stanford defeated Western Kentucky 78–62 in the NCAA Championship game for the program's second title in three years. The freshmen who VanDerveer knew so little about at the start of the season stepped up big, with Rachel Hemmer scoring 18 points with 15 rebounds in the title game to accompany 17 points from Christy Hedgpeth. Paye made four crucial free throws in the final 1:12 of the game. And the stars shined. Whiting, an All-American, scored 16 points with 13 rebounds, and Goodenbour, who was selected as the Final Four's Most Outstanding Player, collected 12 points and 6 assists.

"I call that my bucket of bolts team," VanDerveer said, meaning that in the best way. It ended up being a team that was greater than the sum of its initial parts and an affirmation that the Stanford way was being cemented even as the players changed.

Stanford finished the 1991–92 season with its second 30-win season and another trip to the White House. This time, the Cardinal were there with the Duke men's team and their coach Mike Krzyzewski. As VanDerveer and Krzyzewski were sitting in the hall together, waiting to go into the Oval Office to see President George H. W. Bush, Krzyzewski—who had been to the White House with Duke the previous season—explained how the day was going to go. VanDerveer thanked him for the information, replying, "I've been here already too."

The opportunities for Stanford women's basketball, as Tzu wrote, would continue to multiply.

## Chapter 5

# The Break

**DAYS AFTER THE US WOMEN'S BASKETBALL** team won their eighth straight gold medal in the 2024 Summer Olympics in Paris, Nike ran an ad narrated by six-time gold medalist Diana Taurasi: "It's inspiring when we think about it. Every four years, teams come from around the world to compete . . . for second place." But where did that streak of global dominance start?

The Olympic women's basketball tournament began in 1976 in Montreal, with the team from the Soviet Union winning the first gold medal, besting an American team that included legends Ann Meyers, Nancy Lieberman, and Patricia Head (better known by her married name—Pat Summitt). The US boycott of the Olympics in 1980 in Moscow paved the way for another Soviet Union gold. But the American women won the next two gold medals in 1984 and 1988.

In the run-up to the 1992 Olympic tournament in Barcelona, the US team had taken third place in the 1991 Pan American Games. It turned out to be a portent of a surprising bronze in Barcelona, followed by another third-place finish in 1994 in the

FIBA World Championship in Australia. For USA Basketball, these were unacceptable results that demanded a change in approach.

Up until that point, the US women's basketball team historically spent just weeks together to prepare for major tournaments, while many other countries' national teams trained together for months, giving more time for players to learn, work and play together seamlessly. USA Basketball also solely relied on college coaches to lead their women's teams, with no sustained professional leagues to draw from.

VanDerveer's success at Ohio State, followed by NCAA titles at Stanford in 1990 and 1992, had USA Basketball's attention. "Your name is in the news, you're a candidate [to be a USA Basketball coach]," VanDerveer said.

VanDerveer was already a known quantity to the national federation. She had served on the women's national team selection committee. She had coached for Team USA in a tournament called the Sports Festival in her first season as a head coach at Stanford in 1986. VanDerveer viewed that as a tryout of sorts. "You take your team to a foreign country, a faraway place, and they see how you react and how the team does," VanDerveer said.

She took that first team in 1986 to what was then Yugoslavia—to Belgrade (now in Serbia) and Tuzla (now in Bosnia and Herzegovina). In 1991 she coached the World University Games team, made up of college-aged players, to an 8–0 record and a gold medal. VanDerveer went on to coach Team USA at a World Championships qualifying event in 1993 in Brazil, to a bronze medal at the 1994 World Championships and, two months later, to a gold medal at the 1994 Goodwill Games in Saint Petersburg, Russia.

She was already at the top of USA Basketball's short list when planning commenced for the 1996 Olympic Games in Atlanta,

Georgia, where a gold medal by Team USA was viewed as the only acceptable result. Meanwhile, in New York, NBA commissioner David Stern was laying the groundwork to launch a women's professional league in the United States. The NBA needed a strong showing by the US women's basketball team in Atlanta to justify the investment. They also needed a sustained period of visibility for the players, as the six-game Olympic tournament alone wouldn't be enough to launch a viable women's professional league.

VanDerveer talked with Carol Callan, a close friend and the director of the US National Team. They knew a commitment to win in Atlanta would mean something different than it had in the past. The plan for a yearlong schedule of preparation with the US team was born, and would include a barnstorming tour against the top US college programs and multiple international tournaments and games, culminating in the Olympic tournament. The core of the team would be together for a full year, training and preparing, as was already done in many other countries. This commitment was unprecedented. So was the exposure: there would be media interviews, morning TV appearances, and magazine shoots—not exactly VanDerveer's style. "I don't like being a dancing bear," VanDerveer wrote in her book, *Shooting from the Outside*. "But anyone who says I'm not sensitive to and supportive of public relations doesn't know me."

VanDerveer had also heard the rumblings about starting a new women's professional basketball league in the US, one backed by the NBA. Five US women's professional leagues had already started and failed since the mid-1970s:

- The Women's Professional Basketball League (WBL) 1978–81
- The Ladies Professional Basketball Association (LPBA) 1980–81

- The Women's American Basketball Association (WABA) 1984
- The National Women's Basketball Association (NWBA) 1986–87
- The Women's Basketball Association (WBA), 1993–95

For years, the top players in the women's college game had gone overseas to play professionally when their collegiate careers were over, often unable to speak the language of their teammates and coaches, enduring homesickness and isolation in order to continue their careers in relative anonymity in terms of a US audience.

For a new league to have the backing of the NBA would be a huge opportunity. It would bring financial stability and exposure the previous leagues had never known. It would also be a significant financial risk for the NBA, considering the ignominious history of the prior attempts at professional women's basketball in the United States. A successful Olympics run by the American women could be a springboard for it all.

USA Basketball wanted VanDerveer—and she needed to think about it. It would mean leaving her Stanford program, coming off a Final Four appearance in 1995, for an entire season, something no collegiate coach had ever done. Additionally, she did not want to let down USA Basketball. "This wasn't something I wanted to mess up," VanDerveer said. "For either Stanford or USA Basketball. But it was a once-in-a-lifetime opportunity, and I was going to do it as long as I could get the support from Stanford."

She went to Stanford athletic director Ted Leland. He saw a head coach wrestling with all sides of a difficult decision. "I know she was skeptical to start because she didn't want to leave her team," Leland said. "First off, I think she had a team she loved, and I think she was concerned about this team she had built. I was 100 percent for it." Leland knew VanDerveer was committed to coming back.

He knew they would continue to be nationally competitive in her absence.

In April 1995, just weeks after the close of the 1995 NCAA tournament, VanDerveer announced that she would be leaving the Stanford program for the 1995–96 season to coach the US women's basketball team in the 1996 Olympics in Atlanta. For the then-current Stanford players such as Charmin Smith, there wasn't a worry about whether VanDerveer would return. She said she would be back, and the team had no reason to assume otherwise. "I think we thought, *Wow, cool,*" Smith said. "Like a 'When the cat's away, the mice will play' type of mentality. Not in a negative way, but I think people were excited for something that would be different."

Alongside the announcement of her departure, VanDerveer announced that associate head coach Amy Tucker, who had come with VanDerveer from Ohio State and was the team's lead recruiter, would be taking over the program as interim head coach. VanDerveer felt physically ill at the thought of being away from her team for the season, but those nerves had nothing to do with leaving Tucker in charge. "I knew she could handle the job," VanDerveer said. "She looks easygoing, but just try to beat her at something. I knew she could handle not only the pressure to win but the press, the boosters, the players, the recruits. People responded to her." Tucker said she was "filled with fear" about taking over the program, but that the fear "lit a spark for [her]."

VanDerveer's decision to name Tucker as the interim head coach wasn't without consequences. Assistant coaches Julie Plank and Carolyn Jenkins resigned almost immediately. VanDerveer knew they felt as if they had been passed over in favor of Tucker, the associate head coach. For VanDerveer and Tucker, that was deeply disappointing. "People did what they had to do," VanDerveer said. "The Julie situation was strange, because I was probably going to bring her to the Olympic team with me. But she quit, so that was that."

Of the resignations, Tucker said, "It was disappointing and it was surprising. I mean, that was not the plan. It was a wrench that we weren't expecting. I knew Julie well. She was my teammate at Ohio State. So it was hard. And you feel like Tara already has this hard decision to make, and now it just got a little more complicated. We just had to move forward quickly."

Charmin Smith had a strong relationship with Plank, in particular. Plank had been instrumental in her decision to come to Stanford. "I know we were all sad that Julie and CJ weren't going to be here anymore," Smith said. "But we trusted Tara and Amy."

While VanDerveer was not worried about the team under Tucker's leadership, she knew Tucker was going to need some help. She hired former players Angela Taylor and Ann Enthoven as assistant coaches.

Taylor, who had a relationship with both Plank and Jenkins as a player and had been working the past two years as an assistant coach at Arizona and Texas A&M, credited both of them for encouraging her to take the job when VanDerveer called. "They both told me, 'You have to do this,'" Taylor said. "That Tara was willing to give me that chance, to have voices that understood Stanford and what she wanted—it was not something I had expected, but it was a no-brainer."

Former USC coach Marianne Stanley, who had offered VanDerveer her first head coaching job back in 1976, would also come in to help. Stanley was a pioneer in the game. As a player, she was part of one of women's basketball's first great teams, the Mighty Macs of Immaculata in Philadelphia. She went on to serve as the head coach at Old Dominion, winning AIAW championships in 1979 and 1980 and the NCAA title in 1985. She moved on to coach at Penn before taking the head coaching position at USC in 1989 and recruiting Lisa Leslie to the program. USC already had its own decorated history as the alma mater of legends Cheryl Miller, Pamela and Paula McGee, and Cynthia Cooper.

Prior to the 1993–94 season, Stanley sought a contract. She had taken the USC program from an 8–19 record when she arrived four years earlier to 22–7 in the 1992–93 season. She wanted the same base salary as men's coach George Raveling. USC offered her $54,000 less. After USC refused to budge, Stanley filed an $8 million discrimination lawsuit against the university. When her contract ran out in the summer of 1993 with no resolution, she was out of a job without prospects for a new one. She was labeled a troublemaker. Stanley applied for 25 positions in two years. The price for standing on principle was exile.

She took a job sanding and restoring furniture to make ends meet. For a brief period, she worked in a bookstore in South Carolina for five dollars an hour. Stanley, a single mother, described her situation to the *Los Angeles Times* in 1996: "I lost the security of my retirement. All of my income has either gone to legal fees or to just support myself. . . . I applied for a lot of jobs, and never got a chance because I'd done something taboo in sports. You don't stand up to the status quo."

In 1994 VanDerveer brought Stanley to Stanford in a marketing role in an attempt to help her old friend get back into the game. The only game Stanley couldn't bring herself to attend was the USC game. She left Stanford after a few months to focus on her upcoming trial date; her case would eventually be dismissed.

When VanDerveer was tapped as the head coach of the Olympic team, Stanley had, somewhat ironically, been considered to serve on VanDerveer's Olympic coaching staff before, as Stanley said, "things went south with USC." When VanDerveer announced her Olympic break, VanDerveer knew Stanley was the perfect choice to work under Tucker. Stanley was named a co–head coach in a support role to Tucker, who was the head coach, in charge of the day-to-day operations of the program.

"This is not Be Nice to Marianne Day. Wherever she's been, she's won," VanDerveer asserted. "Marianne felt very strongly about being treated fairly by USC. She was willing to sacrifice the things that meant the most to her—her team and her career." And VanDerveer felt Stanley deserved to coach.

Stanley said she did not feel pressure, even as she was helping to maintain the momentum of one of the nation's elite programs, one helmed by a dear and supportive friend. "For me, pressure was not having a job," she said.

While Tucker assumed the day-to-day administrative duties of the program, Stanley provided experience and support in practices and games. She was heavily involved in game-planning and in-game coaching.

The Cardinal's roster makeup certainly made things easier. There were 11 players on the roster with Final Four experience from the previous season. "I wanted to teach," Stanley said. "It was an experienced team with a really interesting mix of players. I wanted to give them my best stuff. I viewed my role as being supportive of Amy and helping her in any way I could. The players knew the system, and I was there to share with them things I had done that had been successful. But it wasn't me trying to impose myself on the team. I was there to add to what was already there."

Tucker, meanwhile, was getting her first taste of being in charge: scheduling, individual player meetings, tracking the academic success of students, recruiting, budgeting, planning for camps. "You can't possibly prepare yourself. Head coach and assistant coach are two different jobs, and I honestly didn't understand that until I moved over one seat," Tucker said.

In Stanford's first game that season, an exhibition game, the team came to the bench in a timeout, and Tucker found herself standing in the back for one awkward moment. "Then it suddenly dawned on me that I was the one who had to get up there and talk to the team," Tucker said. "It was initially really overwhelming, just trying to feel like you are taking care of everyone and everything. But it really helped that we had a mature, experienced team."

One of the first things VanDerveer said to Tucker before she left for the USA camp in Colorado Springs was to "keep everyone happy." The truth was, the players were already a little happy. "It was like the warden was on vacation," forward Bobbie Kelsey said.

Coming off a trip to the Final Four the prior season, Stanford had an experienced roster that included no freshmen. Kelsey and role player Amy Wustefeld were the lone seniors. The junior class was a heralded group that included point guard Jamila Wideman, defensive standout Charmin Smith, forward Kate Starbird, and forward Tara Harrington. The sophomore class of Olympia Scott, Vanessa Nygaard, Regan Freuen, Naomi Mulitauaopele, and Heather Owen brought both size and skill, all of them at leas than six feet tall.

Notable by her absence on this team was sophomore Kristin Folkl, the budding two-sport star and All-American volleyball player. Folkl, from St. Louis, had made her first impression on Stanford when she came to camp as a ninth grader and dunked a tennis ball in front of Tucker. VanDerveer was out of the country with USA Basketball, and Tucker called her.

"There is a [high school] freshman here who could start for us," Tucker said. VanDerveer thought Tucker needed more sleep. "But as usual, Amy was right," VanDerveer said.

Folkl had played her freshman season at Stanford averaging 9.5 points and 5.5 rebounds per game, off the bench. Most impressive was her efficiency, as she shot 69.1 percent from the floor.

But Folkl announced that she would be taking an Olympic sabbatical of her own heading into the 1995–96 season, accepting an invitation to try out for the US women's national volleyball team. She was one of five collegians invited to try out for the US squad. She would ultimately be named a first alternate to the 1996 Olympic team.

The Cardinal weren't changing much of what they were doing offensively or defensively. That took some pressure off. The players were both familiar and comfortable with what was being asked of them by Tucker and a new staff. "We were going to do the same thing that we'd been successful doing," Tucker said. "We had just come off a Final Four. But I'm not Tara, and so once practice started, it was different. My job was to keep the train on the track. Everyone knew that Tara was coming back."

Tucker had a lighter touch than VanDerveer. She was more willing to laugh and joke at practice. She had established relationships with the Stanford players. But sophomore Olympia Scott said the expectations never changed. "The work ethic was still there, and the energy was a little different, but Amy was the constant, making sure we were still doing things the Stanford way. Some things felt different, but mostly it felt the same," Scott said.

Junior Kate Starbird admitted feeling a little nervous about what was to come. The players were absorbing a lot of change. "My first thoughts were about how we were going to manage this," Starbird said. "Tara was a fantastic coach, and I wasn't really sure what was to happen without her. And there was the loss of Julie, and I think that added to my uneasiness. As it turned out, Tara put people in the right place for us to have an amazing season. Her stamp wasn't gone." But Starbird also relished the opportunity to benefit from a different coaching style. The lighter, more relaxed atmosphere helped build her confidence. "Working with Marianne and Amy was really good for me," Starbird said.

One of the first tasks of the 1995–96 season for the VanDerveer-less Cardinal was facing off against VanDerveer and the US National Team as part of their long exhibition schedule in the run-up to the Olympic Games. Team USA's plane landed in San Francisco two days before tip-off, and VanDerveer immediately arranged a workout for the national team with the Stanford strength and conditioning coach.

The following morning, she learned that the Cardinal signed three of her top guard recruits to letters of intent. She got a haircut and went to her favorite Mexican restaurant. She visited with friends. Her Stanford team came to watch the national team practice that evening. Game day, however, was game day.

VanDerveer felt out of place in the visitors' locker room. There was a catch in her throat as she gave the national team the scouting report on her own college players. It felt a bit like a betrayal. She gave Tucker some advice: "Take care of the ball. Don't let us run."

A sold-out crowd greeted VanDerveer as she walked out onto the floor. They cheered loudly for their coach, as well as Jennifer Azzi and Katy Steding, who were also experiencing a homecoming as the former Stanford stars on the US roster.

As the game began, VanDerveer noticed her Stanford players whipping their heads around when they heard her shouting instructions at the national team players. But they were unfazed. Even with VanDerveer occupying the opposing bench, coaching a roster that included Lisa Leslie, Sheryl Swoopes, and Dawn Staley; a full gym at Maples Pavilion; and the Cardinal facing one of the deepest, most talented women's basketball teams ever assembled, Stanford was within six points at halftime.

Both teams were running the same offense. Stanford was VanDerveer's test case for the national team's offense. At that moment, the Cardinal were running it better than Team USA. "We knew what they were going to do, and they knew what we were going to do," Tucker said.

VanDerveer came out of the locker room after halftime, walked by Tucker on the Stanford bench, and warned, "We are going to put the hammer down." Angela Taylor looked at Tucker with confusion and asked what that meant. Tucker responded, "Just wait and see."

In the second half of the exhibition, the US team turned up the defensive pressure on the Cardinal, stifling Wideman in the backcourt and disrupting Stanford's ability to run their half-court offense. "They basically woke up," VanDerveer said of Team USA.

Smith later recalled bringing the ball up the floor against Teresa Edwards, one of her idols. "I crossed her up, got the basket, and blew the layup," Smith said. "That's what I remember."

The US team defeated Stanford by 37 points with a second-half runaway, and VanDerveer left her team behind, not to return until Thanksgiving break, when she met up with Stanford on the East Coast for their season opener at the University of Massachusetts. The season-opening game was not an auspicious start to the new reality. VanDerveer attended Stanford practice in Massachusetts the day before the game, trying to figure out where she fit in as a bystander. She went to dinner with the team that night, hosted by the family of Massachusetts native Jamila Wideman.

On the day of the game, Thanksgiving Day, VanDerveer sat awkwardly in the press area, close to the bench. And she did not sit quietly. She didn't notice the reporters who were staring at her. One of the UMass officials told her she couldn't cheer in the press box or she'd have to move. She moved closer to the Stanford bench. That only made things worse. "I was yelling and acting crazy," VanDerveer said. "I just wanted them to do really well. I was so invested. I remember Amy turning around and mouthing to me, 'Shut up.'"

The Cardinal lost that game 65–56, marking the program's first season-opening loss since VanDerveer's arrival in 1985. The next day, she read a story from a reporter who criticized her lack of decorum at the game. That stung a little bit. She knew she would have to change her approach to being a spectator of the program she'd built from the ground up. "Those were still my players out there, and I wanted more than anything for them to play well. And they weren't."

VanDerveer invited the players to come to her hotel room later that evening as they absorbed their disappointment over the loss. They didn't talk X's and O's. They talked about perseverance and resilience, and about how they shouldn't let one game define them.

Starbird felt like she could relate to VanDerveer in a different way that season. She described it as a release of tension. "When she was coaching us, you were always trying to impress her, and when she came back that year, it wasn't exactly informal, but it was a different interaction," Starbird said. "It felt less emotionally charged and more like a mentor relationship than a coach. If she gave you feedback, you would internalize it in a different way."

VanDerveer was back in the stands in Lubbock, Texas, over the Christmas break, and Tucker pulled her aside for a conversation before the game. Tucker understood how hard it was for VanDerveer to be a bystander. But it was confusing to the players to hear VanDerveer's frustration. "I told her, 'You cannot sit as close to the bench. You need to move up or you need to be quiet, because they don't need to hear your voice.' It didn't happen again."

Unfortunately, the Cardinal lost that game at Texas Tech that day. VanDerveer was 0-for-2 as a spectator. "I was beginning to think I was bad luck," she said.

Hiccups aside, after a largely successful preseason that included wins over No. 21 Old Dominion, second-ranked Tennessee, and national power Texas, the Cardinal tore through the Pac-10 schedule with an 18–0 record that included two nail-biting wins over UCLA and another over Washington.

The Cardinal cruised through their first two NCAA matchups to advance to the regional in Seattle, where VanDerveer watched from the stands, burning off her own pregame nerves by stopping into the press room to watch the Academy Awards with reporters.

Stanford won a two-point thriller over Alabama in the Sweet 16 and then knocked out Auburn 71–57 to reach a fourth straight Final Four. After the Auburn game, the team cut down the nets accompanied by the family of Naomi Mulitauaopele, who brought drums and sang Samoan war chants. Charmin Smith hopped in to play drums for a bit, while Vanessa Nygaard ran up the bleachers to jam with the Stanford band, a piece of the net hanging out of her mouth.

The season ended the following weekend in Charlotte at the Final Four, with an 86–76 loss to Georgia in the national semifinals. VanDerveer watched from the stands with her sisters Heidi and Marie, and Marie's husband and two children. She went down to the locker room after the game to see the team. They were "low, almost angry," VanDerveer later described. They had come to win and had come up short. The loss was disappointing, but the spirit of wanting more was what VanDerveer wanted to see heading into next season.

Tucker and Stanley were named the United Press International (UPI) National Coaches of the Year, as well as Pac-10 Coaches of the Year. Starbird was named the Pac-10 Player of the Year for a season in which she averaged 21.0 points per game, setting the program record for points scored in a season. The season was bittersweet for senior Bobbie Kelsey, who tore her anterior cruciate ligament (ACL) at the start of conference play in January and ended her career watching her teammates from the bench.

Stanley's return to the game at Stanford revived her coaching career. She was hired the following season as the head coach at Cal. "I will always be indebted to Tara," Stanley said. "She stuck her neck out to give me an opportunity at a really tough time. There wasn't anyone else knocking on my door, so all the credit in the world to Tara for being a good colleague and a good friend."

Tucker became a head coaching prospect, her name associated with openings at Purdue and Florida State. She was offered the head coaching job at her alma mater, Ohio State, and she turned it down. "I knew I really didn't want to be a head coach," Tucker said. "It wasn't a high priority of mine. I liked being behind the scenes more. It just fits my personality." Still, that didn't make it an easy decision, as Tucker's family lives in Ohio. She said, "I felt like I know myself well enough to know that it wasn't [something I really wanted]."

Meanwhile, Tucker indeed kept the train on the tracks for VanDerveer's post-Olympic return. The Cardinal finished the season as the No. 3–ranked team in the country and were set to return their entire starting lineup as well as multiple key players off the bench for the 1996–97 season, where they would set their sights squarely on a national title run.

VanDerveer's job was not done, however. On August 4 in Atlanta, VanDerveer coached the US team to a gold medal in the 1996 Olympics in front of family, friends, and a group of her Stanford players, including Vanessa Nygaard and Christy Hedgpeth. Rita VanDerveer was in the stands, but Tara's father, Dunbar, was not. He was ill with cancer and his condition was worsening. Before Rita traveled to Atlanta, she and Dunbar had been traveling to Buffalo every week for his treatments, more than an hour's drive each way.

The boisterous postgame celebration as the horn sounded was the end of a yearlong odyssey in which Team USA posted a 60–0 record and gained national mainstream attention. Two professional women's basketball leagues were in the starting gates—the Bay Area–based American Basketball League and the WNBA—jockeying for the players VanDerveer had turned into the best team in the world.

Despite her fear that she would let someone down, VanDerveer had elevated the game to historic heights during that year. And her Stanford program had weathered her absence with another Final Four run. She had made the most of her "once-in-a-lifetime opportunity."

The day after the Team USA win, VanDerveer was back on the Stanford campus. "I woke up that morning at home and thought, *Did that even happen?*"

## Chapter 6

# The Dream Team

**TARA VANDERVEER WAS** mentally and physically exhausted after traveling 102,000 miles around the world with the US team, keeping them motivated through a 60–0 season, and dealing with strong personalities, media and marketing demands, and the planning for the two US professional women's basketball leagues happening on parallel tracks.

Being back home, as sweet as it was, did not offer much of a respite; there was nothing slow and easy about VanDerveer's transition back to her head coaching job at Stanford. The day after she arrived home from helping the US women's basketball team win an Olympic gold medal and change the trajectory of an entire sport, she ran the first day of basketball camp at Stanford and then went to the supermarket to get groceries. People stared at the coach they'd seen just days before on their TV screens. A couple of them asked for autographs.

Her voicemail at her Stanford office was full. Media requests poured in, campus groups wanted her to come to their events to assist in fundraising. Her mailbox was full of hundreds of congratulatory letters she was determined to answer. One of them, from legendary UCLA coach John Wooden, quickly went to the top of the pile.

The Cardinal team she had returned to coach was a veteran group, talented, and anxious to get going. They had reached the Final Four under Amy Tucker and Marianne Stanley in her absence. Expectations were sky-high—one more thing that weighed on VanDerveer in the weeks after she returned to campus.

According to NCAA rules, college programs are allowed to take an overseas trip once every four years, and the Cardinal were scheduled to make a nine-day trip to Italy in early September before the 1996–97 season began, although this team didn't really need a European tour to get to know each other. Ten players from the previous season, including the entire starting lineup, were back together and hungry for another shot at a national championship. On the flight to Italy, VanDerveer responded to letters from well-wishers.

By the time they returned from Italy, the players were more deeply bonded by sightseeing and travel, their bellies full of pasta. And with a few exhibition wins under their belts, the players were energized and the head coach still had recruits to visit.

VanDerveer was spent. She needed sleep and a chance to clear her head and recharge. Her dear friend, track coach Brooks Johnson, had noticed, and sent her a note with six words on it: "*REST* IS NOT A FOUR-LETTER WORD." He was telling her to slow down. VanDerveer heeded his advice and took a badly needed week off from basketball just as practice began.

Her name came up as a head coaching candidate for the San Jose Lasers of the American Basketball League, the league founded in Palo Alto by Gary Cavalli and Anne Cribbs, longtime Stanford athletics supporters. Jennifer Azzi was one of the league's founding players. The Lasers were owned by Joe Lacob, a Stanford season ticket holder. Her name was also being bandied about for a coaching opening in the Women's National Basketball Association, the women's professional summer league launched by the NBA.

VanDerveer remembered hearing from coaching colleagues that she would never be able to go back to the college game after her Olympic experience. They said coaching the best team in the world would make everything else seem . . . underwhelming. But she never wanted anything other than her old job. "I had learned things from my Olympic experience that I wanted to take back to my team [at Stanford]," she said.

She brought back an intensity that the players hadn't seen before. She pushed their conditioning, demanded more from them than she had before she left. "I think a lot of people thought at first, *Tara, we are not the Olympic team*," senior Charmin Smith said. "There was a drill we used to do with two balls, and now we had to do it with three. We used to have a certain number of seconds to complete a drill, and now it was less. There was a lot of that."

Tucker saw what was happening, from both sides. "Several players came to me to talk about it, and they definitely felt like she was being too hard on them," Tucker said. "I think Tara thought this team had so much potential, and she had to be demanding of them to get them where they wanted to go. I also think that the change back to Tara was hard on some players because she and I have different personalities."

VanDerveer saw it too. But she had a vision for this team. "After working with the top players in the world, I wanted to bring that training pace back to Stanford. I wanted to share what I'd learned, and I knew our players were capable of playing at a higher level."

VanDerveer was on a mission to prepare them to win a title. This group was special. Not just because of its experience, size, and talent but because this group of players brought a mix of personalities and personal stories that made some of them among the most compelling young women ever to put on a Stanford uniform.

And as their coach upped the intensity, the team grew stronger and closer, according to Smith, united in their quest to prove to VanDerveer that they would take what she was dishing out. "We wanted to win, and we figured out how to do it the way she wanted it," Smith said.

Senior guard Kate Starbird, from Tacoma, Washington, was a lithe, 6'2" wing with a fearless offensive game, honed by playing with—and beating—the boys at the US Army barracks where her father was stationed to work with the Army Corps of Engineers when she was young. She played in the local military pickup games against servicemen and women, spending hour after hour competing against soldiers. "They barely let me in," Starbird said. "I was out there learning to be aggressive, learning how to score, and I had to prove myself every day. That was a huge part of how my game developed."

Starbird was a scorer, but she had something of an unconventional shot. "It was just, well, ugly," assistant coach Amy Tucker said. "Most people start their shot at their waist, when you catch the ball and bring it up and release it. Her shot started really low. It just did not look normal."

Four years earlier on a recruiting trip, Tucker had seen Starbird play at a tournament and reported back: She'd found an "intriguing" player. Her frame was thin, but her skill set for her size was "exceptional," Tucker remembered. "Her ball-handling, her vision, her ability to change direction quickly on the floor with the ball. She was a unique player at her size."

VanDerveer was sold. "I never saw her in person. I saw her on tape, and I knew right away she was really good."

As a high school prospect, Starbird had eyes on going to Duke. But an up-and-coming Blue Devils program wasn't up-and-coming enough for her, and Starbird turned her focus to Stanford.

Starbird's father, Edward, was a colonel in the army and a West Point graduate. Kate was born in West Point. Her mother, Margaret, was a teacher and an author, considered one of the world's foremost experts on Mary Magdalene. Margaret Starbird authored seven books examining the existence of a secret Christian tradition that held that Jesus Christ was married to Mary Magdalene. Her work influenced author Dan Brown while he penned what became the best-selling novel *The Da Vinci Code*. Kate Starbird, meanwhile, was a self-professed computer nerd who was interested in Stanford's world-renowned computer science program.

A benefit of being at Stanford, Tucker said, was that students who had homed in on a field of study—whether it was engineering, law school, medical school, computer science, or anything else—could be routed to some of the world's foremost experts in their field as part of the recruiting pitch. "It was definitely an advantage for us."

After Starbird arrived on campus, VanDerveer and her assistant coaches took the freshman players aside on the first day of practice. Each coach took a player to work with individually. VanDerveer matched with Starbird. "The first thing she asked me when we were alone was, 'Are you going to change my shot?'" VanDerveer said. "I said, 'Not if it goes in.'"

Starbird was thin but strong. Her efforts to put on weight were often fruitless. She tried eating big breakfasts, second helpings, high-calorie shakes. None of it worked. She sustained a knee injury early in her freshman season that limited her playing time. But VanDerveer got glimpses of what was to come, like the day in practice when Starbird abruptly stopped, jumped up, and grabbed the rim with ease. "I said, 'Hello, where did that come from?'"

VanDerveer said, "Kate just wanted to get in the gym, play, win, and then go do her computer stuff." Starbird became deeply immersed in Stanford's computer science program, and spent much of her time away from the team with her fellow computer science classmates designing programs.

The Cardinal's beating heart that season was 5'6" point guard Jamila Wideman. Wideman's journey with her high school team, Amherst Regional High School in Massachusetts, was chronicled by Madeline Blais in the best-selling book *In These Girls, Hope Is a Muscle*. The book included Wideman's six years on the varsity team, beginning in the seventh grade. In her senior year, she led ARHS to the state title, scoring 27 points and making 14 steals in the state championship game. The book was published in 1995, after Wideman arrived at Stanford.

At that point, Wideman's family story was only just becoming known. Jamila Wideman was the biracial child of acclaimed African American author John Edgar Wideman, the first person to win the PEN/Faulkner Award for Fiction twice (for his 1983 novel *Sent for You Yesterday* and his 1991 novel *Philadelphia Fire*). Her mother Judy Wideman, would go to law school and become a lawyer during Jamila's time at Stanford, at the age of 52. Jamila's oldest brother, Danny, was editing anthologies and writing his own fiction and nonfiction works.

The book that VanDerveer read during Wideman's recruitment was John Edgar Wideman's memoir *Brothers and Keepers*, which details the lifelong imprisonment of his brother Robby for being an accessory to murder.

Deepening the Wideman family's tragedy, Jamila's older brother Jake was given a life sentence in an Arizona prison for killing his

16-year-old roommate on a summer camp trip in 1986. Jamila was 10 years old when Jake was arrested. She told *Sports Illustrated* that she had nightmares and insomnia for nearly three years after. In high school, she published poems about the complexities of her biracial identity without mentioning Jake.

Basketball was Wideman's sanctuary. Born at just 2 pounds, 14 ounces, she was always undersized. But opponents quickly found out not to underestimate her because of that, because she could play with quickness, purpose, and wisdom.

VanDerveer remembers a conversation she had with then-recruit Wideman in Stanford's Rodin Sculpture Garden. In the one-acre garden that features some of the French sculptor's most recognized works, they talked about Wideman's life beyond basketball. "We talked about how she just wanted to be able to be herself, and not her father's daughter or her brother's sister," VanDerveer said. "Jamila is just really, really special."

Wideman didn't want to talk about her family history publicly for a long time after she arrived at Stanford. She wanted the focus to be her play on the floor. But the Arizona trips were difficult for Wideman, and VanDerveer would check on her frequently. And her parents often traveled to watch her play with the passion that basketball always brought out in her. On the short list of best floor leaders in program history, Wideman's name is certainly near the top.

Charmin Smith grew up in St. Louis, a self-defined "nerd who loved playing basketball." She was determined to go to college on a basketball scholarship because she knew her parents would struggle to afford her college education. And college programs wanted her too—Smith began getting recruiting letters in the eighth grade. One of them, back in 1989, was from Stanford. The Cardinal hadn't yet won their first national title. Smith didn't know much about the program located way out in California, except that it was a great academic school. But she wanted great basketball. "I just kind of tossed it in the pile," Smith said. "And then it's the spring of 1990, and Jennifer Azzi is leading Stanford to its first national championship. And I'm digging that letter out of the pile."

She told her parents she wanted to go to Stanford's basketball camp. Her father, Charles, "disappear[ed] for a couple of weeks"—while Smith didn't know it at the time, her father was working overtime to make it happen for his daughter.

Smith traveled to California with her friend and fellow St. Louis native, Kristin Folkl, who was being recruited at Stanford as a two-sport athlete in volleyball and basketball. Smith and Folkl had known each other since they were nine years old. Folkl's family made the trip as well. At camp, Smith connected with coach Julie Plank, former All-American Trish Stevens, and Tara VanDerveer's sister Heidi. "After that camp, it was a done deal for me," she said.

Starbird, Wideman, and Smith were VanDerveer's steady seniors. Stanford had a great junior class in Olympia Scott, Heather Owen, Naomi Mulitauaopele, Regan Freuen, Chandra Benton, and the emotional, irreverent forward Vanessa Nygaard.

The 1996–97 season opened with a win over No. 2 Alabama and an 82–65 win over No. 5 Tennessee in Knoxville before the Cardinal stumbled to an 83–66 road loss against No. 4 Old Dominion.

VanDerveer had become a better teacher of the game due to her time with the Olympic team. She was a better tactician as well. And nothing seemed as pressure-packed as what she'd already been through in winning a gold medal.

Twenty games into the season, Mulitauaopele sustained a knee injury, and suddenly the Cardinal were shorthanded inside. Juniors Olympia Scott and Heather Owen would have to hold it down. Vanessa Nygaard could help in the paint but was more useful as a perimeter shooting threat. That didn't leave much room for foul trouble. Or injuries. In addition to Mulitauaopele, Owen, Nygaard, and reserve power forward Regan Freuen had all missed time with various ailments.

Smith and Wideman took it upon themselves to fix the problem. They paid a visit to their former teammate Folkl, who had finished her final volleyball season by leading Stanford to a national title and wasn't planning to play basketball again. They told her they needed her. And then Folkl got a phone call from VanDerveer. Suddenly, Folkl was back in the basketball business.

Folkl's athleticism and strength were extraordinary. She could jump out of the gym, as the saying goes, and she was an efficient scorer with a high field-goal percentage. But she hadn't played basketball in a year and a half, after taking time away to try out for the 1996 Olympic volleyball team. She needed some time to shake off the rust.

As it turned out, she didn't need that much time. In 10 games, in a reserve role, Folkl averaged 10.7 points a game and led the team with 8.2 rebounds per game. "She comes off the bench and she's averaging almost a double-double," Smith said. "We felt like we were magical that year. We were the best team in the country."

The Cardinal certainly played like a title favorite. After an 18–0 run through the Pac-10 in which only three teams—USC, Washington State, and Oregon—came within single digits of the Cardinal, Stanford won the first four games of the NCAA tournament by an average margin of 32.75 points. The Cardinal looked like a buzzsaw on the way to a title.

Up next was the national semifinal game against the Old Dominion Monarchs, the same team that had handed the Cardinal their only loss of the season, by 17 points back in December. But Stanford had Folkl now, and they were largely a healthy team coming in on a roll. Meanwhile, the Monarchs were coming in at

33–1 and had a great coach in Wendy Larry; one of the nation's top point guards in Ticha Penicheiro, a Portuguese star; and an underrated post in 6'5" Clarisse Machanguana, who had come to ODU from Mozambique. "They were a formidable opponent," Tucker said. "I think we thought we were better. We were looking forward to playing them again."

Starbird had butterflies as Stanford headed to the arena in Cincinnati. The team had lost one game all season, and they were one win away from the place that they had counted on being since the day the season began. The game was the first of the night at Riverfront Coliseum, in front of more than 16,700 fans, and it started fast and physical, up-tempo and a little out of control. The following day, *The New York Times* called it "downright brutish."

Starbird, who had been named the Naismith National Player of the Year, hit four of her first five three-point attempts as Stanford weathered the bruising play to build a lead. But Folkl, coming off the bench, picked up two early fouls. The Cardinal built a 15-point lead in the first half, but by halftime, ODU had cut the Cardinal's lead down to seven points. Starbird scored 21 points in the first half.

The Monarchs started the second half with an 8–0 run, giving them the lead. Machanguana hadn't scored in the first half, but she was picking up steam. The second half saw 13 lead changes with neither team leading by more than four points. Stanford took a 72–67 lead with two minutes left in the second half before the Monarchs rattled off nine straight points in 1:35 to go up 76–72.

Stanford forced overtime on a Mulitauaopele layup and two free throws by Smith with 10 seconds to play but went into the five minutes of extra time without Folkl, whose impact was limited by foul trouble (she fouled out on what appeared to be a clean block with 1:46 to go in regulation). Folkl still finished with 18 points (going 8-for-8 from the floor) and 10 rebounds.

ODU forced Stanford into 29 turnovers, 17 of those by steals. They trapped guards at half court and forced three turnovers when Stanford took the ball out of bounds. After her 21-point first half, Starbird scored just five points in the second half as the ODU defense clamped down.

In the last 12 seconds of overtime, Wideman and Nygaard missed crucial shots. The ball fell away each time, and with it, the Cardinal's national title dreams. The final score: Old Dominion 83, Stanford 82. Starbird dropped to her knees on the floor in tears, Old Dominion's coach Wendy Larry comforting her.

The Stanford locker room after the game was a scene of disappointment, emotion, and grief unlike any other in program history. Some players went to cry in the shower stalls, their sobs audible through the tile walls. Players sat by their lockers and in corners on the floor, some with their head in their hands, others just staring into space.

Before the media entered, Wideman talked to her devastated teammates. "Pick your heads up," the captain instructed. She told them she would rather lose with them than win with anyone else, that the pain of the loss would not replace what they had accomplished together. Wideman then walked out onto the floor and collapsed into her mother's arms, sobbing, just a few feet from where Tennessee and Notre Dame were warming up for the next game.

Starbird barely talked above a whisper at the postgame press conference as she answered questions. Folkl, usually unfailingly polite, responded to a question about how it felt to lose this game with an uncharacteristic, "How the hell do you think it feels?"

Nygaard was inconsolable. She couldn't bear to take her jersey off. When the team got back to the hotel, she grabbed teammate Chandra Benton and walked aimlessly in the rain in downtown Cincinnati for hours. At one point, she took off her basketball shoes and flung them in the Mississippi River. The pair walked until 4:00 AM, stopping in a diner for breakfast. They made it back to the hotel just before the team boarded the buses to go home.

Tennessee, a team that had collected 10 losses throughout the season, including a regular-season loss to Stanford, defeated Old Dominion for the national title, which Stanford felt to its bones it should have won. "That's probably the most talented team we've had that did not win a championship," Tucker pointed out. Every member of the starting lineup of that team went on to play in the new WNBA.

"Old Dominion," assistant coach Angela Taylor said. "Even saying the name, I feel it in my body. You have to put that game on a shelf with all of the things you never want to revisit."

"It happens to teams," VanDerveer said of that game 27 years later. "There's an expectation that you are a national championship–quality team, and there is a certain amount of pressure that comes with that. For the kids on that team, that was a really close group. And I wanted it for them because they wanted it so badly. It would have been really fun to win it with that team."

VanDerveer left Cincinnati the next morning to go to her parents' home in Chautauqua to spend time with her father, who was dying of cancer. It provided her some much-needed perspective through the pain of defeat.

But to this day, in the history of the Stanford program, the Old Dominion loss has become a barometer for all of the other tough days. "Was it as bad as Old Dominion?" is always the question after a painful loss. The answer, nearly always, is no.

## CHAPTER 7

# The Harvard Game

**THE MAGIC OF MARCH MADNESS,** the NCAA basketball tournament, lives in the upsets. It lives in the teams that aren't supposed to win—the emergence of a Cinderella story. But being the opposite side of someone else's Cinderella story does not feel like a fairy tale.

Every year since 1998, in the middle of March, the same grainy video of a pre-HDTV sports broadcast has shown up on television screens like clockwork. "Every time it's on, my phone blows up with screenshots," said Milena Flores, who played point guard at Stanford in the 1997–98 season.

The video is from March 14, 1998, and depicts the Harvard women's basketball team rushing the floor and celebrating a historic 71–67 win on Stanford's home court—the first time in the history of the NCAA tournament that a No. 16 seed defeated a No. 1 seed. It is an ignominious distinction. It took two decades for Stanford to have a partner in notoriety. The University of Virginia men's team was knocked off as a No. 1 seed by the 16th-seeded University of Maryland, Baltimore County (UMBC) Retrievers in the 2018 tournament. Yes, UMBC took Stanford partially off the hook, but it felt like much longer than two decades for the Stanford players and coaches whose program was associated with that loss for years.

For a moment that unusual to materialize, unusual things have to take place. The circumstances that led to the March 14, 1998 game—the Harvard Game, as it is known in Stanford history—began seven days earlier on March 7 with a sequence of unfortunate events.

Stanford was closing out its Pac-10 regular-season schedule on a Saturday in Corvallis, Oregon, against the Oregon State Beavers, a team that had won only seven games all season. In contrast, Stanford had been to six Final Fours and won two NCAA titles in the previous eight seasons. Now, with a 20–5 record, Stanford was poised to be a No. 1 seed in the NCAA tournament, which was just a week away.

Stanford had a big lead in the game against the Beavers, but as the minutes wore down, Oregon State closed the gap. Senior forward and team captain Vanessa Nygaard left the bench and went back into the game to stem the Beavers' run. Ball in hand, Nygaard planted her leg and turned her body to deliver a pass. Then she buckled and fell to the floor, letting out a scream. She grabbed her right knee, writhing in pain. Her teammates had to carry her off the floor. Nygaard knew right away it was a significant knee injury, mostly because it was not her first. She had torn the ACL in her other knee in high school. The intense, burning pain was familiar in the worst possible way.

When Nygaard got to the locker room, the only doctor available to assess her was a local veterinarian. Oregon State did not have a physician on-site. Nygaard managed to laugh about that later, but only that. In the moment, she was inconsolable. Even the memory still hurts.

Stanford won the game, but all they felt was loss. The players and coaches boarded their flight back to Palo Alto with Nygaard on crutches. The worry was that Nygaard's injury would derail their championship hopes. She would need to be examined again once the team returned home, but the team needed to pivot immediately to the drama of Selection Sunday, mere hours away.

On Selection Sunday, the NCAA brackets are finalized by the NCAA Selection Committee and then revealed on national television. The NCAA Selection Committee, made up of representatives from conferences across the country, is sequestered for several days in a room in Indianapolis each year and chooses the field of 64 teams that will play for the NCAA championship.

Stanford had already earned an automatic NCAA bid as the Pac-10 regular-season champions. Their seed, however, was up to the discretion of the committee members. And those members were having a hard time figuring out whether Nygaard's injury, and possible absence, should compromise Stanford's seeding. They needed more information about Nygaard's situation to make an informed decision. They only knew what they saw on paper.

Heading into the final weekend of the regular season, Stanford was in line for a No. 1 seed. The committee felt Stanford had the résumé to justify a top seed, with a regular-season record of 21–5.

Coming off the Old Dominion loss in the Final Four six months earlier, the Cardinal had started the season well-stocked with a senior class that had been the top recruiting class in the country when they arrived on the Farm—Nygaard, Olympia Scott, Kristin Folkl, and Heather Owen (Naomi Mulitauaopele, who had averaged 10.2 points and 5.5 rebounds the previous season, had knee surgery in the summer and would have to miss the entire 1997–98 season). Those players comprised the core of a team making a run at the program's third title, and looking to atone for coming up short against Old Dominion the previous spring.

A young backcourt, with three sophomores and two freshmen in the guard spots—none of whom had significant experience—was slow to gel, and the Cardinal dropped its first conference matchup in 48 games with a loss against the University of Arizona in January. On top of all that, Nygaard's injury could threaten to derail an NCAA title quest, and needed to be taken into account.

At NCAA headquarters, there was not a lot of information about Nygaard's diagnosis, her ability to play, or the implications for Stanford. Nygaard was in the hospital getting her MRI, relentlessly hounding the radiology technician to tell her what he saw, to give her a hint about her future, to no avail.

Meanwhile, the chair of the selection committee, Jean Lenti Ponsetto, was on the phone with Stanford's sports information director, Beth Goode, trying to get an answer about Nygaard's status for the tournament while the committee sat in their sequestered space at NCAA headquarters filling out the tournament brackets. Goode didn't have information to give them. Ponsetto said that at the time of Nygaard's injury on Saturday, the NCAA bracket was nearly complete and ready for Sunday's reveal.

By Sunday morning, the calls to Stanford were getting frantic. Ponsetto tried to call VanDerveer, who was out walking her dog. Ultimately, they would not connect before the committee had to make a decision. On Sunday evening, the Stanford players watched the selection show in VanDerveer's living room. Nygaard sat there with her anxious teammates awaiting both the NCAA's announcement and her doctor's call. Stanford would remain a No. 1 seed, Nygaard's injury be damned.

The call from the doctor came just a few minutes after the Cardinal's No. 1 seed was revealed. Nygaard's ACL—the band of tissue that connects your thigh bone to your shinbone—was completely torn. It was the worst-case scenario.

ACL injuries are a common occurrence in women's sports, particularly in sports such as basketball and soccer that include a lot of cutting, stopping, and sudden changes in direction. Research indicates that female athletes are four to six times more likely to suffer an ACL tear during their careers and that as many as 80,000 female high school athletes suffer an ACL tear each year.

The structure of the knee joint in women plays a significant role in putting them at higher risk for ACL tears. Women's joints generally have more looseness and range of motion than men's and also have less muscle mass around the knee, contributing to more instability, which can lead to a ligament tear if the ligament gets overstretched. Many ACL injuries occur without physical contact, and the vast majority of ACL injuries require surgery and a six-to-nine-month rehabilitation time, sometimes longer.

Nygaard's initial reaction to the news about her second career ACL tear was not grounded in reality. She'd played the game since the second grade, she thought, and her career wasn't going to end like this. "I'm playing anyway. I'm getting a brace and I'm playing," Nygaard insisted. Former Stanford quarterback and NFL star John Elway had once played on a torn ACL, she pleaded. The doctor said no. Nygaard asked to sign a release saying that she would play against medical advice. Again, no. Nygaard asked for a brace, and they appeased her. "They all knew there was no way I was playing," Nygaard said. "They were humoring me with the brace."

Still, when Nygaard joined VanDerveer on a media call moments after the NCAA bracket reveal, she was asked about her injury, and much to the surprise of her head coach, she declared she would play.

VanDerveer knew better—she knew she would be preparing for the start of the NCAA tournament in six days without her team's emotional leader and best three-point shooter.

On the other side of the country, Harvard's coaches and players saw their name come up on the screen in the bracket with Stanford, and they were not happy. They were a No. 16 seed for the third year in a row, and the Crimson, who had a 21–5 record for the season, felt strongly they were significantly better than the lowest seed in the bracket, particularly at the end of a season when their star forward, Allison Feaster, was leading the nation in scoring, averaging more than 28 points per game. The chip on their shoulder was quickly forming.

On Tuesday, two days after Selection Sunday, Stanford returned to practice to prepare a game plan—which would not include Nygaard—against Harvard, a matchup that would take place on their home court on Saturday night.

Practice had just started, and the team was running a standard five-player weave drill. It was what Folkl—the team's leading scorer and rebounder heading into the tournament—described as a "five down, three-on-two back." Folkl filled the lane on the right side, cut to the three-point line, took the ball, and made one dribble to go in for the layup. She landed on a teammate's left foot, which Folkl described as "the most normal amount of contact ever." Her ankle rolled and her knee popped. Another awful scream echoed through the gym. It was the most intense pain Folkl had ever felt. She thought she might throw up. VanDerveer's first thought was, *This is a nightmare.*

Point guard Milena Flores heard a buzzing sound in her ears. Nygaard sat on a chair, gripping her crutches, watching in disbelief as Folkl, who had never had a significant injury during her two-sport college career, was carried to the training room the same way she had been only three days before. VanDerveer immediately ended practice. Only a few players stayed behind in the stunned silence of Maples Pavilion, working on their free throws.

A reporter from the *St. Louis Post-Dispatch*, Folkl's hometown paper, was sitting in the bleachers—there to cover the local girl bound for the WNBA—and watched the whole thing happen. It was only a matter of time before the news of the latest Stanford injury broke.

Folkl sat on a table in the training room, sobbing as the doctor on-site grabbed her leg, moved it back and forth, and pronounced, "Yep, your knee is shot. There's nothing there," referring to her ACL. Folkl's college career was over in a moment. Her mind raced as she lay on the table while the doctor made arrangements to take her to the hospital. She was supposed to play in the NCAA tournament, graduate, and prepare for the WNBA. Now what?

In 72 hours, Stanford's season had come crashing down. The Cardinal struggled to gather themselves. Players who had watched their teammates go down were suddenly very aware of playing not to get hurt. VanDerveer was running noncontact practices in the lead-up to the Harvard game. The Cardinal couldn't afford any more injuries. The team's enthusiasm about the NCAA tournament—which was supposed to redeem them after the previous year's Old Dominion loss—had vanished.

VanDerveer knew she would need to rely heavily on senior center Olympia Scott—so much so that she penned a four-page handwritten letter to Scott, which the forward summed up concisely: "You have to put this team on your back." Scott said, "I was already thinking like that anyway. This was the year our senior class was supposed to come in and win it all. All of a sudden, we lost three seniors [in Mulitauaopele, Nygaard, and Folkl], and the gap between who we thought we would go into the tournament with and the younger players who were going to have to step up, but were much less experienced, was big."

That VanDerveer would send that letter showed what a long way their relationship had come since she recruited Scott out of Los Angeles four years before. Scott had been a closed book for much of her recruitment, not giving VanDerveer much more than short answers when she tried to engage. The coaches took turns calling Scott to see if one of them could get her to open up. No one succeeded. "It was a little painful," assistant coach Amy Tucker said. "She was very reserved—stoic, even."

VanDerveer did not know where she stood, even when, at the end of her campus visit, Scott told her she was coming to Stanford. VanDerveer stopped her and said, "I don't feel like I know you very well." Scott told her she had made intentional choices not to get close to any of the coaches who were recruiting her, because she didn't want those feelings to influence her choice. She kept everyone at arm's length until she made her choice.

"She was a kid who did not need a lot of attention," said Tucker. "She was self-sufficient from the get-go. She played really hard the first day of practice and then walked up to Tara and said, 'What do I need to do to start?'" VanDerveer gave her some ball-handling drills and sent her on her way. Scott earned VanDerveer's trust and went on to start all four years at Stanford.

Across the country, at Harvard, Stanford's injury news was greeted with something of a shrug. "We all have injuries," said Harvard coach Kathy Delaney-Smith. "I don't remember feeling happy or sad for them. To be honest, I would have taken the last five players on their team."

Two days before the game, Harvard arrived in California and headed to campus for their designated practice session on Stanford's home floor. VanDerveer ran into Delaney-Smith in the parking lot as she was heading home for the day and began to tell her about the injuries. Delaney-Smith couldn't muster up any sympathy.

On game day—a week to the day after Nygaard's injury at Oregon State—the Harvard players made their way into the Stanford visitors' locker room, and the locker room attendant said, "Welcome to the world of real basketball." That comment stuck with the Crimson, playing in their first nationally televised game, for the rest of the evening.

In the home locker room, Nygaard dressed in her uniform and went to the bench during warm-ups with a brace on. "In my stupid mind, I was going to play," Nygaard said.

When the ball went up at tip-off in front of a packed and tense Maples Pavilion, the Harvard game plan quickly became obvious. The Crimson would triple-team Scott, every time she touched the ball. "Everyone else was going to have to beat us," said Harvard guard Suzie Miller.

In the meantime, Feaster began to dominate, and Harvard quickly ran out to an 18–7 lead that stunned the sold-out crowd at Maples Pavilion who tried to inspire the Cardinal with their nervous energy. It was so loud that Delaney-Smith had to hold up flash cards to call plays.

Without Folkl and Nygaard on the floor, VanDerveer started freshman forward Sarah Dimson in an attempt to slow down Feaster, a move that didn't work well. Scott also struggled with Feaster when VanDerveer made the defensive switch to see if size would make a difference. No matter what they tried, Stanford struggled to defend Feaster's size and couldn't find the right matchup to shut her down. And the Cardinal couldn't shoot Harvard out of its zone. At halftime, Harvard led by nine points.

"We weren't our normal selves. I remember pushing and playing my hardest, but we [couldn't] just manufacture a new identity out of nowhere," Scott said. "As much as I tried to put the team on my back, the team [wasn't] used to being 100 percent on my back. We weren't set up for that, whereas Harvard was set up for Feaster, and they were doing what they did."

The Cardinal found the fight to get back into the game. With 3:58 to go, Stanford had rallied back to within three points, trailing 65–62.

Scott battled to keep up the energy through a grinding comeback. "I was a believer until the end," Scott said. "It's a team game, and we were really good at playing together [before the injuries]. When players went down, we just weren't together. At that moment, we were so young and inexperienced."

Nygaard and Folkl sat at the end of the bench with their crutches and braces, feeling helpless. "I remember thinking, *We're gonna turn it around. It will be OK,*" Folkl said.

The two teams traded the lead until a crucial Feaster steal manifested a huge shot in the corner for Suzie Miller with 46 seconds to go. Miller buried the three-pointer, sealing the win for the Crimson and sealing Stanford's fate as the first No. 1 seed to exit in the first round of the NCAA tournament. Feaster finished the game with 35 points and 13 rebounds. Stanford, which came into the tournament as the nation's best shooting team at nearly 53 percent, shot just 33.3 percent from the floor and were outrebounded by the Crimson. What was supposed to be a redemptive title run for the Cardinal was over after just one miserable game.

Delaney-Smith compared the joy she felt about her team's upset to how she felt on her wedding day. She asked ESPN analyst and basketball legend Ann Meyers-Drysdale not to let her say anything embarrassing on TV in the postgame interview.

In the minutes after the game, as a disappointed crowd quietly filed out of Maples Pavilion, the Stanford players looked shocked.

Scott called it a "cloud of devastation." Flores felt embarrassed, as if they'd damaged the legacy of the program. "You go to Stanford to be a part of great teams every year—that was the expectation," Flores said. "You feel like you've let down the entire program, your teammates. We did not play well. That is not to take anything away from Harvard, because they played a fantastic game."

In the aftermath of the loss, which also ended a 59-game home winning streak that dated back five years for the Cardinal, there was a lot of grief. Folkl said she worried that people were "freaking out" and that some players might quit the team. "It was so depressing. It felt that bad," Folkl said.

Meanwhile, the NCAA tournament went on without Stanford. Two days later, Harvard returned to Stanford's home floor and lost to Arkansas. The NCAA had chosen Oakland as a regional site for the Sweet 16 and Elite Eight rounds, clearly hoping that the presence of a top-seeded Stanford team would be a big draw for ticket sales and media attention from Bay Area fans. Instead, Bay Area fans watched Arkansas, Duke, Florida, and Kansas. The Razorbacks earned their first trip to the Final Four out of Oakland. Arkansas coach Gary Blair joked that his team "ruined the Oakland region" by succeeding once the Cardinal were unexpectedly knocked out.

Nygaard didn't sleep well for weeks after the Harvard game, even after the rest of the country had moved on from the college basketball season. "It was the end of my career, and there was no shot of redemption for me," Nygaard said.

Scott found a way to be philosophical about it, saying, "It just wasn't meant to be us."

Scott, Folkl, and Nygaard, once they had graduated with their Stanford degrees, all went on to play in the WNBA. Folkl played for four years with the Minnesota Lynx and the Portland Fire. Nygaard played six WNBA seasons, became one of California's most successful high school girls' basketball coaches, and spent one and a half seasons as head coach of the WNBA's Phoenix Mercury. Scott played in the WNBA from 1998 to 2007, with Utah, Detroit, Indiana, Charlotte, Sacramento, and Phoenix. She became the first player in WNBA history to win WNBA titles with two different teams—Sacramento and Phoenix.

Feaster, still the greatest women's player the Ivy League has ever produced, played a decade in the WNBA and is now the vice president of team operations and organizational growth for the Boston Celtics.

Flores went on to coach at both Princeton and Yale, and every season when those Ivy League teams played Harvard, she had to walk past a trophy case that included photos of that awful night at Stanford.

Miller, who hit the game-winning shot for Harvard, was interviewing for her residency in emergency medicine at Stanford when one of her interviewers brought it up. He was at the game. She still got the job.

VanDerveer moved on from the experience as well. And she wouldn't mind if everyone else did too. It remains a sore spot. She said the loss of that game wasn't even close to the most painful loss that she experienced at Stanford. "It was the loss of the players. I don't think [Harvard was] a 16-seed, and we weren't a 1-seed. The seeds were wrong. They were a very good team—they had a great player, an excellent coach, and I think it was the perfect storm." Still, she's never watched the tape. No point in remembering that brutal week. It wouldn't change anything.

"You've got to play the game—you don't go into a game with a No. 1 seed and get a 20-point head start," VanDerveer said. "You've got to come out, play the whole game, and you've got to play really well."

But the loss transformed the way VanDerveer looked at her team's postseason prospects. Seeds suddenly didn't matter as much. Where Stanford played didn't matter. The health of her players mattered most of all. "All that matters this time of year is that our team is healthy," VanDerveer said year after year when she went to the podium to discuss her team's NCAA prospects.

It's a thing that a lot of coaches will say. VanDerveer and the Cardinal experienced it in a way that has seared it into the program's history and its philosophy to this day. "They weren't talking a lot about mental health back then—maybe a little bit," Nygaard said. "But I think that experience cemented that Tara doesn't think about her players as pieces of a puzzle but as people. I mean, I'm almost 50 years old, and she is still sending me birthday cards."

Folkl will always remember the Harvard loss as a far more complicated situation than has ever been portrayed in those grainy media clips that seem to show up every year in March. Just back in 2023, ESPN displayed the record of No. 1 seeds in the first round of the women's tournament—335–1. And an unforgettable one it was, even if none of the players on the current roster were even born when it happened. "They can never tell the whole story in those 10 seconds they show on TV," Folkl said.

## CHAPTER 8

# The Drought

**IF THE 1997 LOSS TO OLD DOMINION** by a team built for a championship was the equivalent of a high-impact crash, and the 1998 historic first-round loss to Harvard was a very loud thud, what came next for the Cardinal was most troubling of all—a period of time when the program turned into background noise.

Between 1997 and 2008, there were no Final Four trips for Stanford. While Connecticut and Tennessee took turns dominating the women's game over that decade, and while programs such as Baylor and Notre Dame ascended, VanDerveer's Stanford program played catch-up.

VanDerveer had come to Stanford in 1985 to build a program. Two years after her Olympic break, she needed to rebuild it. The 1996 Olympic team spawned two professional leagues and inspired new levels of interest in women's basketball, but the Cardinal program paid a price for the sacrifice of their head coach. Partially because of a loaded roster, and also because of VanDerveer's absence, Stanford did not sign a single recruit in the fall of 1995, and for a year, VanDerveer— who was officially not considered

Stanford's head coach because of her position with Team USA—could have no contact with the country's best high school players. Not only was she unable to communicate with potential Stanford recruits, she was not allowed to be involved in the scouting and recruiting of the 1996 recruiting class.

By the start of the 1998 season—following the pain and embarrassment of the Harvard loss—those gaps became more apparent. The Cardinal didn't have the kind of leadership on the floor they needed to guide them into a new era.

Stanford opened the 1998–99 season with a 2–5 record, dropping out of the national rankings for the first time in 12 years. It was the first time Stanford had lost five of its first seven games since VanDerveer had arrived on the Farm. The incoming freshmen classes of 1995, 1996, and 1997 included just one elite-rated recruit—center Carolyn Moos. VanDerveer lost out on a top recruit, Stephanie White, who ended up at Purdue. And the crowd sizes at Maples were tapering. "I think [the Olympic break] hurt our program at Stanford," VanDerveer said.

To highlight the Cardinal's downturn further, several years earlier, the NCAA had chosen nearby San Jose as the site for the 1999 Women's Final Four, hoping to capitalize on the Bay Area's interest in the women's game, largely driven by Stanford's success. That put even more pressure on a program that wasn't, at that moment, playing up to the level that would get them there.

The Cardinal went 18–12 in the 1998–99 season—the season following the Harvard upset—the most losses the program had recorded since the first two years of VanDerveer's tenure. They finished third in the Pac-10 standings, and the season ended for the second year in a row with a first-round NCAA tournament loss, this time to Maine. Stephanie White, the player VanDerveer had tried and failed to convince to come to Stanford, led Purdue to a national title in San Jose that season.

The women's basketball landscape was changing, and the number of schools landing the top players in the country was beginning to increase. Purdue won the 1999 title against Duke, a team with a similar academic profile to Stanford that was beginning to rise under head coach Gail Goestenkors. The Blue Devils reached the Final Four three times between 1999 and 2003. Notre Dame, another strong academic school capable of landing the nation's top student-athletes, was becoming a national factor under head coach Muffet McGraw, winning the 2001 NCAA championship. Oklahoma, the school whose program briefly ended during the 1990 Final Four, reached the national championship game in 2002.

"I think at Duke and Notre Dame, they saw us get really good in the early '90s and thought, *Why can't we do that?*" said Stanford assistant coach Amy Tucker. "We are a similar profile, and even though our admissions requirements were stricter, I don't think recruits really understood that. And I think those schools started investing more in their programs."

Stanford felt the impact most acutely with East Coast and Midwestern recruits. Those areas of the country had been "fertile ground" for Stanford for a long time, Tucker said. "Now those kids had an option to stay close to home and be on really good teams," Tucker said.

The University of Connecticut had become the program of choice for the nation's top recruits as the Huskies won three straight titles from 2002 to 2005 with players such as Diana Taurasi and Sue Bird, the latter of whom VanDerveer worked hard to recruit. Stanford was one of Bird's final three choices, along with UConn and Vanderbilt. When two point guards announced their commitment to Connecticut, Bird, a New York native, hesitated to accept the Huskies' scholarship offer. But when one of those guards withdrew her commitment, Bird was bound for UConn.

Losing a player of Bird's caliber was particularly painful at Stanford because the program's most glaring needs were in the backcourt, a place where Stanford had excelled over the previous decade with star guards such as Jennifer Azzi, Sonja Henning, Molly Goodenbour, Kate Paye, and Jamila Wideman.

In the absence of All-American-caliber floor leadership, the Cardinal finished 40–20 over the 1999–2000 and 2000–01 seasons with a pair of second-round losses in the NCAA tournament. "It's too easy to say that because Tara was gone for a year in 1996 that we got so far behind," Amy Tucker said. "There was a lot more to it. There were some kids we couldn't get into school, and our margins are so thin that you can't manufacture backup plans if you don't get them in. There were others we recruited who didn't turn out to be quite what we hoped they would be. There was no back door to get into Stanford. We didn't get to make the decisions about who came in. Everyone had to go through the front door with admissions, and we were at the mercy of that."

It was the arrival of a unique talent in guard/forward Nicole Powell that began to turn Stanford back toward its place among the national elite. Powell arrived at the start of the 2000–01 season, and VanDerveer immediately asked the 6'3" Arizona product to bring the ball up the floor as a point guard. Powell was nicknamed Magic by the players on the Stanford men's basketball team for her blend of size, agility, and ball-handling. Her skill set was "not like any player we've ever had here," VanDerveer said. Powell was a precursor to the style of "positionless" basketball that is much more a part of the current game at the college and pro levels.

Powell was regarded as the best girls' basketball player ever to come out of the state of Arizona. And she had been walking around wearing a Stanford hat since the sixth grade. "That's never a real good sign for us," said Arizona State coach Charli Turner Thorne at the time, who actively recruited Powell as well. Powell was also recruited by Duke, Notre Dame, Tennessee, Vanderbilt, and Kansas.

In high school, Powell played center. After initially moving her from the post to the wing, by the start of the Pac-10 season, VanDerveer was asking her to play point guard. She shifted out of necessity. Jamie Carey, a highly rated guard recruit out of Colorado, had her career cut short by concussions. Susan King, the point guard from Minnesota, had endured a season-ending knee injury on a road trip to Oklahoma. Powell was the best option in every way.

Powell earned the first triple-double of her career as a freshman against Washington State. By the end of her first season, she ranked in the top 10 in 8 of the Pac-10's 12 statistical categories, and she was a front-runner for the Conference Player of the Year. "I know I've been put into a new position, but I feel like a lot of excuses have been made for me—things like, 'She's good for a freshman' or 'She's never played point guard before.' I don't want to hear that anymore," Powell said.

Powell's stellar play salved the wound caused by the loss of Carey. Carey had been a standout in her freshman season at point guard. She was named the Pac-10 Freshman of the Year, averaging 11 points per game. She set the school freshman record for three-pointers in a season. So it was devastating—for the team and Carey—when her concussions ended her playing days at Stanford.

Carey sustained her first concussion in seventh grade. She estimated she had "a few more" in high school. At the start of her sophomore season at Stanford, Carey sustained another, hitting her head on a teammate's leg during practice. This time, the symptoms were severe, they lingered, and they were alarming. The dizziness, headaches, and memory loss not only sidelined her from playing basketball but impacted her ability to go to class, sometimes even to get out of bed. She lost track of her car in a parking lot and sometimes couldn't remember whether she'd paid for something at a store.

Concerned about the risk of future injury and potential permanent brain damage, Stanford doctors refused to clear her to play. "Those were the hardest words to hear. My heart went straight into my stomach," Carey said. "As soon as I got into the elevator [at the doctor's office], I cried."

Carey sat at a table in front of a gathering of media to announce her "retirement" from basketball. Her teammates stood in the back of the press conference and cried. What the world outside of her team didn't know that day, and Carey wouldn't reveal publicly until years later, was that as she suffered with her concussion symptoms in California, her older brother Josh had died by suicide while away at college.

Carey's devastating situation took its toll on the entire team, and Powell's arrival brightened the Cardinal's morale and their prospects. In Powell's sophomore season in 2001–02—on a roster that also included a bevy of highly rated recruits, including New Jersey's Kelley Suminski and Oregon's Lindsey Yamasaki—the Cardinal won 30 games, earned a No. 2 seed, and got past the first weekend of the NCAA tournament for the first time since 1997, advancing to the Sweet 16 before falling in an upset loss to Colorado in Boise, Idaho.

The Stanford comeback felt like it was beginning in earnest. For Stanford athletic director Ted Leland, he never looked at the early NCAA exits or the double-digit-loss seasons as "failures." He said, "We were still close to the top of the Pac-10, we were getting into the NCAA tournament every year, and our kids were graduating. Tara was so darn competitive, and maybe she looked at those seasons as disappointing. But I never judged the program by how far they went into the tournament or the national ranking. We had tough, tough admissions requirements, but we had great coaches and we were getting great players. As far as I was concerned, we were a successful program."

The 2001–02 season was also noteworthy for the start of the Pac-10 postseason tournament. The first tournament was held in Eugene, Oregon, at the University of Oregon's McArthur Court (known as Mac Court). VanDerveer was not a fan, even though other conferences were already holding postseason tournaments. Subjecting her team to three games over three days in a tournament format to compete for a tournament title (and an automatic NCAA bid) seemed risky at the cusp of the NCAA tournament. It felt to VanDerveer like a good way to get someone hurt. And she worried that the Pac-10—already viewed as "Stanford and everyone else"—would pay a price in NCAA seeding and placements for tacking on a postseason tournament in which every team in the field would go into the NCAA consideration process with a loss except for the team that won the conference tournament.

The Cardinal, playing without leading scorer Lindsey Yamasaki, who'd had an emergency appendectomy days before the first Pac-10 tournament began, lost that first conference tournament in Eugene to Arizona State despite winning the regular-season title with an 18–0 record. But the Cardinal would go on to win 15 Pac-10 tournament titles in the 23-year history of the tournament. Still, VanDerveer never really warmed up to the format.

The Stanford resurrection continued. A second-round loss against Minnesota in the 2003 NCAA tournament at Maples Pavilion felt like a short-term setback for the program, but instead proved to be a huge motivator with Powell's senior season looming.

Riding Powell's All-American talent, the Cardinal took a 27–6 record, and another Pac-10 title, into the 2004 NCAA tournament, where they reached the Elite Eight in Norman, Oklahoma, against a familiar foe—the Tennessee Lady Vols. It was a back-and-forth contest in which Powell dominated the proceedings, trying to will her team to a Final Four berth. But the three-point attempts that were the bread and butter of the Cardinal's most successful teams wouldn't fall. Stanford finished 3 of 16 from beyond the arc, all by Powell. And the Cardinal, the best free throw–shooting team in the nation that season, attempted only three free throws in that game. Powell's contested three-point heave at the buzzer banged off the rim as her incredible college career ended with Stanford's 62–60 loss to Tennessee. Powell scored 31 points with 10 rebounds in the game, the only Cardinal player in double figures.

Still, Powell's presence on the Stanford roster reopened a recruiting door for Stanford. The 2004–05 season, the first in the post-Powell era, marked the arrival of the program's first transfer, sophomore Brooke Smith. Smith was a Marin County product who had been a McDonald's All-American in high school, who came to Stanford from Duke after playing one season with the Blue Devils in 2002–03. Undergraduate transfers were rare for Stanford admissions, much less its athletic teams. Smith had initially chosen Duke over Stanford when making her final decision, a choice she reconsidered after her first season in Durham, North Carolina.

Smith said she had viewed Stanford as "the easy choice because it was close to home." She thought that being across the country was a challenge she needed. But she averaged only 9.3 minutes per game as a freshman at Duke, and she was homesick. Even her mother spending a week at a time with her in Durham didn't blunt the feeling that she'd made a mistake.

She reached out to VanDerveer about coming to Stanford, and VanDerveer went straight to admissions, which said yes. Per NCAA rules, Smith sat out a season before making her Stanford debut in 2004.

Brooke with the Hook became an immediate contributor, a traditional post with size, strong footwork, and a lethal hook shot that would become her trademark. The 2004–05 season also marked the arrival of the nation's No. 1 recruit in guard Candice Wiggins from San Diego, who would become one of the most decorated players in program history.

Over the next two seasons, with Smith and Wiggins anchoring the team from both the post and the backcourt, Stanford twice made a run at the Final Four, only to fall just short. The 2004–05 season ended with a 76–69 loss to Michigan State in Kansas City, the Spartans a team that had never made it past the second round in five previous tournament appearances.

The 2005–06 season included another long NCAA tournament run in which Stanford faced Oklahoma and its record-setting star Courtney Paris in the regional semifinal, the winner to face LSU in the Elite Eight. Smith outdueled Paris in the regional semi matchup, going 14 of 16 from the field with a career-high 35 points. Stanford guard Krista Rappahahn finished with 15 points, all on three-pointers, and the Cardinal bested Oklahoma and looked primed for a long-awaited breakthrough.

LSU, a team anchored by future Hall of Famers Seimone Augustus and Sylvia Fowles, awaited Stanford in the regional final. Augustus capped a back-and-forth game by taking a game-saving charge on Wiggins with 4.8 seconds to go to lift the Tigers past Stanford 62–59, a call that rankles VanDerveer to this day. At the point of contact, Wiggins passed the ball to Rappahahn, who drained what would have been a game-tying three-pointer when the offensive foul was called. "It was a horrible call," VanDerveer said. "It was a disappointing way to lose."

It was yet another year when the Cardinal failed to get over the hump. Making three straight trips to the verge of a Final Four before falling short in the Elite Eight was a tough pill to swallow after all the work that the Cardinal—and VanDerveer—had put into getting the program back on track. "In the back of your mind, you wonder whether we will ever get back to a Final Four again, whether we will be in a position to win a national championship again," Tucker said. "You can't help but think about it."

VanDerveer and her coaches couldn't help but hear the chatter that Stanford was "falling off the map." But Stanford's new athletic director, Bob Bowlsby—who came to Palo Alto from the University of Iowa—didn't buy it. Bowlsby became Stanford's athletic director in 2006 and said he never hesitated to re-sign VanDerveer to a quick contract extension. He admitted that the first conversation with the "iconic" head coach was an interesting one. "I think, at that time, she was wondering how long she was going to continue doing it," Bowlsby said. "I don't think she was playing games with me when she said, 'I don't know how long I'll be here.' I think she was generally questioning whether she wanted to do it over the long haul. Nobody loves Stanford more than Tara. But I think she was probably face-to-face with the reality that it's just harder at Stanford. I didn't want her to go anywhere. I saw the players we had coming in, and I knew we were going to get really good pretty fast."

Bowlsby convinced VanDerveer to sign a contract extension, and she went back to work—hard work. "It's disappointing to lose some of those games, because you are so close. Sometimes there's a little luck involved," VanDerveer said. "We kept knocking at the door, and at some point, we were going to push through."

The knocking was getting louder and louder.

## Chapter 9

# The Return

**IN 2008, ON A RAINY,** chilly early spring night in Spokane, Washington, Candice Wiggins dribbled off the final 10 seconds of the clock, her eyes and smile wide. When the horn sounded, the dam broke. Stanford players poured onto the court in a joyous dogpile, where Wiggins lay with her hands over her face, sobbing. Tara VanDerveer pumped her first into the crowd, her glasses fogging up from the tears in her eyes. After 11 years and 349 games of frustration, disappointment, and "almost there," the wait was over—Stanford ended their Final Four drought with a 98–87 win over No. 1 seed Maryland.

The postgame interview Wiggins gave that night circulated widely, going viral before that was even a thing. "I'm so happy," Wiggins said, crying happy tears in her postgame interview. "I just love this team and I love Tara and I love Stanford. I can't believe this is happening . . . I'm sorry, America." No apologies necessary, Candice.

Wiggins had scored 41 points against the Terrapins, and as a result, she and her teammates had broken the spell. Stanford was returning to the Final Four. After three straight trips to the Elite Eight in four seasons, the Cardinal had busted through the barrier. Wiggins admitted to feeling the pressure that night—for the program, for VanDerveer, and for her own future WNBA prospects.

Wiggins, who led her high school team, La Jolla Country Day School in San Diego, to a pair of California state titles, came to Stanford on the heels of Nicole Powell, the game-changing three-time All-American. Her impact for Stanford was immediate, and her personal story was riveting.

Her father, Alan Wiggins, was a second baseman and leadoff hitter for the San Diego Padres team that played in the 1984 World Series, and he set a club record with 70 stolen bases. He died in 1991 at age 32 from complications of AIDS after years of drug addiction, the first known Major League Baseball player to succumb to the disease. Candice was only four years old when he passed, and her memories of him were hazy. She called him a "mythical figure" in her life.

She was asked about him multiple times each season throughout her college career. On the surface, she appeared to handle it all with grace, but inside it burned. She thought she was being judged. She had to prove she was worthy of her own attention, which she always was. As a six-year-old, she scored 30 points in a game against third and fourth graders. By the fifth grade, she was playing on boys' teams to keep a competitive pace. In seventh grade, she played on the same Amateur Athletic Union (AAU) team as her brother Alan. She started, and he came off the bench.

At 5'11", she was lithe and agile and aggressive. She was a skilled driver and three-point shooter. She was an energy boost every second she was on the floor. VanDerveer saw a player who exuded "electricity"—an exuberant, fist-pumping, high-jumping bundle of constant motion and emotion. "She was the type of player who would make other people better because they would see how hard she was going," VanDerveer said.

Wiggins had first impressed VanDerveer as a high schooler at Stanford's annual youth basketball summer camp. "She did drills all day with the campers, and no one could guard her," VanDerveer said. "And at night, after a full day at camp, she would play with the counselors, and no one could guard her in those games either. She was incredible."

Wiggins got chills the first time she put on a Stanford uniform. As a freshman, she and her Stanford teammates would scrimmage at practice, red jerseys versus white jerseys. Wiggins was on the white team, stealing passes, grabbing rebounds, hitting shots. The white jerseys were winning handily. VanDerveer blew the whistle and switched Wiggins to the red team. Wiggins huddled up her teammates. "She said, 'All right, now let's take care of the ball,' when she was the one who had been stealing it from them the whole time," VanDerveer said. "And now the red team won. That's Candice."

Wiggins, who later admitted that her father's death brought periods of "darkness" into her life, was shaped by her Stanford experience in every way—the competition on the floor, the competition in the classroom, the expectations of VanDerveer, with whom she developed a close player-coach relationship. "Stanford was a place where I could thrive and prosper, and I credit Tara for that," Wiggins said. "She was instrumental in the person I became. I became a good person. I liked who I was as a teammate, who I was as a player, even who I was as a student. . . . When I was playing, you could see how happy I was, which was really a result of the environment I was in."

Four years after Wiggins's arrival at Stanford, and led by her relentless excellence, the 2008 Stanford team was well-built for where it was headed—a shot at the national championship. But as

VanDerveer knew too well, that doesn't always mean that you get there. "Sometimes things just have to be right," VanDerveer said. "There are no guarantees."

In addition to Wiggins, the program's one and only four-time All-American, the Cardinal had a formidable interior presence with Jayne Appel, a Bay Area native, and one of the top recruits in the country, and Kayla Pedersen, a freshman from Arizona who went straight into the starting lineup and never left for four years. Jillian Harmon, from Lake Oswego, Oregon, was the starting small forward, a heart-and-hustle player who will forever be considered one of the best "glue" players in program history.

Wiggins was complemented at guard by another Oregon product, JJ Hones, as well as Rosalyn Gold-Onwude, the Queens, New York, native whose mother, Pat, was VanDerveer's first college roommate at SUNY Albany. Gold-Onwude was both a defensive star and a three-point shooter, who had her share of battles of will with the head coach.

Stanford had it all—stellar guard play led by Wiggins, dominance inside with Appel and Pedersen, and all of the requisite supporting pieces. This was the team VanDerveer would take to Tampa to compete in the program's first Final Four in more than a decade.

Plus, the Cardinal could draw from the previous season's sting of defeat. In March 2007, with a roster anchored by four seniors—Brooke Smith, Kristen Newlin, Clare Bodensteiner, and Markisha Coleman—Stanford exited the NCAA tournament in a 68–61 second-round loss to Florida State on their home floor. "That was devastating," Jayne Appel said.

As spring practice began after that loss, the 10 returning Cardinal players were stinging, and VanDerveer wanted to make sure they felt it acutely. "We did a lot of running, and Tara would run with us and say, 'Don't let me catch you,'" Appel said. "We would run laps around the football practice field, and we just kept running. At one point, she told us to go for a jog around campus, and we should stop when she found us. We ran all over campus, and you couldn't stop because you didn't want her to find you and you weren't running. . . . It was a culture shift of hard work and how much harder we had to work to get to that next level."

It was also the season when former point guard Kate Paye joined the staff. Paye had WNBA experience as a player, and it showed. In the Cardinal's first practice of the 2007–08 season, guard Melanie Murphy swung into the key to drive to the basket, and Paye, playing defense, moved in to take the charge. The coach ended up with a bloody nose. Everyone stopped. After wiping her nose, Paye said, "C'mon, let's keep going."

"I thought, *Oh, boy*," Appel said. "It was like turning on the jets on a whole culture change."

VanDerveer brought in leaders from across campus—professors and heads of industry—and other coaches to talk to her team. The topic was always team chemistry. The sense of urgency was palpable. "We didn't want to feel like we felt against Florida State ever again," Appel said.

Stanford was ranked No. 7 to start the 2007–08 season. Measuring-stick games came early, such as a tough 60–58 win on the road against Rutgers in the second game, a win sealed by a pair of free throws by Wiggins with a tenth of a second on the clock. Wiggins finished with 19 points. Appel and Pedersen each had double-doubles.

It took double overtime to beat an unranked Utah team in Salt Lake City before the team headed to the Virgin Islands to take on No. 2 Connecticut in a Thanksgiving Day game, the first time the two programs had played outside of the NCAA tournament since

1997. With freshman sensation Maya Moore on the Huskies' roster, Connecticut won 66–54, handing the Cardinal their first loss of the season.

The week before the holiday break, which usually followed Stanford's final exam break every season, the Cardinal notched two defining wins—an 87–63 win over No. 10 Baylor followed by a 73–69 overtime win over No. 1 Tennessee in front of a packed and raucous Maples Pavilion. The latter was a duel with national attention, a matchup between Candice Wiggins and Tennessee superstar Candace Parker. Ice and Ace. Gold-Onwude scored 9 of Stanford's 10 overtime points, and Wiggins hit a key free throw with 28.6 seconds to go to seal the win. "I just want to say one thing," VanDerveer declared after the game. "Tonight, *Candice* is spelled with an *i*." It was Stanford's first win over Tennessee since 1996, and it affirmed what the Cardinal already knew: this was a team that could play for the title. But there was still a long way to go.

Road losses in early January in Los Angeles to USC and UCLA at the start of the Pac-10 schedule were quickly remedied by a run of 18 straight Pac-10 wins, including the Pac-10 tournament title.

Stanford received a No. 2 seed in the NCAA tournament, the losses in Los Angeles costing them a chance to be a No. 1. As always, VanDerveer dismissed the "diss" of a No. 2 seed and said nothing was more important than taking a healthy team into the postseason.

After defeating Cleveland State to open the NCAA tournament at home, next up was the second-round game that loomed so large after the previous season's second-round stumble. In Wiggins' final home game at Stanford, she tied a school record with 44 points, leaving no doubt that the Cardinal were moving past the previous year's disappointment with an 88–54 second-round win over UTEP. Her 44-point game ranked as the third-most points scored by a single player in NCAA tournament history.

The Cardinal traveled to Spokane for the regional, facing Pittsburgh in the Sweet 16, a game they ground out to win 72–53. Appel led the way with 22 points, with Pedersen adding 10 points and 15 rebounds in a game where rebounding proved huge. Stanford finished with a 54–30 rebounding edge, grabbing 37 of the first 57 rebounds in the game.

The trip to Spokane had already been memorable thanks to a celebrity sighting in the team hotel. Cuba Gooding Jr. and Christian Slater were in town filming a movie titled *Lies and Illusions*. Gold-Onwude went to McDonald's and brought a fish sandwich back for Gooding. But the best memory was still to come.

Stanford faced a titanic matchup with Maryland in the regional final, widely viewed as the toughest game to win in an NCAA tournament run because of the stakes. Maryland, coming off their program's first national championship the previous season, was loaded with size and experience, including All-Americans Crystal Langhorne, Marissa Coleman, and point guard Kristi Toliver.

Wiggins led the "underdog" Cardinal from the start. Stanford led by 10 at the half, shooting 61.3 percent from the floor and sinking eight three-pointers. The offensive barrage continued in the second half, Stanford putting up its season-high in points in the biggest game of the season.

VanDerveer focused her defensive game plan on slowing Langhorne, greeting her every touch with a double-team—another example of her long-standing and highly effective strategy of limiting the impact of the team's best player. Langhorne scored 13 points on 4-of-6 shooting. She only got off six shots—mission accomplished. In the meantime, Stanford's offense ran through Appel who, while scoring only 11 points, dished the ball out to Wiggins and Hones and Pedersen.

Wiggins finished the game by becoming the first player in NCAA tournament history to score at least 40 points in back-to-back games. Her line: 10-of-22 shooting, five three-pointers, and 16 of 19 free throws. Sophomore guard JJ Hones added a career-high 23 points, with Pedersen adding 15 points, 7 assists, and 6 rebounds.

"Growing up on the West Coast, a lot of us know what a great institution Stanford is, what a power it is in basketball," Wiggins said after the game. "We wear that with so much pride, and we did have [returning to the Final Four] as our mission. Especially in my last year."

After cutting down the nets, the players and coaches went back to the locker room, sat in a circle, and held hands. They were going to the Final Four. In fact, Stanford's return to the Final Four in 2008 was the first time any NCAA team west of Texas had competed in the sport's biggest showcase since the last time the Cardinal had done it back in 1997.

The Final Four trip to Tampa was a "sweet" experience, Appel remembered. "Tara talked about what it would be like because she'd been there before," Appel said. "But to have our families there, and to have so many of the alumni come, and we had a big ice cream social; it was an experience like no other." Appel also has another lasting memory of that trip. "Every time we sat down for a meal in the hotel, there was this jazzy version of 'Smooth Operator' playing," Appel laughed.

Maybe it was a sign of what would come next. The Cardinal arrived in Florida to face the star-studded Connecticut team that had already beaten them on Thanksgiving. It was a roster that included not only Maya Moore but All-American post Tina Charles and WNBA-bound guard Renee Montgomery.

Again Wiggins led Stanford to new ground. With 25 points and 13 rebounds from their star, the Cardinal punched a ticket to the national title game with an 82–73 win over UConn coach Geno Auriemma's loaded team. Stanford led by seven points at the half before the Huskies cut the lead to one in the second half. Hones and Pedersen hit big shots down the stretch. The tinkering that VanDerveer did to the offense after the Thanksgiving Day loss against the Huskies paid off, revolving the offense around Appel and Pedersen inside and opening up offensive possibilities for players such as Hones and Gold-Onwude, while Wiggins took the brunt of the defensive focus. "We needed them to miss some shots, and they didn't," Auriemma said after the game. "Every shot they missed in the Virgin Islands, they made today. Every one."

The Cardinal were playing for a national title for the first time since 1992. And they would be facing a familiar foe in defending champion Tennessee, who had beaten LSU in the other national semifinal.

As the Cardinal had prepped to avenge their earlier loss to Connecticut, Pat Summitt and Tennessee were prepping to do the same against Stanford. The Vols immediately clamped down defensively on Stanford and never let go. Just a week after scoring 98 points against Maryland, the Cardinal were held to a season-low 48 against the Vols. "It felt like we could barely get the ball past half-court," Appel said of Tennessee's stifling defense, led by post Nicky Anosike, who finished the game with six steals. Candace Parker, dealing with a shoulder injury, finished with 17 points and 9 rebounds. Guard Shannon Bobbitt harassed Cardinal ball-handlers, forcing Stanford into 14 turnovers by halftime; the Cardinal had 25 turnovers by the end of the game. "The turnovers absolutely killed us," VanDerveer said after the game. "The game wasn't indicative of the season we had." Tennessee held Wiggins to 14 points, going 6-for-16 from the field before VanDerveer took her out to a standing ovation in the final moments of her college career.

After the game, on the other side of the floor, Tennessee celebrated its eighth national championship under Pat Summitt. It would be the legendary coach's last title.

For the Cardinal it was a new beginning, one in which the Final Four was no longer a quest but once again an expectation. The culture change VanDerveer had initiated the previous spring had taken hold. Between that season and the end of VanDerveer's tenure in 2024, the Cardinal would play in nine more Final Fours, including two National Championship Games, winning it all in 2021.

"All those years, we kept knocking at the door," VanDerveer said of the 11-year drought, full of frustrations and near misses. "[In 2008] we were able to push through."

## Chapter 10

# The Dethroning

**IN THE WINTER,** it's cold in the cement-walled concourse at Maples Pavilion, Stanford's home arena. It was especially so on the night of December 30, 2010. But there was too much energy coursing through the hallways for anyone to notice. More than 7,000 people were filing in for a moment it seemed the whole country would be watching. The local Bay Area sports cable station had set up a live pregame show in the corner, with Stanford alum and recent WNBA Draft pick Jayne Appel providing commentary. The *New York Times* and *USA Today* were in town. ESPN was televising the game nationally.

Stanford was hosting top-ranked Connecticut, a game with coast-to-coast interest because the Huskies were coming in with an NCAA-record 90-game winning streak that had started the season after the Cardinal defeated the Huskies in the 2008 Final Four and eclipsed UCLA men's basketball's 88-game winning streak from 1971 to 1974. UConn was utterly dominant during the streak, winning by an average margin of 33 points. Only two teams had gotten within single digits—one of those games was the 2010

NCAA title game against the Cardinal, which Stanford led 20–12 at the half and eventually lost 53–47.

When the December 30 game tipped off on national television, the Cardinal's home gym was filled to its rafters and vibrating with anticipation. VanDerveer said it felt like being in the Roman Colosseum. "You felt like the lions were coming out at any moment," VanDerveer said.

If there are two teams that have been a barometer of Stanford's elite status in women's basketball, they are Tennessee and Connecticut—not surprisingly the two programs with more NCAA championships than any other in the sport's history. The difference between the two national rivalries is that while Stanford's regular-season series with the Lady Vols was a collegial, but defining moment of every season for 34 years, a chance to find out where you stood as a team, it was the Huskies who became a rival and impediment to the Cardinal's national championship ambitions. The Cardinal met the Huskies in the Final Four five times during VanDerveer's tenure and in the national championship game in 2010. Stanford won only one of those games. "I've learned a lot from competing against them," VanDerveer said.

While Stanford scheduled Tennessee every season for 34 years, their postseason history was considerably less prolific—the two programs faced each other only once in the Final Four in 1991 and in the national championship in 2008. The Tennessee series, while intense, always had a friendlier feel. VanDerveer had a close relationship with Tennessee's Pat Summitt. They were contemporaries, colleagues, and friends.

Since VanDerveer lured Jennifer Azzi from Tennessee to play at Stanford, the two powerhouse programs played a yearly preseason game—a progress report for both teams, usually right before the holiday break in December. The two teams alternated home courts,

Stanford relishing the opportunity to play in the Lady Vols' women's basketball hotbed in Knoxville. And when Tennessee came to town, Stanford fans savored the moment when the always-steely Summitt walked out onto the floor just before tip-off. "We always knew what kind of Christmas it was going to be after we played Tennessee," Jayne Appel said.

But VanDerveer's relationship with UConn head coach Geno Auriemma was more complicated. The ascension of Connecticut's program under Auriemma began in earnest in Auriemma's sixth season, when the Huskies reached the 1991 Final Four—the year between Stanford's national championships. Four years later, in 1995, Auriemma and UConn won the first of what would be the program's 12 national championships.

The star of that 1994–95 Connecticut team was a lanky forward named Rebecca Lobo, whose freshman season with UConn had been in 1991–92. Lobo, a Southwick, Massachusetts, native, got a taste of success in her first two seasons, but in 1993–94, the Huskies—led by Lobo, point guard Jennifer Rizzotti, and center Kara Wolters—built their first 30-win season and a national following.

The next season, with the addition of Connecticut high school player of the year Nykesha Sales, UConn went 35–0, including an 87–60 blowout win over Stanford in the Final Four, the first NCAA meeting between the two teams. VanDerveer, asked by a reporter after the game, predicted after that game that Tennessee would beat Connecticut for the national title. Connecticut won the championship game and became the sport's new pace car. Auriemma never forgot VanDerveer had picked Tennessee to win the title game: "Now, we've just beaten her ass, and you might think that might have made an impression on her," he wrote in his book *Geno: In Pursuit of Perfection.*

Following UConn's championship season, Lobo was selected to the US National Team roster—the team VanDerveer would be coaching for a year in the lead-up to the 1996 Summer Olympics in Atlanta. Lobo was the youngest player on that team, chosen by the USA Basketball selection committee without input from the head coach. Lobo's national name recognition—UConn had become a national sports story—and association with the most popular college program in the country made her an appealing pick. But Lobo didn't have the international experience or the quickness and physicality of other players on the roster.

When the national team played an exhibition game in Storrs, Connecticut, VanDerveer did not start Lobo. The coach was roundly booed on the Huskies' home floor. "This has been a big adjustment for Rebecca," VanDerveer said to the press before the game. "She's definitely a role player, and I wouldn't expect her to have significant minutes." That statement rankled most of the state of Connecticut. And it rankled Auriemma, though he kept his feelings largely to himself.

Auriemma wasn't afraid to joust with opposing coaches. He'd certainly proved that in back-and-forth moments with Summitt and Notre Dame's Muffet McGraw through the years. And VanDerveer and Auriemma had competed for recruits such as Jayne Appel and Chiney Ogwumike; even Sue Bird and Diana Taurasi were interested in Stanford before landing at UConn, adding to the rivalry narrative. "I would like to say that Geno likes to get in little battles with people," VanDerveer said before the two teams met for the final time in VanDerveer's career in the 2022 Final Four. "I like him, and I think we get along really well. I've never felt we were adversaries in a negative way, but more competitors in a good way."

But as Connecticut became the biggest brand name in the sport, VanDerveer's Cardinal struggled to find their way back into the national elite. The two teams did not face each other between 1997 and 2005, a period of time that began when VanDerveer returned after coaching the Olympic team. When Connecticut and Tennessee ended their annual series in 2007—the most viewed non-NCAA game every season—there was space for a new rivalry. Was Stanford ready to fill that bill? First, the Cardinal had to figure out how to get back to the Final Four after more than a decade.

As detailed in the last chapter, the beginning of the end of Stanford's decade of frustration turned out to be a 2007 loss to Connecticut in a tournament in the Virgin Islands. VanDerveer and the Cardinal applied the lessons of that loss to the rest of the season, and defeated the Huskies in their first trip to the Final Four in 11 years in Tampa later that season.

Over the next 10 years, starting with that game on St. Thomas, Stanford and Connecticut played 12 times. Five of those games were in the NCAA tournament. "Too many times," Jayne Appel said with a laugh.

In 2006, Appel was being recruited heavily by Stanford, Connecticut, and Tennessee as a high school star out of Pleasant Hill, California, about 50 miles from the Stanford campus. She brought her father, Joe, on her recruiting trips, which went through the Midwest and South, and culminated in Connecticut. Joe insisted they go in the winter so that Jayne could experience the East Coast winter. They went to Duke, Notre Dame, Tennessee, and ended at UConn, where they were going to watch the annual UConn-Tennessee game in Hartford.

They were making their way to the practice gym in Hartford to attend a pregame shootaround and struggled to find the entrance to the gym. Joe Appel went up the steps to try a door that turned out to be locked, and as he walked back down the steps, he slipped on black ice and dislocated his ankle. Jayne called 911, and he was taken to the hospital in an ambulance for an injury so severe that he would need emergency surgery. "He had eight screws and a plate put in that are still there," Jayne Appel said. "I walked into the practice gym with a police officer, crying, and as soon as Geno saw me, he knew something had happened."

Connecticut team officials had to call the NCAA to get approval for Jayne to ride on the team bus to the game, and participate in the pregame meal—things they were not normally allowed to provide a recruit on an unofficial visit.

While her dad underwent surgery, Jayne sat alone at the game behind the bench. She flew home alone as well, her father returning home a few days later after surgery. "I'm not sure that was the ultimate reason I didn't go to Connecticut, but it was definitely a big factor," Jayne said.

The last game of Appel's All-American Stanford career was that 2010 NCAA title game loss to Connecticut in San Antonio, a haunting day for her. She had injured her right foot at the end of the regular season, heading into the Pac-10 tournament. She wanted to play through it. "Awful luck, terrible timing," Appel said. She had a boot specially made to wear off the court. VanDerveer did what she could to limit her game minutes in the conference tournament and the early rounds of the NCAA tournament, and she wasn't practicing at all. (Neither Appel nor VanDerveer let on to the media how serious the injury was. It wasn't revealed until after the season that Appel's foot was fractured.)

The Cardinal reached the April 6, 2010, NCAA title game in San Antonio with a loaded roster that included Appel, Jeanette Pohlen, Kayla Pedersen, and Nneka Ogwumike. In a sluggish game, Stanford led Connecticut 20–12 at halftime, the lowest-scoring half in the history of the NCAA title game. Coming out of the locker room after halftime, the Cardinal struggled without Appel's offensive contributions. Maya Moore and Tina Charles—the latter of whom Appel had played against in AAU since she was 11—began to dominate. VanDerveer likened the game to a heavyweight fight.

In Appel's final game, she went 0-for-12 from the floor and Stanford lost 53–47. Appel, in tears, walked to the bus with VanDerveer, telling her head coach that she didn't want to take her uniform off. "[Losing that last game of my career against UConn] doesn't take away from my time at Stanford or playing for Tara, but it would have been really sweet to get that," Appel said. "And I'm convinced that if I didn't have a broken foot, we would have won that game. It was one of the worst games of my career, and there was nothing I could do about it."

Appel was back at Maples eight months later, on December 10, 2010, sitting as a spectator along the baseline next to former teammate Candice Wiggins and other alumni, some of whom had flown in to be at this nationally televised game against UConn with historic implications. Former secretary of state Condoleezza Rice was in the crowd, as was Stanford football coach Jim Harbaugh and VanDerveer's mother, Rita.

The Orange Bowl–bound Stanford football team, including quarterback Andrew Luck, was crowded into the tunnel area where the Huskies and Auriemma came onto the floor. "Our football team was heckling Geno," said point guard Jeanette Pohlen. "The student body wasn't there because it was the holiday break, but anybody who was anywhere near campus was there that night."

For Nneka Ogwumike, the sound in the gym was swallowed up into a "vacuum," she said. She couldn't hear it. VanDerveer's meticulous game plan was the loudest thing in her head. "For me, the thing I will always remember about that game is the preparation," Ogwumike said. "The intensity of that game that people witnessed was about the seven days before that."

Stanford had come off a rocky road trip before the game, losing back-to-back games to DePaul and Tennessee before rebounding with a home win over Xavier. VanDerveer was still trying to erase the sting of that road trip. She pumped crowd noise into the speakers of Maples Pavilion during practice to simulate what the environment would be like on game day. She dissected the Huskies' offense and defense, their strengths—namely stars (and future WNBA All-Stars) Maya Moore, Tiffany Hayes, and Stefanie Dolson—and their weaknesses. "It was surgical," Nneka Ogwumike said. "Playing the game was the easiest thing that happened that week. And it wasn't easy. But our preparation was even harder."

That noisy, wall-shaking night belonged to Pohlen. She had bided her time as a role player in her first two seasons but earned the starting point guard spot in her junior season. Against the Huskies, she was transcendent, and led the Cardinal to a start-to-finish advantage in the game. She finished with 31 points (including 5 three-pointers), 9 rebounds, and 6 assists.

Nneka Ogwumike and her sister Chiney, a freshman, teamed up to play lockdown defense on Moore, holding her to 14 points on 5-of-15 shooting. Moore did not score her first points until 17 minutes into the game. "I wasn't even looking at the ball," Chiney Ogwumike said. "I just followed [Moore] everywhere. Tara told me that I needed to know what kind of toothpaste she used. It was the most electric environment I've ever been in as a player in my life."

Stanford's defense held Connecticut to 32.8 percent shooting and outrebounded them 43–36 on the way to a 71–59 streak-snapping victory. Nneka Ogwumike leaped into the air and pumped her fist as the Maples crowd roared. Wiggins led the alumni in rushing the floor. It was Stanford's 52nd win in a row at home, in an atmosphere unlike almost any other in program history.

Almost four years later, the Cardinal played spoiler again, beating Connecticut in overtime on November 17, 2014, to end a 47-game Huskies winning streak. Connecticut would counter that loss by winning 111 games in a row, including another victory over Stanford in the 2014 national semifinals in Nashville.

What would be the last matchup between VanDerveer and Auriemma took place in 2022 in Minnesota in the national semifinals, with the Huskies knocking out Stanford—the defending national champions—63–58.

While Connecticut was collecting 11 national titles and pumping out world-class talent, such as Moore, Bird, Taurasi, and Breanna Stewart, VanDerveer held a small lead over Auriemma in the category of all-time coaching wins. And so the Cardinal coach became the winningest coach in the history of college basketball first, passing Mike Krzyzewski's previous record in January 2024. Auriemma passed Krzyzewski's record two weeks later.

Auriemma had joked at the start of the 2024 season that, because of VanDerveer, he would never own the all-time wins record. The running narrative on social media was that he and VanDerveer would hang around and wait each other out in order for one of them to lay an ultimate claim to the record. But with VanDerveer's retirement at the end of the 2024 season, Auriemma passed her on November 20, 2024, becoming the winningest coach in the history of the game.

## Chapter 11

# The Sisterhood

**NNEKA AND CHINEY OGWUMIKE** went together to their first organized girls' basketball practice in denim shorts. Nneka Ogwumike, 11 years old, was wearing her glasses; Chiney, nine years old, was wearing a halter top and some canvas sneakers. Not long after the practice began, Chiney was in the bathroom crying, refusing to come out after getting confused running the three-player weave drill.

Just a few years later, both of them were on the radar of Tara VanDerveer and the Stanford coaching staff, outstanding students and two of the most athletic, dynamic players in high school girls' basketball.

Nneka's arrival on the Farm in 2008 set into motion a new era in Stanford women's basketball culture, a "sisterhood" built on the presence of three sets of siblings on the roster over the next 14 years.

First it was the Ogwumike sisters, who played together for two years. Chiney finished as the leading scorer in program history, with Nneka at No. 3. Chiney is also the No. 1 rebounder in program history, with Nneka at No. 4.

They were followed into the program by the sharp-shooting Samuelson sisters, first Bonnie (2011–15) and then Karlie (2013–17), who ended up being ranked sixth and fifth respectively in the school record books for three-point shooting.

And in 2018 the Hull twins, Lexie and Lacie, arrived from Spokane to become the team's heart-and-soul players and leaders through the COVID pandemic and the Cardinal's first national championship in 29 years.

"There is something special about having sisters on your team," said Kate Paye. "With your sister, you know you are going to have your sibling's back, no matter what. You might be competing against one another in practice, or for playing time, but at the end of the day, you love that person, would do anything for them, and want them to be successful. And I think having actual sisters on our team was a living, breathing, everyday example of the type of relationship that we want everybody on our team to have."

Nneka Ogwumike was a raw talent headed into high school, and her family was unfamiliar with the club circuit that ends up being the college recruiting pathway for most young basketball players. From the age of 11 to 14, Ogwumike improved rapidly, and she found her way onto the radar of some of the nation's top programs. "That's when I learned that I could get a full sports scholarship," Ogwumike said. "I was learning along with my family. We didn't know about these things, and we didn't know anyone who did besides one person who understood what it meant to get a sports scholarship."

The family's Nigerian friends in Houston gave Nneka and Chiney's parents, Peter and Ify Ogwumike, grief about letting their girls play basketball. "Sports were viewed as a distraction, especially for girls," Chiney said. When Nneka got a letter from Stanford, it got the family's attention. "As a Nigerian kid, Stanford is everyone's holy grail," Chiney Ogwumike said.

*Tara VanDerveer (back row, center) plays her first season for the University of Indiana women's basketball team in 1972. VanDerveer played at Indiana from 1972 to 1975.* (Tara VanDerveer personal collection)

*Tara VanDerveer (far right) poses with her parents, Rita and Dunbar VanDerveer, and younger sister and fellow coach, Heidi VanDerveer, in front of their family home in Chautauqua, New York.* (Tara VanDerveer personal collection)

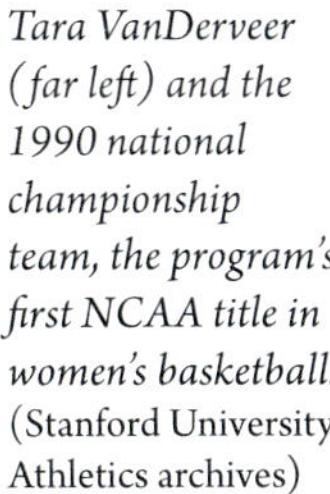

*Tara VanDerveer (far left) and the 1990 national championship team, the program's first NCAA title in women's basketball.* (Stanford University Athletics archives)

*Left to right: Tara VanDerveer, Chris MacMurdo, Val Whiting (center), and Molly Goodenbour celebrate the 1992 NCAA title, the program's second national championship in three seasons.* (Stanford University Athletics archives)

*Longtime associate head coach Amy Tucker took over the Stanford program in the 1995–96 season as head coach when Tara VanDerveer took a year off to coach the 1996 Olympic Team. Also pictured: Stanford guard Milena Flores.* (Stanford University Athletics archives)

*Left to right: Stanford players Naomi Mulitauauopele, Vanessa Nygaard, Heather Owen, and Kate Starbird react to losing to Old Dominion in the 1997 Final Four, the most devastating loss in program history.* (Associated Press/Amy Sancetta)

*Tara VanDerveer (left), stands with coaching legends Geno Auriemma (left center), Van Chancellor (right center) and Pat Summit (right), as she is inducted into the Women's Basketball Hall of Fame in Knoxville Tennessee in April 2002.* (Tara VanDerveer personal collection)

*(Left) Tara VanDerveer and three-time All-American Nicole Powell, one of the most decorated players in program history, celebrating winning the 2003 Pac-12 Tournament Championship.* (Stanford University Athletics archives)

*(Below) The 2007–08 Stanford team (left to right: Jeanette Pohlen, Candice Wiggins, Kayla Pedersen, Jayne Appel, and JJ Hones) celebrates defeating Maryland in the Elite Eight of the NCAA Tournament to return the program to the NCAA Tournament for the first time in 12 years.* (Associated Press/Elaine Thompson)

*An emotional Tara VanDerveer and four-time All-American Candice Wiggins celebrate returning Stanford to the Final Four for the first time since 1997. (Associated Press/Elaine Thompson)*

*The Stanford bench and a sell-out crowd celebrate Stanford's December 30, 2010, win over No. 1 Connecticut, 71–59, ending the Huskies' 90-game winning streak.* (Stanford University Athletics archives)

*Always the teacher, Tara VanDerveer hits the floor to coach guard Amber Orrange during the 2014 NCAA Tournament.* (Associated Press/Steve Helber)

*Tara VanDerveer's coaching staff frequently includes former players, such as Kate Paye (far left) and Bobbie Kelsey (far right), both of whom played in multiple Final Fours for the Cardinal between 1992 and 1997.* (Associated Press/Michael Macor)

*Sisters Nneka (30) and Chiney Ogwumike (13) rewrote the Stanford record books during their time playing together for the Cardinal, each becoming the Pac-12's all-time leading scorer during the playing careers, which overlapped for two seasons. Each went on to become the No. 1 pick in the WNBA Draft, Nneka in 2012 and Chiney in 2014.* (Associated Press/Paul Sakuma)

*Tara Vanderveer (left) coaches against her former All-American Jennifer Azzi (right) as Stanford faced Azzi's University of San Francisco team in the first round of the 2016 NCAA Tournament. Azzi is one of the many former Stanford players who have gone on to successful coaching careers.* (Stanford University Athletics archives)

*Tara VanDerveer teaching the offense to freshman Nadia Fingall heading into the 2016-17 season. At the end of the previous season she seriously pondered retirement, but reconsidered and went on to coach eight more seasons and win another NCAA title.* (Associated Press/Ben Margot)

*Stanford celebrates winning the 2021 NCAA Championship, the program's first title in 29 years. Tara VanDerveer (center) broke the NCAA record for the longest period of time between championships.* (Stanford University Athletics archives)

*Lexie Hull (left), Cameron Brink (center), and Hannah Jump (right) break down in celebration and relief after winning the 2021 NCAA title in what will be known as the COVID season, in which the Cardinal spent the majority of the season on the road, living out of hotel rooms, and isolating from family and friends during the height of the COVID pandemic.* (Stanford University Athletics archives)

*Stanford players past and present came to Maples Pavilion on January 21, 2024, to celebrate VanDerveer becoming the winningest coach in the history of college basketball, passing Duke head coach Mike Kryzkewski with 1,203 wins.* (Stanford University Athletics archives)

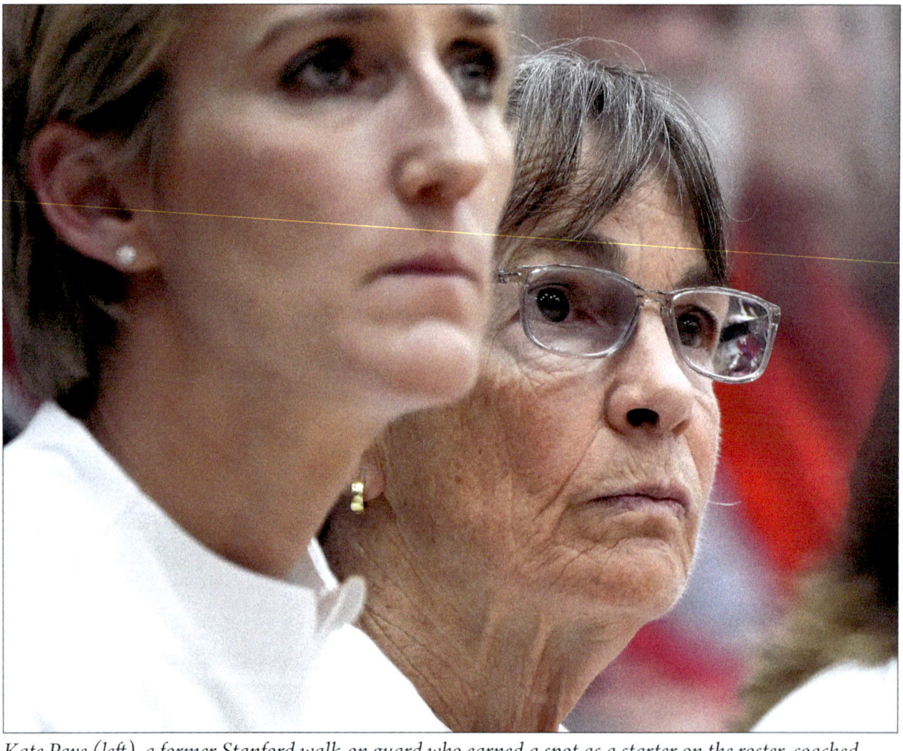

*Kate Paye (left), a former Stanford walk-on guard who earned a spot as a starter on the roster, coached alongside VanDerveer (right) for 17 years before being named the Cardinal's head coach following VanDerveer's retirement in 2024.* (Associated Press/Tony Avelar)

Ify, an educator, set the terms for Nneka's home visits with coaches. She stipulated that visits could last no longer than two hours. Tara VanDerveer, who knew she was competing with Duke, wanted to be as prepared for her visit as possible. She was looking at a shelf of board games when she came up with an idea: they would play "Nneka-opoly," based on the game Monopoly. Within days, assistant coach Kate Paye created a game board and a set of cards based on Stanford trivia and all the things the staff knew about Nneka—the things she liked to eat, her favorite music, etc. The Stanford coaches walked into the Ogwumike home, Paye with the game in a box under her arm. They didn't talk much about basketball. They played the game with Ogwumike, her mother, and Chiney. And after two hours, as VanDerveer and her assistant coaches were getting ready to leave, Ify Ogwumike asked them to stay.

The low-pressure pitch appealed to Nneka, who found the recruiting process stressful as she tried to take in all the information she needed to make the biggest decision of her life. "Tara made it easy for me," Nneka said.

VanDerveer told Ify her and her husband, Peter, that Nneka would not be making a four-year decision to come to Stanford but a 40-year decision, one with the potential to impact the rest of her life. "That was it for me," Ify Ogwumike said.

Chiney's recruitment was somewhat less stressful. "I always knew I was going to Stanford," Chiney said with a laugh. Chiney had accompanied the family on Nneka's campus visit and built a relationship with the coaching staff. She watched Nneka play in Final Fours, and in 2010 for the national championship. But she engaged in her own process when the time came, including considering offers from Notre Dame and Connecticut. "I made those visits to make sure. But I always knew it was going to be Stanford," Chiney said.

Stanford sealed the deal on her final recruiting visit, taking her into a VIP tent during a Stanford football game. There she met Hall of Fame quarterback John Elway, chief justice of the Supreme Court John Roberts, and former secretary of state Condoleezza Rice. "Here I was in high school, and to me, it was like my nerd Super Bowl," Chiney said.

Nneka was already an All-American by the time younger sister Chiney arrived. Their games were not dissimilar—they were both agile players with high efficiency on the offensive end and a nose for rebounds. Personality-wise, they could not have been more different. Nneka was reserved, even a bit introverted. Chiney was the extrovert, the "spitfire," as VanDerveer called her—expressive and emotional. The Cardinal coaches were already aware of these differences before Chiney joined Nneka on campus. Their high school coach, Ann Roubique, had told VanDerveer, "They are very different." Paye joked that the difference could be boiled down to this: "Nneka will always ask for permission, but Chiney will just do something and ask for forgiveness."

VanDerveer decided, after a couple of intense practice dust-ups, that the sisters could not be on opposing teams during practice. During games, they were perfect complements. Initially, VanDerveer wasn't sure how much she would put Chiney on the floor as a freshman on a team loaded with accomplished post players—Nneka, Jayne Appel, and Kayla Pedersen. But in Stanford's first exhibition game of the season, Chiney pulled down 25 rebounds. "So she was going to play," VanDerveer said. "Nneka was always helping Chiney, sometimes calming her down. They played hard for each other, and you knew that they did not want to let each other down. And that was great for our team."

The Ogwumikes were Stanford prototype athletes, accomplished academically and leaders on the entire campus. On the floor, they rewrote the program record books. In the six years one or both of the Ogwumikes played at Stanford, the Cardinal reached the Final Four five times.

Nneka laid a path for excellence on the court that Chiney fit into nicely. And then Chiney laid her own path, including the Nerd Nation movement in Stanford athletics, celebrating "nerd culture" with glasses and a "Nerd City Kids" rap video that went viral.

Chiney joked that she used to get nervous at the thought of making 10 free throws in a row, which was the ticket out of practice for the day. She admitted she felt a much different, more acute sense of pressure after Nneka graduated. She felt the weight of the program on her shoulders, and she wanted to set her own course off the court. Condoleezza Rice pushed Chiney to become more of an active participant in her classes, to become a leader on campus. Chiney ended up changing her major to international relations and studying abroad in her family's home country of Nigeria. "Those things gave me perspective, to realize that I am not the summation of the points I score or the rebounds I pull down," Chiney said. "I feel like that's where I stepped into my purpose."

As the Ogwumikes moved to the WNBA in 2012 (Nneka) and 2014 (Chiney)—the first set of siblings to be No. 1 draft picks—the Samuelsons, from Huntington Beach in Southern California grabbed the sibling baton.

Bonnie Samuelson, who set school records in high school, arrived on The Farm first, a role player and specialist for much of her career, until her senior season when she became a starter and the team's leading perimeter threat. Her sister Karlie was a two-year starter who has since carved out a long WNBA career as a player who is always ready to contribute when called upon.

The Samuelsons were born into a basketball family. Their father, Jon, played college basketball at Cal State Fullerton and played professionally in Europe. Their mother, Karen, played netball, a game similar to basketball, growing up in England. The girls were playing basketball before they started elementary school. Jon would take his daughters shooting every day, always on the hunt for open gyms to use, ducking into churches and schools where the gym door might be cracked open. He would coax them to get up to 200 shots a day, which was often met with groans from the girls. But basketball rarely carried over into family time. The family rule was always, "Leave it at the gym."

Bonnie—a McDonald's All-American who led Edison High School in Huntington Beach to three California state title appearances—arrived at Stanford first. Karlie admitted that the opportunity to play alongside her sister was a huge pull to join her at Stanford two years later. At Stanford, the Samuelson sisters' bond was apparent immediately. They would take the court together for pregame warm-ups and would walk back to the locker room side by side, joined at the hip at all times, according to Bonnie. "They had radar for each other," VanDerveer said. "Karlie always knew where Bonnie was going to be, and vice versa."

And they were lights-out shooters. Between the two of them, they made a combined 486 three-pointers in their Stanford careers. Bonnie Samuelson was the program's first stretch four, a power forward who can shoot beyond the three-point line and is known for their shooting ability rather than post play. She had size, and her ability to extend defenses away from the paint, making room for the Cardinal's post players to operate. Karlie was more of a true shooting guard with one of the highest basketball IQs VanDerveer had ever coached.

The third and youngest Samuelson sister, Katie Lou—also in the family business of three-point shooting—was recruited by Stanford but chose to go to Connecticut. It was an initial disappointment to

Karlie, who wanted to play with her younger sister, the way she'd been able to play with Bonnie. Katie Lou went to Connecticut as the No. 1 recruit in the nation. In 2017, the two sisters found themselves together at the Final Four in Dallas on opposite sides of the bracket. Stanford got eliminated by South Carolina, and Connecticut got knocked out by Mississippi State before they had a chance to play against one another.

The Hull sisters—identical twins Lexie and Lacie—from Spokane, Washington, comprised the next set of sisters to play at Stanford. They always did everything together. They began playing basketball in kindergarten, and they played soccer and volleyball together when they were young. Even then, they were competitive. So much so that their mother, Jaime, split them up in elementary school so they would be in different classes, to have their own experiences and to avoid comparisons. But if one of them were shooting in the driveway, the other would inevitably come outside in order to avoid getting left behind. Often, one-on-one games ended in tears. "They hate losing," their father, Jason, said. "But they hate losing to each other more."

Lexie and Lacie weren't set on going to college together. They got individual recruiting letters and had separate conversations with coaches. But ultimately all of the schools they considered—Gonzaga, Washington, Oregon, and Stanford—were appealing to them for the same reasons, making them a package deal. "It was never explicitly said that we could go to the same school, but I've always said that if we had done the entire recruiting process separately, we would have ended up in the same place because we liked and loved the same thing about every school we visited," Lacie said. "We value the same things."

It was a compelling package. The Hull sisters dominated high school girls' basketball in Spokane. Behind the twin sisters, Central

Valley High School in Spokane Valley went 83–1 in the Hulls' final three seasons, winning a pair of Washington state titles.

Not only did the 6'1" Hull sisters obviously resemble each other physically, but their games had the same type of poise and grit. Their toughness, in particular, appealed to VanDerveer, who had coached twins before at Ohio State—Jane and Joan Cowdery. "Twins are different," VanDerveer said. "They say that twins are closer than sisters or mothers and daughters. And they are used to battling it out."

The Hulls proved this statement true quickly after their arrival at Stanford. "There are literally no boundaries," Lacie Hull said. "Everyone on the team [is] competitive, but when it's Lexie and I against each other, we throw each other to the ground." There was the occasional shove or dust-up. And lots of time spent on the floor scrapping with one another for the ball. "They battled the hell out of each other," said guard Hannah Jump.

Not unlike the approach she took with the Ogwumikes, VanDerveer stopped putting the Hull sisters on opposite teams during practice and warned them that if they were going to spend their time wrestling one another on the floor, they were going to sit on the bench. That did the trick. Jump lamented that she always ended up having to guard one of them after they weren't allowed to guard one another anymore.

Whatever happened in practice stayed in practice for the Hulls; that was always the point. "We are always the most competitive with each other, but then off the court, we love each other, and being able to be that example for our teammates was huge. You put aside your emotions and just focus on the task at hand when you are on the court. But your love and care for each other never wavers."

The Hull twins, born 20 minutes apart, were pacesetters in terms of their work ethic and hustle. Floor burns and bruises were badges of honor. They were also connectors, bringing their teammates together, particularly during the COVID season of 2020–21, which ended with the Cardinal winning a national title. They were a center of gravity for a team that needed one badly that season. "They put the team before themselves," said Kiana Williams, a senior guard on the 2020–21 national championship team. "They held each other accountable, but it came from a place of love, and that spread through the team."

Forward Fran Belibi was so close to the Hulls that they often called her "the third twin." Belibi joked that things would get awkward when Lexie and Lacie argued during practice. Belibi, like so many others, had siblings of her own. "We understand the ties that go along with that level of intensity, that really not liking (your sibling) in a moment but still always having your back," Belibi said. "Even in those moments when they were going at it, they showed all of us that you can battle but step out of that space and still laugh and joke and support each other. It was a constant reminder that even if we weren't flesh and blood, we treated each other like sisters."

In their senior season in 2022, the Hulls returned to Spokane to play in the Sweet 16 and Elite Eight games that would return Stanford to the Final Four in defense of their national title. Lexie had scored a career-high 36 points against Kansas State in the second round to get the Cardinal back to their hometown for the regional. Both finished their careers as Academic All-Americans and left Stanford with their bachelor's *and* master's degrees in four years.

"I never had a bad day coaching Lexie and Lacie," VanDerveer said. "They had such motors. They were some of the top defenders that ever played here. They were glue players, the kind that keep your team together, and they were such hard workers."

Lexie and Lacie combined for 355 steals and won four all-defensive honors in the Pac-12. Still, Lacie said, "We are different people who play different games."

That was something VanDerveer always understood. When coaching sisters—whether the Ogwumikes, the Samuelsons, or the Hulls—she was intentional about treating them as individuals, building distinct relationships with all of them. "I tried never to compare them. They are individuals, and I coached them as individuals," VanDerveer said.

But the "sisterhood" culture that these six young women brought to Stanford stuck, and VanDerveer leaned in to the label. "We've always had teams with great chemistry, teams that loved each other and played for one another," VanDerveer said. "That 1990 national championship team—they were extremely close, for example. They are all still in a book club together. But when you have blood-relative sisters on your team, it makes it really obvious that creating a sisterhood is your goal."

The sisterhood ethic continues under new head coach Kate Paye, even without siblings on the roster. "It's totally kind of embedded in our everyday common language that we use with our team and our program, and in our office with our staff," Paye said. "When we speak to our alums, and when we recruit, we talk about sisterhood all the time. We always will."

Lindy La Rocque—the current head coach at UNLV—played with the Ogwumike sisters and with Bonnie Samuelson. She saw the Ogwumikes' sibling rivalry, and its benefits, firsthand, and experienced its ripple effects in her own relationships with teammates. The changes in the game have made building a tight team culture even more important. With the emergence of the transfer portal, players can more easily move from program to program. Cementing the culture of sisterhood has become more important, and more challenging than ever. "I remember days when Nneka and Chiney would literally rip each other's hair out at practice and then go to dinner. They were good with it, and we were good with it. I think it propelled us in a lot of ways, because there was so much trust," La Rocque said. "There is still unconditional love among us as teammates. We are bridesmaids in each other's weddings. Our kids play together. We are always going to be sisters."

## Chapter 12

# The COVID Season

**THE VIBE AT THE** 2020 Pac-12 tournament in Las Vegas was, in a word, weird. The airport was oddly quiet for one of the most popular tourist destinations in the United States. Lines at the hotel check-in counter, usually snaking through the stanchions and across the marble floor, were nonexistent. Hand sanitizer stations were set up every few feet. The activity on the casino floor was muted, the bells ringing from the slot machines sporadic at best.

As the tournament took place from March 5–8, 2020, inside the Mandalay Bay Events Center, basketball was happening with a nervous energy in the air, as the coronavirus—a highly contagious respiratory virus that had originated in China but was spreading rapidly across the globe—became worldwide news. Following Stanford's last game of the tournament against Oregon in the title game, Tara VanDerveer walked through the handshake line offering her elbow rather than her hand. "As a team, I think we thought that was a little bit more of a joke," said sophomore Fran Belibi. "Like, why would they do that? Nothing is going to happen."

The Oregon Ducks won the 2020 Pac-12 tournament with a loaded roster that included All-American Sabrina Ionescu, Ruthy Hebard, and Satou Sabally, all of whom later headed to the WNBA. The Ducks were on a path to be a No. 1 seed in the NCAA tournament and a favorite to win the program's first national title.

After the Pac-12 title game, Oregon coach Kelly Graves stepped off the podium and asked what was happening in California around the coronavirus. He wondered whether people were overreacting. He wasn't alone. Other coaches finished their conference tournament runs trying to figure out what would happen next with the NCAA tournament starting in two weeks. They assumed everything would have to go on as normal. Right? "I don't think any of us understood the magnitude of what was about to happen," said Stanford guard Hannah Jump.

But cases of coronavirus—later to be known as COVID—had begun to multiply rapidly, and the sense of alarm was building. Hand-washing while counting to 20 or singing the ABCs became the first line of defense. Travel restrictions were increasing. Cruise ships were being held in ports, their passengers unable to leave. Schools, including Stanford, were starting to consider closing in-person classes.

In Utah, on March 9, 2020, NBA player Rudy Gobert made a joke of touching microphones at a press conference. Then, on March 11, three days after the Pac-12 tournament title game, everything changed: the World Health Organization declared a global pandemic; Gobert tested positive for COVID; the Utah–Oklahoma City NBA game was canceled; and within 45 minutes of that cancellation, the NBA canceled the rest of its season.

The next day, on March 12, for the first time ever, the NCAA officially called off its men's and women's tournaments, along with the rest of their winter and spring seasons in all divisions. Just like that, the basketball season was over. "Everything happened so fast," said Hannah Jump, then a sophomore guard. "We had been making jokes before we went to the [Pac-12] tournament about not being able to touch each other. And it went from that, in just a few days, to Tara calling us into the locker room to tell us that they canceled the NCAA tournament."

VanDerveer had gotten the call from the NCAA, but not before the players began to see the news on Twitter and Instagram. She called an emergency meeting in the team's locker room, sat the players and staff in a circle, and delivered the news that most of them had already heard at that point. But hearing it come directly from their coach made it real. "I told them, 'We've had a great year, and it's OK to be really sad about this. You have to enjoy every day you are with your team, every day in practice,'" VanDerveer said.

The tears began to flow immediately. For the Cardinal seniors—Nadia Fingall and Mikaela Brewer—this was an abrupt end to their college careers. They took a moment to address their teammates. The players sat together and shared their favorite memories of the season. Reality was setting in. "We would never be the same team again, because our seniors were leaving," Kiana Williams said. "And there was really no time to think about it because everything was happening so fast."

VanDerveer gave her players time to process their immediate feelings together. But there was more news to deliver. There would be no hanging out for the remainder of the spring, no team workouts, no weight room sessions. Stanford was shutting down, and everyone was being sent home to finish the quarter with online classes. "I encouraged them to go somewhere they wanted to be, because they were going to be there for a while. We didn't know how long," VanDerveer said. "I think we thought it might be a month or two. Little did we know." The Cardinal was told that the team's performance coach, Ali Kirschner, would be in touch in a couple of weeks to begin to make individual workout plans.

An hour later, the players left the gym and packed to leave campus, leaving most of their possessions behind in their dorm rooms. Hannah Jump had the luxury of living close by, only 17 miles down the road in San Jose. Before she left, she briefly talked with VanDerveer in the hallway about improving her conditioning during the break. Haley Jones was headed over the hill to Santa Cruz. Belibi had a flight home to Colorado within a couple of hours. For Williams, it was a long flight back to San Antonio, thinking about what to do next, thinking about whether she would have a senior season by the time next fall came around.

VanDerveer got in one last swim at the Stanford pool and then headed for her family's summer home in Chautauqua, New York, to be close to her mother, Rita.

What came next for the players was finding the motivation to work out on their own, without access to a gym or a pickup game. Jump's neighbor had a pool with a tether that allowed her to swim in place for long stretches. Williams tried online workouts with teammates. Belibi's parents, both doctors, own a medical clinic in Colorado and were able to set up a workout room for her there. Working out for what? That remained to be seen. "Nobody knew anything," Belibi said.

"You are working out because you love basketball. You want to stay in shape," Kiana Williams said. "But there's no end goal in sight, and you have to find the motivation. We didn't know if we needed to be ready to come back in two weeks or two months. It was hard to get ready for something that was unknown."

Belibi woke at 7:00 AM every day, got in some lifting, and went for a run. Then she would log on for a summer class in physics and go back to the clinic for another workout. "Honestly, there wasn't much else to do," Belibi said.

The pandemic, with its threat of serious illness and death, brought the world to a halt. It was so much bigger than basketball. But basketball was what the coaches and players could control to an extent.

Through the spring and summer, VanDerveer organized weekly team meetings on Zoom. They held their team end-of-season banquet on Zoom as well. "I didn't even know what Zoom was before that," VanDerveer said.

Those video calls were a chance to bond, share experiences, and play games online. VanDerveer did individual meetings with players to check in on them—on their classes, on their workouts, and on how they were coping mentally. At one point, the team captains—Alyssa Jerome and the Hull twins, Lexie and Lacie—asked each of their teammates to do a slide presentation on something that no one else knew about them. Williams did hers on her obsession with barbecue sauce. Sometimes the players organized meetings on their own, just to stay connected.

"We just always wondered when we were going to come back. Did we have a date? Would we get to play? And the date kept getting pushed back," Williams said. "It was hard living with the uncertainty."

The murder of George Floyd by police in Minneapolis, which propelled the nation into coast-to-coast protests against police brutality and racism, added to the backdrop of instability. Belibi said her teammates began talking to one another even more. She called them "deep conversations." "I learned a lot more about people during that time," Belibi said. "It gave us space to talk about our experiences, and I think it gave us greater understanding to empathize with one another."

Meanwhile, spring had turned to summer and basketball was leading the way back to some form of normalcy. The two US professional leagues, the WNBA and the NBA, paved the path forward for a return to the court, with both the WNBA and the NBA setting up "bubble seasons." The WNBA players convened in Bradenton, Florida, at the IMG Academy in what would become known as "the Wubble." The league's 12 teams and 144 players were holed up together, along with WNBA staff and referees, putting on a campaign that would be viewed as the season that saved the league.

The players were isolated with one another (and a few spouses and children), testing constantly, observing physical distancing on their benches, and figuring out how to make a season work while publicly advocating for racial justice. There would be no confirmed cases of COVID among players, team personnel, or officials during the season and playoffs.

At the same time, the NBA began its own bubble season. Major League Baseball began a 60-game season in mid-July, playing games in empty stadiums. The NFL began its season on time in September, the league allowing players to opt out of the season and holding games in front of small crowds, while maintaining huge national television audiences. The NFL would ultimately play all 256 regular-season games over 17 weeks with no cancellations. The sports world was proving it was possible to move forward safely, and that was welcome news for VanDerveer and her players.

VanDerveer got a call at her cabin in Minnesota in mid-August that Stanford was permitting some student-athletes to return, including her team. The Cardinal players returned to campus in September 2020, with California—and Santa Clara County, in particular—having some of the strictest quarantine rules in the country. The players immediately went into a five-day quarantine, each of them with a roommate in a two-bedroom suite. There was no hanging out in the common space. Each player had to keep to her own room.

On night four of quarantine, with everyone on the team continuing to test negative, some of the players decided to go play some pickup at an off-campus gym. The next day, one of the Cardinal players tested positive. No one wanted to say anything at first. Someone suggested just sending the coaches a text. Williams said that as a team leader, she knew what they had to do. "We had to tell Tara," Williams said. "We shouldn't have gone, but we were itching to play basketball and to be around each other. And normally, we wouldn't be in trouble for going out to play in a pickup game, right? But we knew we were supposed to stay in quarantine."

VanDerveer insisted on talking to her captains on the phone, and Williams said it was a conversation she will never forget, especially the disappointment in VanDerveer's voice. "She's not really a yeller, but she couldn't believe we couldn't wait one more day, and we felt that," Jump said, "It was definitely a wake-up call."

VanDerveer acknowledged that what they were asking the players to do was hard. But "people were dying, and they had to be disciplined enough to wait one more day." That five-day quarantine quickly turned into two weeks because of the exposure. Not the way the Cardinal wanted to start the season.

Williams and fellow senior Alyssa Jerome vowed at that moment that they would lead the team in "the right way." They knew they were putting their own health and the health of others on the line by playing at all. They had to make the season "worth it," as Williams put it.

VanDerveer arranged for outdoor practices, turning nearby tennis courts into basketball courts. An outdoor weight room was set up nearby. Everything was done with masks on. Student-athletes from multiple sports lined up in the predawn hours down the block at the Arrillaga Center, Stanford's athletics building, for regular testing. The first test of the day, at 6:00 AM, would get you into your practice that day. The second test, the one with the long swab that was nicknamed the "brain tickler," was your ticket into practice the following day. Unless, of course, your morning test the next day came out positive. Fans, and that included family and friends, would not be allowed to attend games.

On November 28, 2020, with COVID cases spiking coming off the Thanksgiving holiday, Santa Clara County announced stringent new social-distancing measures. Those measures included a three-week ban on contact sports, which applied to all professional, collegiate, and youth sports teams. That included practices and games. On top of that, anyone who traveled farther than 150 miles outside of the county would be required to quarantine for 14 days upon their return.

The county's health officer, Dr. Sara Cody, was a college rower at Stanford, and her husband was a professor of medicine and health policy at the university. She knew what her decisions would mean for many. She said at times she would get choked up during a press conference thinking about the "full force" of the restrictions she was putting in place.

The Cardinal, ranked No. 2 in the country and a national title contender, had played one game at home on November 25 before the ban was announced. Their next two games had been canceled. They suddenly needed a plan B, or they would face the cancellation of a large portion of their season. "It was a quick pivot," said former Stanford athletic director Bernard Muir. "We had a couple of days to figure out on the fly what would work for the county, for our school, for the student-athletes."

The plan to move not only the women's basketball team but men's basketball and other winter sports out of Santa Clara County for an extended period of time came together. Muir and VanDerveer discussed where the team could stay, practice, and compete and still be safe. The student-athletes from multiple sports gathered on a conference call and told Muir that they wanted to move forward no matter what. "We knew they all wanted to play, but you don't always account for the wear and tear on everybody's mental health, the isolation, and the testing. We were ready to throw whatever support systems we had—academic, sports psychologists, medical staff, trainers—at our teams," Muir said.

VanDerveer brought up Las Vegas as a possibility, and Muir agreed to let her figure it out. "We just wanted to play, and we didn't care where it was," Williams said.

VanDerveer reached out to former guard and assistant coach Lindy La Rocque, who was in her first season as the head coach of UNLV, her hometown team. At first, VanDerveer wanted to set up a game against La Rocque's team on the Rebels' home floor. But what came next changed the trajectory of the Cardinal's season. After discussions with the UNLV administration, president, and athletic director, La Rocque offered VanDerveer a home base to play games, live, and practice during the ban, which was supposed to last three weeks. The Cardinal would ultimately be gone from campus for nine weeks. They would stay in more than a half dozen hotels in six states and take 12 flights, living for weeks out of the bags they took with them when they first left on December 2, prompted by a text that read, "Pack your bags, we're leaving today. We probably aren't coming back."

In her dorm room preparing to leave, Belibi stared at her duffel bag, trying to figure out what to take and what to leave behind, what was important and what was not, and whether they would have the opportunity to return to campus to swap out their belongings at some point. "I packed my basketball stuff, of course, but I have so many shoes, and I love every single pair," Belibi said. "I thought, *This bag is going to be so heavy*. I had real things to pack. I think I ended up with one bag of shoes and the other bag with the stuff I needed."

Upon arriving in Las Vegas, the adaptations to life on the road began immediately. When team meals weren't available, players became adept at ordering from food delivery apps. Haircuts were do-it-yourself. They held movie nights in large ballrooms, with room for social distancing. Daily walks for coffee, soon called Coffee Club—which were open to all, whether one was a coffee drinker or not—turned out to be necessary opportunities for human interaction with teammates. In Los Angeles, they got to walk on the beach. Stanford also brought in its resident "happiness professor," Dr. Fred Luskin, and the team's sports psychologist.

The Cardinal celebrated being the nation's No. 1 team for a week on December 7, 2020. They celebrated again when, on December 15, VanDerveer became the winningest coach in women's college basketball history with her 1,099th win, against Pacific, 90 miles from Palo Alto in Stockton. Belibi ordered the coach a knee-length fleece jacket with the name T-Dawg embroidered on the back as a gift from the team. The team marked the occasion quietly, together in the locker room and then in an area near the concession stands in an empty arena, where there was cake and balloons. "It made it really special in a way that it would not have been, I think, had a lot of other people been around," VanDerveer said. "Instead, it was intimate and very meaningful."

They played in Berkeley and Santa Cruz, staying in hotels tantalizingly close to the Stanford campus and their normal lives but just beyond Santa Clara County borders. Haley Jones showed her teammates around her hometown in Santa Cruz. They practiced in a high school gym, and a winter storm knocked out the power, leaving the players to work out in the dark.

They celebrated Christmas at a hotel near campus and just beyond the Santa Clara County line. Players were allowed to go to campus one by one to retrieve some of their belongings. Family members arrived at the hotel to spend socially distanced time with their daughters, only after they had been tested. Some brought Christmas stockings and home-cooked meals for players whose family was unable to visit. Some players connected with family on video calls.

For Alyssa Jerome, it was her first Christmas away from home. There was usually cold weather or snow in Toronto, where she was from, and this was a decidedly different experience. Belibi had never not been home for Christmas. Her parents came to visit, and everyone sat six feet apart. "It was a lot of masking," Belibi said. "And it was really awkward."

Following the Christmas holiday, two coaches and two staff members tested positive for COVID. Stanford traveled to Arizona for games against Arizona and Arizona State with just VanDerveer and assistant coach Katy Steding on the bench. The team stayed in Arizona for a week.

On that trip, Jerome hugged a fellow Canadian player whom she knew well following the game. The player later tested positive for COVID. The Stanford coaches had to go through the game video to determine who was near that player for more than 10 seconds at a time, and they were required to quarantine. "It was challenging," VanDerveer said.

Players and coaches struggled with their mental health. "Flexibility" had been the team mantra, but as the weeks wore on, it was getting harder. Everyone was isolated in their own rooms. The seniors began checking on their teammates. Players held mental health talks and validated one another's struggles with anxiety and the daily fear that it could all blow up with one mistake. Every day the isolation and a lack of normalcy brought new challenges. Energy levels ebbed and flowed. Getting away wasn't an option. "There were times when I know I said, 'I don't know if I can do this another day. I don't know if we can do this another week,'" VanDerveer said. "We were nomads with suitcases, going here and there. We were in nice hotels and we were eating well, but you were always sitting six feet apart."

The players were trying to keep up with their studies through a computer screen at one of the world's premier academic institutions. "The isolation part of it was all-consuming," Jump said. "You could never get away from it. In a normal year, in the season, you are able to step away from it when needed—go see your friends, spend time with your family, and rejuvenate yourself. To not be able to do that was really, really hard. Being together as a team was the only thing that got us through."

Hard days were amplified by the isolation. There were no comforts of home, whether *home* meant family or a dorm room on campus. The Hull sisters had something no one else had—family. "I'm grateful to have gone through that with my sister," Lacie Hull said. "Every part of that experience was difficult, and even though our team is like family, having your actual sister with you is different. We were lucky in that way."

Little moments of joy proved vital. In mid-January, the Cardinal made the trip to Boulder, a game that is usually attended by VanDerveer's mother, Rita. Instead, the team went to Rita. The bus pulled up at her apartment building, she came outside, and they stood across the parking lot for her annual photo with the team. Rita cried. The weather was warm enough for Rita to have a short outdoor visit with her daughter.

When Stanford played in Pullman, Washington, for back-to-back games, Lexie and Lacie Hull's parents brought their dogs to visit the team. Ashten Prechtel's parents brought their family dog when the team was in Colorado. Cameron Brink's family drove 16 hours to bring their dog from Oregon to L.A. The dogs made things feel normal.

On Hannah Jump's birthday, she was quarantining at home after being exposed to COVID. The team made their way from Santa Cruz, where they had been practicing, to her home in San Jose, where they sang "Happy Birthday" to her through the window of her bedroom.

But the restrictions remained limiting. Players and staff had begun wearing monitors that would indicate if they were standing within six feet of another person when they weren't on the court. That brought a new level of stress to everyone. "One time, Fran and I were in separate hotel rooms where we were sharing a wall, and the sensor was pinging," Jump said. "They would collect them and run the data in case someone tested positive."

The stress of testing positive for COVID was all too real. Williams said she worried about getting COVID, because vaccines were only starting to become available at that point. She mostly worried about spreading it to her team and risking the season they had sacrificed so much for already. "I did not want to be the reason we couldn't play," Williams said. "Nobody wanted that."

"I don't remember how many swabs we had up our noses, but the stress of getting your test back every day, twice a day, hoping that it wasn't positive—that produced a lot of anxiety," Lexie Hull said.

By the end of the Cardinal's late-January 2021 trip to Washington, the restrictions had been lifted. It was time to go home. All told, Stanford played 17 straight games on the road, winning 15 of them. They wouldn't play at home again until February 5, 2021, 72 days after their last game at Maples Pavilion.

Belibi was thrilled to be reunited with her shoe collection. Players were able to cook their own meals, drive their cars. They would be able to play on their home court and finish the season in a familiar place. As happy as the players and coaches were to be home, something had been built over those previous two months—a reservoir of resilience that would serve the Cardinal well as the season hit its home stretch.

The NCAA had announced that the entire three-week NCAA tournament would be played in San Antonio, Texas, in a bubble. Teams would be isolated, living many of the protocols that Stanford had already experienced, including daily testing and social distancing. There would be no team outings. The number of fans would be limited, but family and friends would be allowed to attend. Being bubbled in San Antonio for three straight weekends would be "nothing" for the Cardinal, VanDerveer said.

On the court, Stanford had found its groove. The Cardinal had veteran guards with Williams, Haley Jones, Anna Wilson, and the Hull twins and some of the best depth in the country inside with Belibi, Prechtel, and freshman Cameron Brink. After losing back-to-back games in January to Colorado and UCLA, Stanford had reeled off 11 straight wins heading into the Pac-12 tournament in Las Vegas, and they ran through the conference tournament with three wins, the closest margin being 20 points. As good as they were offensively, the Cardinal had also turned into one of the best defensive teams in the nation.

Still, at that moment, VanDerveer would not take anything for granted. "I'm always a worrier," she said after the Pac-12 title game. "I am always looking for things that we can do better. I can't say that I'm ever, like, really confident. Maybe the insecurities motivate me to work harder. We need[ed] to continue to stay healthy; [We were] always day-to-day . . . [had] to test negative."

For Williams, the tournament's location in San Antonio was a gift; she would play her final college games in her hometown. She was elated to make the trip. Everyone she loved—her family, friends, former coaches, and teammates—would be able to be there, to see her lead her team on the quest for a national title. She didn't care about the bubble. "To visibly be able to see them, to see them cheering us on—it was everything," Williams said.

When the team arrived in San Antonio, the Williams family's home cooking began immediately. Literally. Williams's father delivered homemade BBQ to the families who had traveled. Her great-aunt made her famous enchilada pie for the team and even made a vegan version.

The team put together a "fun committee" of players to plan ways to keep themselves entertained, and organized a Ping-Pong table in the hotel ballroom and played an intersquad competition that lasted the entire tournament. The mood was much more relaxed than what they had experienced in the winter. "We knew we had an advantage over people," Jump said. "There was a lot of comfort in already knowing how it was going to go."

Even as Stanford opened the tournament with two decisive wins over Utah Valley and Oklahoma State, the tournament itself was not without controversy. Before Stanford's first game, Stanford's performance coach, Ali Kirschner, tweeted a photo of the men's weight room facilities in their bubble in Indianapolis in a side-by-side collage compared with the women's. The men's weight room was fully equipped, with rows and racks of barbells and hand weights. The women's facility was, by contrast, lacking; it included a set of light hand weights next to a table stacked with yoga mats.

Oregon center Sedona Prince, with a large social media following, quickly amplified the post on TikTok, getting millions of views and drawing national media attention and outrage. Sporting goods companies jumped in to supplement the women's space with equipment. Then it was revealed that the women's teams had different, less reliable COVID testing protocols than the men. The men were using more accurate, medical-grade PCR tests, and the women were given antigen tests akin to the home tests that were being sold and distributed widely. The NCAA had to release a statement of apology, and on the eve of the biggest tournament of the season, VanDerveer and other coaches had to address it with the media.

VanDerveer was furious about the whole situation. The difference in facilities and amenities wasn't surprising. She'd been around for a long time. But the difference in COVID testing protocols between the men and women was beyond the pale. "That was never justified to me," VanDerveer said. "I felt like they didn't care about the women. I mean, I'm 68 years old at that point. It felt like they didn't care about me."

Still, the Cardinal refused to be distracted. A 27-point win over Missouri State in the Sweet 16, a game they led by as many as 38 points in the fourth quarter, sent the message that Stanford was gunning for a title. Next up was an Elite Eight matchup against Louisville for a trip to the Final Four. The Cardinal opened with one of their worst halves of the season and were down by 12 points when the third quarter started. Stanford rallied in the second half, however, led by Lexie Hull's 21 points and 9 rebounds. Prechtel came off the bench to go 6-for-6 from the field, with three huge three-pointers to finish with 16 points. It was enough for a convincing 78–63 victory.

Stanford had earned a date with Dawn Staley's South Carolina program, a rematch of the 2017 Final Four game in Indianapolis, which Stanford had lost after leading at the half. The rematch was a knock-down, drag-out battle ultimately decided by a single point, when South Carolina's young star center Aliyah Boston missed a shot under the basket after an offensive rebound, handing the Cardinal a hard-fought 66–65 win. Haley Jones led the way with 24 points, including a jumper with 32 seconds left to give Stanford the lead. Williams struggled to finish with eight points, missing 10 of 14 shots, but her teammates had her back. Lexie Hull finished with 18 points, 13 rebounds, and 4 assists.

The Cardinal were headed back to the national title game for the first time since 2010, when they had fallen to Connecticut. And in the second semifinal matchup, it was the Huskies who were heavily favored over Pac-12 upstart Arizona and their newly crowned star, senior guard Aari McDonald. But it was the Arizona Wildcats who came away with the upset, setting up an all-Pac-12 national title game for the first time in history.

Stanford built a 31–24 lead at halftime of the NCAA title game, before Arizona came storming back behind some stingy defense and McDonald's scoring. While the Wildcats shot just 28.3 percent for the game, their defense forced Stanford into 21 turnovers, and the Cardinal hung on for dear life to the final shot. Stanford had built a nine-point lead in the fourth quarter before Arizona cut it to one point on a three-pointer by McDonald that made the score 51–50. Jones responded with a three-point play that would be Stanford's last basket of the game. McDonald got Arizona within one again by converting three free throws, making it 54–53. The Cardinal could not get a shot off after their last timeout, returning the ball to Arizona with 6.1 seconds to go. McDonald's last-second contested shot hung in the air for what felt like forever before bouncing off the rim. Stanford's celebration exploded.

For the first time in 29 years, Tara VanDerveer and Stanford were national champions. None of the players on this team were even born the last time the Cardinal had won an NCAA title. This team had accomplished something "miraculous," as Muir called it, under the most extraordinary circumstances. They were the first team in history to win an NCAA title with a pair of one-point wins in the Final Four. VanDerveer hugged every player and staff member as they ascended the ladder to cut down the nets.

There was elation and a deep sense of relief that it was finally over. "Everything we've been through, it feels like it was worth it," Williams said after the game. "Everything just lined up. Feels like it was written."

The 29-year gap between titles for VanDerveer was the largest ever in Division I collegiate athletics. Yet VanDerveer demurred when asked about what it meant to close the circle with a title after nearly three decades, to silence the doubts that as great as she was, her teams couldn't win titles in this new era of college basketball. "This isn't why I coach," VanDerveer said after the game. "I want to be a teacher, and each year is a great year."

She wasn't afraid to call her team a little bit lucky, because to win a national championship, VanDerveer said, always involves a little luck. And in this case, a lot of grit after 86 nights in hotel rooms and chaos and uncertainty where routine should have been. It was a challenge unlike VanDerveer, the coaches, the staff, and the players had ever experienced. "It was an incredible testament to everyone's determination and their resilience and the unbelievable sacrifices everyone made," VanDerveer said.

Jump later admitted she has questioned, even with a national championship, whether it was worth what they all ultimately sacrificed. "Looking back, you could see the toll that it took on everyone's mental health," Jump said. "I think that is when people were like, 'Damn, that was hard.'"

Lexie Hull later said that if the ending of Stanford's extraordinary season had been written any differently, she might feel the same. "I wouldn't trade it . . . because we won," Lexie said. "If we had lost, honestly I think the way I look back on that season would be different. It's crazy to say that about the outcome of one game, but that's the reality of it."

VanDerveer said that if the 2021 title has an asterisk next to it in the NCAA annals because of COVID, she thinks it will be for the right reasons. "In some ways, I think it was the hardest championship," VanDerveer said. "To maintain your health . . . with all the issues that were going on and the challenges of that. How we survived that and stuck together is a real testament to the resilience, determination, and passion of the young people on our team."

After the game, the head coach thanked Arizona and the Pac-12 conference teams that had prepared them. She thanked the litany of players she coached between 1992 and 2021 who never got to experience this championship moment. In the end, VanDerveer felt like the Cardinal won this title "for all the great players that have played at Stanford." She said, "I know that these women are kind of on the shoulders of those women. Former players would be so proud to be part of this team because of the resilience they've shown, because of the sisterhood that they represent. I'm just thrilled for this team, but also for all the women out there that played at Stanford."

As a bookend to the way the season started, the Stanford players returned to the hotel to celebrate their title. They were still not allowed to interact with friends and family because they had to fly back on a charter the next morning. One of Williams's friends texted and suggested that she meet up with them at a local bar. "I'm the instigator," Williams said. "I let them convince me to go to this small bar around the corner from the hotel. I told my teammates, and they wanted to come. We literally ran past security and down the street. We were only there for like 30 minutes, and hardly anyone was there. But then we heard the coaches and the NCAA officials were looking for us."

When the players got back to the hotel, Stanford's director of basketball operations Eileen Roche and NCAA security were waiting for them in the lobby. In the elevator, Roche turned to the players. "Did you at least have a good time?" she asked them. The answer, finally, after the hardest year of everyone's lives, was a resounding yes.

A couple years later, Belibi found herself in a premed graduate school class at Harvard, among a group of students who didn't know one another. The instructor asked them to share something interesting about themselves. Belibi didn't know where to start. So she started with winning a national title during COVID. "I think I sometimes forget how awesome it was that we did that, and the way we did it, and how hard it was," Belibi said. "We really did that."

## CHAPTER 13

# Taraisms

**THE WISDOM AND INFLUENCE** of Tara VanDerveer comes in many forms, all of which can be summed up by the term *Taraism*.

> **Taraism (Tar-uh-izm), noun**: A saying or phrase coined and consistently repeated by Stanford coach Tara VanDerveer to her team during practice or in-game huddles, or to the media during press conferences; a philosophy of leadership that includes innovation, advocacy, and personal evolution.

The first definition is one that every Stanford player knows too well.

*"Do you want to have fun? Try winning. That's fun."*

*"You are a Ferrari! Stop driving like a Volkswagen."*

*"Some days you are the dog, and some days you are the hydrant."*

*"The S isn't for* stupid."

*"The hungry lion hunts best."*

*"They already made the movie* Dumb and Dumber, *but you're not in it."*

She saved other special gems just for the media:

*"We are a cake, and we aren't quite baked yet."*

*"We are like an orchestra, and [fill in star player's name here] is playing a solo."*

*"We are a puzzle, and we don't have all the pieces yet."*

Stanford players all have their favorites. Vanessa Nygaard, the shooting guard who played from 1994 to 1998, made a YouTube video back in 2017 with her young children reciting the classics, joking that she was preparing "the next generation" for the way of life her former head coach had drilled into her.

VanDerveer shrugged off the entire concept. "Some of it is just the stupid stuff that pops into my head," VanDerveer said. "It comes from a place of wanting people to play with intelligence and purpose, not just running around out there doing knuckleheaded stuff."

The effectiveness of the Taraism is not just the turn of phrase; it is also in the delivery—that flat, nasal tone. The dry wit. The intent to be funny while sending a message. "There's just kind of a Tara voice," Jennifer Azzi said. "I don't know that I could do it, but if you ask any former player what is the 'Tara voice,' they will all know what that is. It can be kind of serious, a little bit sarcastic."

But *Taraism* is not solely defined by quirky adages and clever quips. *Taraism* is also a philosophy that has guided VanDerveer throughout her coaching career. It is a lifelong quest for knowledge coupled with unbending commitments to activism and feminism. All of it flows from a sense of regret that, despite a deep passion for the game, her own young basketball career was stifled by the realities of a time before the passage of Title IX; before the NCAA ran a tournament for women; before women's professional basketball; before being a college athlete was viewed, by young women, as anything more than a hobby on the way to another career. She always wanted to give others what she never had, to make sure that opportunities were not wasted.

When VanDerveer was inducted into the Naismith Memorial Basketball Hall of Fame in 2011, she quoted the Malcolm Gladwell book *Outliers,* citing his theory that successful people are built from "heritage, patronage, opportunity, 10,000 hours of practice, and legacy." "I passed 10,000 practice hours a long time ago," she joked from the podium in Springfield, Massachusetts, that night.

VanDerveer's vision always reached miles beyond her own opportunity. She has been a basketball innovator and an evolver, the master teacher who saw the benefit of the three-point shot before the others, the tactician who was willing to adapt her offense—whether the triangle, the Princeton, or pro-style pick-and-roll—to suit her players rather than the other way around. The strategist whose defensive scout preparations were a national standard, her ability to take an opposing team's best player (or two) out of the game a given.

The late Pat Summitt once told her biographer, Sally Jenkins, that playing VanDerveer's Stanford team would always expose every one of her team's weaknesses. And that she used to relish the opportunity to match wits and game plans with her friend.

As much as VanDerveer shape-shifted her coaching style with the evolving women's game, VanDerveer also prioritized personal evolutions, including taking up the classical piano at the age of 48. Her openness to professional and personal evolution has defined how she sees the world, and it has compelled her to use her influential voice and her considerable platform. The Hall of Fame coach has rarely shied away from a statement, an interview, or an opportunity to answer a difficult question. She has initiated more than a few tough conversations—with her team, with individual players, and with a bevy of reporters in front of her. She has said what she thinks needs to be said on topics ranging from the quality of play of her team on a given night to the state of the world, which she has traveled extensively, thanks to basketball.

VanDerveer has consistently paved a path for young female coaches, both by bringing them on to her own staff—hiring exclusively female coaches during her 38 seasons at Stanford—and supporting and mentoring fellow coaches across the country and helping to pave a career path for young female coaches through the Women's Sports Foundation.

Heidi VanDerveer has watched her older sister form a worldview through the lens of basketball, and fly in the face of perceptions about her single-mindedness in the process. "I think there are a lot of misconceptions about Tara that she is all about basketball," Heidi said. "Basketball is the conduit to a lot of things for her."

UCLA coach Cori Close attended VanDerveer's Stanford camps as a teenage player who grew up 15 miles away in Milpitas, and worked as a camp staff counselor during her college years. "I remember thinking about Tara, *Wow, she is so serious. She is so all about basketball,*" Close said. "She was so stately, although I'm sure that's not the word I would have used then. When I worked at camp, the staff would always go out at night, and she was never there."

It wasn't until Close began her career as a coach at UC Santa Barbara and Florida State before coming to UCLA that she began to see VanDerveer in a different light, with a warmth and humor that belies her professorial exterior.

Close, then–Utah coach Lynne Roberts, Washington coach Tina Langley, and VanDerveer were recruiting at a tournament together in the spring of 2023. Close had a private plane available to take her to the next recruiting stop. She offered Roberts, Langley, and VanDerveer a lift since they were all going to the same place. The two-hour plane ride was full of laughter and insight. VanDerveer supplied most of the laughs. "I rode with Lynne to the hotel after the flight, and we both said, 'We didn't know Tara was that funny.' But it was not just that she made us laugh, but she let us into her life outside of basketball," Close said. "We talked about how the game has grown. I don't think any of us wanted to move or talk, because you knew you were getting so much wisdom and having so much fun."

Kate Paye has heard the same story more than once about VanDerveer—the unexpected earnestness from a coach who many viewed as buttoned-up or even aloof. "Head coaches, assistant coaches will tell me that they were out recruiting and Tara sat next to them, and she just started talking," Paye said. "She asks questions; she's interested in what they have to say. It's not what they expect, I guess, based on the perception of what a legendary Hall of Fame coach is supposed to be like, or what they think Tara might be like. They don't expect how down-to-earth and personable she is."

Former Stanford athletic director Bernard Muir felt that same sense of intimidation when he took the job at Stanford. His impression as he prepared to arrive at Stanford was that he might have to brace himself to deal with the legendary head coach, who seemed so stern and single-minded on the sideline and during his brief interaction with her during his interview process. He had already gone through several rounds of interviews when he landed in front of the search committee, which included VanDerveer. "There were 12 or 15 people around the table, and I thought I had given a pretty good effort at answering their questions," Muir said. At the end, one of the search committee members asked Muir how he felt about the process. He began talking about his own full-circle moment, that after being a student-athlete at Brown, he had always dreamed of being an athletic director at a major institution. "Tara stopped me and said, 'Yeah, Bernard, that's great. But here's what is different at

Stanford: we win.' All I could say was, 'Good point.' From that time on, Tara has always been my truth-teller and the one I go to for perspective. She's always going to keep it real."

Close said VanDerveer's demeanor is reminiscent of the legendary UCLA men's coach John Wooden, considered perhaps the greatest coach in the history of college basketball. "It's a sense that they have a keen awareness that it's not about them," Close said. "I think her personality is a reflection of her selflessness. For her, it's been about teaching the game and teaching life lessons and impacting young women and further opportunities for women."

VanDerveer's willingness to cede her own role as teacher and become a student again back in 2001 opened one of the more colorful chapters of her career. The person in perpetual control gave it up to learn something she'd always wanted to try—the piano.

VanDerveer has loved music since childhood. She played the flute until she was a teenager. She always thought she would like to learn to play the piano. VanDerveer and her sister Heidi were doing some pre-holiday shopping at an electronics store back in 2001, when VanDerveer approached a portable keyboard, started tapping the keys, and told her sister that she was putting it on her Christmas list. Heidi fulfilled the request. VanDerveer decided she would teach herself how to play. She figured she would read a couple of books and figure it out. "Obviously, I had no idea what I was getting myself into," VanDerveer admitted.

A Stanford season ticket holder told the coach that she knew a good piano teacher and made a call to Jodi Gandolfi, who told her friend that she didn't usually take beginners. "She told me that I should say yes, and that I would find it interesting," said Gandolfi, who has a doctorate in music from Stanford. She had no idea her new student had coached teams to national championships and an Olympic gold medal.

Before she had her first lesson, VanDerveer had a baby grand piano wheeled into her home. She took weekly lessons for several years. "This is the closest thing to being coached that I can think of," VanDerveer said. "Sitting on this bench by yourself, you are very vulnerable, and I never understood it like I do now." She even brought a keyboard on recruiting trips, much to the entertainment of fellow coaches. She practiced every chance she got, booking team hotels for road trips based on whether there was a piano available, and playing during team meals. Gandolfi became a regular at women's basketball games, a new fan. VanDerveer made three collections of music, burned them on CDs, and gave them out as gifts to family and friends.

VanDerveer has also always had a keen awareness that she has a platform as a head coach with a national profile that allows her to advocate and amplify causes that are important to her. For years, she has served on the board of Humane Society Silicon Valley, a devoted dog lover helping to place rescue dogs throughout the region.

During the COVID pandemic, VanDerveer used the visibility of breaking Pat Summitt's all-time women's coaching win record to organize a donation campaign to the Second Harvest Food Bank in Santa Clara County, knowing how many families were struggling to meet basic needs. "It's a matter of taking advantage of a moment to do some good," VanDerveer said.

When Russia invaded Ukraine in 2022, VanDerveer turned the attention of the NCAA tournament into an opportunity to raise money for humanitarian relief, pledging $10 for each three-pointer made during the NCAA tournament and challenging other coaches to do the same. It was a plan she came up with over breakfast. Georgia Tech coach Nell Fortner, who coached with VanDerveer on the 1996 Olympic team, accepted the challenge. WNBA star Breanna Stewart and NBA Hall of Famer Charles Barkley also made the pledge, as did NBA star James Harden and current USC coach Lindsay Gottlieb. "I have been to Ukraine with the US team. We played them so much in 1996 that I called them our cousins," VanDerveer said at the time. "Maybe I have an affinity for the country, and watching what's happening has been really, really, very hard." She raised more than $300,000.

During Brittney Griner's nearly yearlong detention in Russia in 2022, it was VanDerveer and South Carolina coach Dawn Staley who, during their nationally televised matchup, wore T-shirts and spoke about Griner's plight and the importance of keeping attention on her and returning her home. At the time, VanDerveer said, "I think more and more people feel like because sports are so visible, it can be used to make positive change. I admire [Golden State Warriors coach] Steve Kerr for using his platform to talk about gun violence and gun control, and I think that's great. Wearing a T-shirt for a game is the least I can do, but if someone thinks it's helpful, that's awesome."

VanDerveer has encouraged her players, through the years, to find their own causes. "Alanna Smith talked about human trafficking and brought some attention to that. Jayne Appel brought attention to mental health," VanDerveer said. "How fortunate we have been to be at Stanford, and so I think it's important to think about giving back."

"Giving back" came in many forms for VanDerveer, who, as mentioned in chapter 12, felt that it was her duty to speak up when she saw the women's game receiving inferior treatment by the NCAA during the 2021 NCAA tournament, held during the COVID-19 pandemic. After issuing a statement that was picked up nationally, VanDerveer, Connecticut's Geno Auriemma, and Dawn Staley—three of the most powerful voices in the women's game—served on an ad hoc committee formed by the Women's Basketball Coaches Association to make recommendations on needed changes.

The negative attention spurred the NCAA to begin a gender-equity investigation that concluded five months later, at which time an independent review board released a scathing report confirming that the NCAA had fallen short of upholding its commitment to gender equity. The report led to changes to the women's tournament that included allowing the women to use the March Madness moniker for its tournament branding, expanding the tournament field to 68 teams, expanded fan events, equal pay for officials in the men's and women's tournaments, and addressing resource discrepancies between the two tournaments to the tune of millions of dollars. It was just more evidence to VanDerveer that she could not rely on others to do the right thing.

Over 38 years at Stanford, VanDerveer hired only women on her coaching staff. Only once in her coaching career, while she was at Idaho in her first year as a head coach, did she have a man on her staff: Lubomyr "Luby" Lichonczak, who went on to coach women's basketball in the college ranks as a head coach at Radford and the University of Texas–San Antonio.

Hiring only women did not begin as an intentional effort. Even now, VanDerveer believes that all basketball staffs would benefit from a mix of female and male coaches, and she would happily advocate for women coaches on men's coaching staffs. But through the decades, as she watched more men move into women's basketball coaching with little to no reciprocation on the men's side, her intention to elevate women coaches in the women's game began to solidify. "Until men's programs start to hire women, then I felt like I had to give the opportunity to women, to get experience, to learn, and to be able to get jobs," VanDerveer said. "And I think for the most part, I've made some really good hiring decisions. Some great ones. We don't accomplish the things we do without the staff I've had. They are role models to our players in their own right."

For years in the Bay Area, as men's college coaching vacancies opened, some writer or broadcaster would inevitably say, "Hire Tara." Andy Geiger, the athletic director who hired VanDerveer at Stanford, said in 1990 after Stanford won its first national title: "I think Tara's tremendously capable of coaching any team. But women's sports needs Tara VanDerveer. Tara's staff was the only all-women coaching staff at the Final Four. We need to emphasize that and build careers for women coaching women. Let's deal with that first." VanDerveer said she never got any serious inquiries to coach men's basketball. But she wouldn't have done it anyway.

VanDerveer did more than fill her own staff with women's coaches and create a Stanford pipeline into the coaching ranks. In 2019, she collaborated with the Women's Sports Foundation to create the Tara VanDerveer Fund for the Advancement of Women in Coaching. Through 2024, the fund has provided $1 million to 38 colleges and universities for coaching fellowships, benefiting 43 coaches across 12 sports. VanDerveer got a call in 2019 from Billie Jean King, the founder of the Women's Sports Foundation, who wanted to come out to the kickoff celebration. "That was thrilling for me," VanDerveer said.

VanDerveer has also helped friends in need, such as Beth Burns and Marianne Stanley. Burns had lost her job at Ohio State in 2004 when VanDerveer brought her to Stanford to serve as the team's strength and conditioning coach for two seasons. Burns eventually returned to a head coaching job at San Diego State. Stanley was unemployed and in a legal battle with USC over equal pay when VanDerveer brought her to Stanford to coach with Amy Tucker during the year she stepped away to coach the 1996 Olympic team. Her career rejuvenated, Stanley moved on to become the head coach at Cal and then transitioned into the WNBA. "We've tried to be a place for people who need a reboot," VanDerveer said.

Burns said VanDerveer is all about the adage "Lean on me." "She's good at making people feel valued," Burns said.

Meanwhile, VanDerveer has never lost sight of how to afford girls the opportunities she never had. At Stanford camp, sometimes speaking to as many as 100 campers at a time, some as young as eight years old, she would tell stories about the early days. "I told them about how I never played, how I had to bring the best ball to play with the boys," VanDerveer said. "I never had JV, varsity, nothing. I never had a scholarship. We were never on television.

"One girl, after I give this whole litany, raises her hand and says, 'Coach, why was it like that?' I didn't really know how to answer that. So I asked, 'Can anyone else answer this question?' And another little eight-year-old right away raises her hand. She goes, 'Sexism!'

"I tell that story a lot because girls from a very young age know how things are in the world," VanDerveer said. "And they are the ones who can change it."

In her mind, making change for the better is the ultimate Taraism.

CHAPTER 14

# The Power Players

**IT WAS A BEAUTIFUL MID-SPRING** evening in Palo Alto on May 8, 2018, as the Women's Sports Foundation hosted a tribute dinner for Tara VanDerveer, honoring the Hall of Fame coach by announcing the Tara VanDerveer Fund for the Advancement of Women in Coaching, a fund providing fellowships to aspiring female coaches in all sports.

The next day, the WNBA announced the promotion of former Stanford women's basketball player Bethany Donaphin to the head of WNBA league operations. Just a few weeks later, VanDerveer attended a board meeting of the Women's Basketball Hall of Fame to discuss her coaching endowment. Who did she find herself sitting next to? Donaphin. VanDerveer was happy to brag about the photo they took together that day. "It's awesome," VanDerveer said. "And it's not a surprise. Bethany is one of those bright, motivated, get-things-done women."

VanDerveer knows a lot of them. And many have one big thing in common—time spent in Stanford's women's basketball program. Donaphin's promotion at that time was just the latest elevation of a former Stanford women's basketball player into a leading role in the professional ranks of a variety of fields.

The list is long and distinguished:

- Jennifer Azzi—Las Vegas Aces (WNBA), chief business development officer
- Christy Hedgpeth—Current: president of Playfly Sports Properties; Previous: WNBA's chief operating officer
- Amy (Wustefeld) Brooks—NBA, president of new business ventures
- Bethany Donaphin—WNBA, head of league operations
- Jayne Appel-Marinelli—Women's National Basketball Players Association (WNBPA), senior vice president of player relations
- Nneka Ogwumike—WNBPA, president; More Than a Vote, organization leader
- Sonja Henning—Nike, senior director of business affairs and league relations (retired); Urban League of Portland board of directors; Women's National Basketball Players Association, former president
- Rosalyn Gold-Onwude—ESPN broadcaster, host, and public speaker
- Heather Owen—Santa Clara University, director of athletics
- Angela Taylor—Washington Mystics (WNBA), general manager, 2008–10; Atlanta Dream (WNBA), general manager and team president, 2014–16
- Chiney Ogwumike—First WNBA player to be hired as a full-time broadcaster at ESPN; President Biden's Advisory Council on African Diaspora Engagement
- Dr. Kate Starbird—University of Washington Center for an Informed Public, cofounder and director

- Jamila Wideman—Washington Mystics (WNBA), general manager; NBA, senior vice president of player development
- Becky Bonner—Orlando Magic (NBA), director of player development and basketball operations
- Susan King Borchardt—the Athlete Blueprint, director and founder; US women's national basketball team, performance coach

Beyond this group there are dozens more success stories: doctors, lawyers, authors, researchers, educators, engineers, business owners . . . . The woman who became the winningest coach in college basketball history before her retirement takes no credit for her players' considerable professional successes. But they will give her credit for fostering and empowering a group of leaders who turned their basketball experiences into a springboard for leadership off the court. "It's like cooking," VanDerveer said. "You have to have really good ingredients to begin with. And then you have a recipe, and you still have to cook it right."

"She didn't wake up every day and come to practice and say, 'Be a leader,'" said Appel-Marinelli, who ended her WNBA playing career in 2016 after seven seasons and moved to a position with the WNBPA, where she leads the union's player-relations efforts, including internships, partnerships, and transitional programs. "But she showed us examples of her service to the game all the time. She has invested so much of her own life into it, and we pulled from that."

Nneka Ogwumike, the 2016 WNBA MVP, and Appel-Marinelli, work closely together. Nneka has served three terms as the president of the WNBPA, beginning in 2016. There have been three WNBPA presidents in league history, and Stanford can claim two of them. Sonja Henning was the union's first president from 2001 to 2003.

Nneka Ogwumike is credited with leading the WNBA through a groundbreaking collective bargaining agreement in 2020 that increased player compensation, gave players more freedom of movement in free agency, and improved health and wellness initiatives, including advancements in child care, maternity leave pay, and family planning. She led the players through their social-justice-fueled "bubble season" during COVID in 2020–21, and she helped push the WNBA to offer charter flights for its players, which began in the 2024 season. And she led the players into another critical CBA negotiation in 2025, a contract expected to reset the financial model for the league. In addition to being one of the league's most accomplished players, she is among its most revered for her commitment to improving the conditions for the league's players.

VanDerveer asked Nneka to be a team captain in her sophomore season, and Nneka did not think she was ready. The coaches assured her they would support her and guide her. "And now she is a fabulous leader of the WNBA players," VanDerveer said. "Leadership skills are real things to learn. And I hope we taught them."

Nneka's younger sister Chiney Ogwumike became the first Black woman to cohost a nationally syndicated ESPN radio show, and regularly appears on *NBA Today*, *SportsCenter*, and *First Take*. In 2024, Chiney was named to President Joe Biden's Advisory Council on African Diaspora Engagement as the panel's youngest female member. Both sisters have long been involved in international advocacy work in Nigeria. Chiney Ogwumike was an international studies major at Stanford, and for the work in her major, she was required to spend a term overseas, an opportunity that student-athletes often must skip because of the requirements of their sport. She went to VanDerveer with trepidation about asking to be away from the program for an extended period of time, but she was surprised when her coach was immediately supportive.

"That's not even a hard decision," VanDerveer said. "I think the players maybe had a tendency to view me as inflexible, but I think I'm the opposite. You have to make decisions that are best for each player, because ultimately you want them to be successful and thrive." It was VanDerveer who connected Chiney with former secretary of state Condoleezza Rice, who would serve as Chiney's advisor through her time at Stanford. "It's part of how Tara 'raised' us," Nneka said. "She taught us how to weave things together in terms of the things we wanted to do outside of basketball and our commitment to the team."

Kate Starbird found her balance at Stanford too. The 1997 National Player of the Year spent her non-basketball time working with professors on research projects and with her computer science classmates. "I remember a time when Hillary Clinton was coming to the Stanford business school, and I heard her say, 'I can't wait to meet Kate Starbird,'" VanDerveer said.

Starbird's career as an academic and one of the world's leading experts on misinformation and disinformation is a reflection of the ways she was allowed to flourish away from the floor. It's also been a difficult journey—she has been exposed to harassment and death threats for her groundbreaking work.

Susan King Borchardt's path was entirely different. The former point guard from Minnesota, who sustained two ACL injuries during her Stanford career runs the Athlete Blueprint, a sports performance business, along with her husband and fellow Stanford basketball star Curtis Borchardt. The two met while both rehabbing injuries at Stanford more than 20 years ago. King Borchardt, who served as Stanford's strength and conditioning coach in 2011–12, has worked with some of the most accomplished athletes in women's sports, including Sue Bird, Nneka Ogwumike, Megan Rapinoe, Kelsey Plum, Breanna Stewart, Skylar Diggins-Smith, Jewell Loyd and 2024 Stanford graduate Cameron Brink. She also serves as the performance coach for the US women's national basketball team.

Rosalyn Gold-Onwude left Stanford wanting to start her broadcasting career. She quickly found work as a fill-in, calling games when more established broadcasters were unable to work. After one of her early broadcasts, she got a call from VanDerveer asking her to come to her office on campus, so Gold-Onwude, still living near campus, stopped by. "[Tara] said, 'Sit down.' She presses play on the monitor, and suddenly we are watching the game broadcast I just did. And for the entire first half, Tara is pressing start and stop. She would say, 'I like what you are trying to say, but can you do it with less words?'

"It's such a beautiful way that she shows that she's not done with you just because you finished playing on the basketball court with her. And it was a real investment of her time. I didn't necessarily ask her to do that. And it was a really useful critique and feedback."

Gold-Onwude has gone on to broadcast college, NBA, and WNBA games for national outlets as a sideline reporter and an analyst.

Amy Brooks stood near the podium to honor VanDerveer at the May 2018 Women's Sports Foundation event. Brooks was named among the most powerful women in sports by *Forbes* magazine in 2018. She has worked for the NBA since 2005 and has led the development of the NBA's global business initiatives, as well as the league's marketing and business operations. Brooks was Amy Wustefeld when she played at Stanford, and she was a player, she admits, who came off the bench in the closing minutes of games that weren't exactly close. "I was a walk-on who averaged 1.8 points a game," Brooks said, joking that her role during a game was to know which way the possession arrow was pointing. "But for me, being at Stanford was transformative. I graduated with this confidence that I could do anything. . . . It's cliche that team sports teach you all of these great things about leadership, but it's supercharged at Stanford."

Brooks was a senior at Stanford in 1996 when VanDerveer stepped away from her program to become the coach of the US national team, leading to a gold medal in the 1996 Olympic Games in Atlanta. That team was credited with spurring the formation of two professional women's basketball leagues, including the WNBA. "The lesson for us was that there is nothing more important than the game, and we all saw that," Brooks said. "How could you not live up to your responsibilities after that?"

Christy Hedgpeth, the former point guard who was part of Stanford's national championship team in 1992, said her experience in VanDerveer's program made her understand a "higher purpose." Hedgpeth moved from the NBA executive ranks to become the president of Playfly Sports Properties, an emerging company specializing in marketing, media, and technology.

"Women's basketball, in particular, is still growing and needs support and help, and it's serendipity that leads so many of us back to the sport, beyond the coaching side," Hedgpeth said. "Tara always taught us to see the bigger picture. We played for a pioneer, and we saw that there is work to be done."

Appel-Marinelli points out that she is surrounded by her Stanford sisters at every turn. While working for the WNBPA, she often interacts with Donaphin, Wideman, and Brooks. And technically, Nneka Ogwumike is her boss. "Stanford is everywhere," Appel-Marinelli said.

Chiney Ogwumike said VanDerveer has taught her players lessons on leadership that are both implicit and explicit. "People always asked me why I didn't go to UConn, why I chose Stanford even when Stanford hadn't won a championship in a long time, and I feel like [it was because] I always understood that basketball is a small piece of your life," Chiney said. "You will play for a quarter of your life if you're lucky. But that Stanford degree matters for the rest of your life. You can always define your success by so much more than basketball."

In Donaphin's position with the WNBA, she oversees all on-court basketball operations, including rules, scouting, scheduling, and venues, as well as the administration of player-related policies and programs.

She said she followed the example of fellow Cardinal alums like Brooks and Azzi. "I feel like we are champions of the game and champions of the things we care about," Donaphin said. "The way Amy [Brooks] approaches leadership, the way Jennifer approaches it, wanting to have an impact and do good in the game and hold yourself to high standards. You want to follow that example."

Jennifer Azzi credited VanDerveer's example of leadership as one that so many players have followed, often whether they realize it or not. "Tara's example as a very ethical, authentic leader had an impact on all of us," she said

Former Stanford athletic director Bernard Muir called VanDerveer a "promoter of people." "She wants to win, but she also wants people to be the best version of themselves," Muir said. "I've never seen anyone that up close that really just cares about just making sure that people are better."

VanDerveer dismissed the idea that she's had anything to do with the chain of powerful, influential women beyond being fortunate enough to coach them. "Stanford, in a lot of ways, self-selects these types of women," VanDerveer said. "They come here very driven and high-achieving, and they leave with a lot of confidence. And that's a big part of being successful in the real world."

CHAPTER 15

# The Tree

**AT THE END OF** her basketball career, Lindy La Rocque took her Stanford degree and went to work at a financial software company. The Las Vegas native had stayed in the Bay Area after graduating with her bachelor's degree in 2012 in science, technology, and society, and when she had free time, she would pop into the women's basketball office on campus. Every time she left, assistant coach Kate Paye would yell after her, "See you soon!"

It was a secret to no one that the scrappy guard who appeared in four Final Fours with the Cardinal, the daughter of a basketball coach, the veteran who knew every play in the playbook and every drill in practice, wanted to get into coaching. La Rocque lasted at the software job until Christmas break. She called Paye, walked into the Stanford coaches' conference room, and admitted, "OK, work sucks." She later said, "I remember them all sitting there laughing their asses off, and I said, 'What's so funny?'" The coaches had made a friendly little wager about how long she would last before she showed up wanting to pivot to coaching. Some said six months, others eight. She lasted five. They had been waiting for her arrival.

At that moment, La Rocque, known during her playing days for her hustle and leadership, joined the Stanford coaching tree, working first as a graduate assistant at Oklahoma in 2014. She moved to Belmont University in Nashville to be an assistant coach in 2016 before VanDerveer brought her home to be a part of the Stanford staff in 2019. Two seasons of Stanford training ground later, and La Rocque was hired as the head coach at UNLV, her hometown team. In four seasons (through 2023–24), she led the Lady Rebels to three straight Mountain West Conference titles, two consecutive 30-win seasons, and three straight trips to the NCAA tournament. La Rocque is considered one of the country's best young coaches.

"There are people that you can see are meant to be coaches from a mile away," VanDerveer said. "Lindy was a no-brainer."

And she wasn't the only one. La Rocque is only one among the 15 former VanDerveer players and assistant coaches who have gone on to head coaching positions either at the collegiate level or in the WNBA.

Heidi VanDerveer called her sister Tara a connector, a trait that has paved the way for coaching careers for so many of her players and coaches. Sometimes it is VanDerveer making the direct connections to help get someone a job. Sometimes it's a letter of recommendation. Sometimes it is sage advice in an important moment. "She is tuned in to what other people need," Heidi said. "And she wants them to be successful."

Charmin Smith, who got her first recruiting letter from Stanford as a budding basketball star in St. Louis in the eighth grade, played for the Cardinal from 1993 to 1997, helping Stanford to three Final Fours and three Pac-10 titles. She earned her bachelor's and master's degrees in civil and environmental engineering, respectively. Coaching wasn't the obvious option. She thought she would become an engineer.

But upon her graduation in 1997, playing professional basketball was an option, with two leagues to choose from—the American Basketball League and the WNBA. Smith initially played one season with the ABL's Portland Power before the league folded. She then spent four seasons in the WNBA playing for the Minnesota Lynx, Seattle Storm, and Phoenix Mercury, plus one season of basketball overseas before retiring.

After playing a journeyman's role in the WNBA with three teams in four seasons, Charmin knew she was not done with basketball, even when her last roster cut came. "I called Tara and said 'I don't know what to do,'" Smith said. "And Tara said, 'I think you'd be a really good coach.' My first reaction was to say no. I didn't know how to do what she did. I wasn't sure I wanted to coach. But she made the call to Boston College, and they hired me. We won the Big East tournament in 2004, and it was amazing."

After Smith spent one season as an assistant coach at Boston College, VanDerveer brought her back to Stanford, where she served as an assistant coach until 2007. "Tara was always there for me as a former player. I could call her, and she wrote me letters of recommendation, but in terms of getting to know her as a person, it wasn't really until I worked with her," Smith said. "For me to see the other side of Tara—as a player I was intimidated by her. To get to know her in a more personal way and learn from her [was] a different experience."

Smith also noticed ways in which her former coach had softened through the years. "There were times when I thought, *We never would have gotten away with this.*" Smith said. "But things change and the game changes and players change, and the way we coach has to change—and I learned that lesson too."

In 2007, Smith moved to rival Cal to serve as the associate head coach under new coach Lindsay Gottlieb, helping Gottlieb to lead the Golden Bears to their first-ever Final Four in 2012. In 2019, she was hired as the Bears' head coach, the first head coaching job of her career.

Rivalry aside, VanDerveer never ceased to be a mentor for Smith. Smith called VanDerveer during the COVID season, when Cal had to cancel games and at times Smith had only five healthy players. She needed both advice and encouragement. "There were times when I called her to ask how she would handle things," Smith said. "She called me after some of the losses we had during that time to encourage me and to let me know she was watching."

Smith said they rarely talked about game plans. "I just want[ed] to hear about her experiences," Smith said. "There [were] a lot of times when she [was] the first one on my phone to text or call. For someone who didn't think they'd ever be a coach to have the career I have now, I feel extremely lucky. And she is a huge reason why I am in the position I am right now."

Vanessa Nygaard, whose playing career at Stanford ended with the agonizing knee injury just a week before the Cardinal's historic loss to Harvard in 1998, played five years in the WNBA and has coached at every level over the past 25 years. She spent nine years at Windward School in Los Angeles as a high school coach, leading her team to three California state titles. She has coached USA Basketball with the Under-16 and Under-17 programs. She was the head coach of the WNBA's Phoenix Mercury from 2022 to 2023, and now she is serving as an assistant coach for UC San Diego under VanDerveer's sister Heidi.

Two things about playing for VanDerveer have always stuck for Nygaard—work ethic and a love of practice. "Tara is incredibly hardworking, so the first thing I learned as a coach is never to leave anything unturned," Nygaard said. "I turn over every stone. I watch every video I can. I prepare my students in every way possible for them to be successful, because this is their opportunity. Tara never shorted herself or her team on putting in the work."

Nygaard "couldn't get enough" of practice as a Stanford player. "They were three hours long and so hard and mentally and physically draining in every way, and I loved it so much," Nygaard said. "And if you love to practice, there's no other job than being a coach."

Nygaard still turns to the notebooks she had as a player at Stanford. "I read [them] every year," Nygaard said. "The same rules apply."

When the opportunity came up for Jennifer Azzi, the former Naismith Player of the Year, to take a coaching job at the University of San Francisco, VanDerveer was one of her first phone calls.

Coaching had never really been on Azzi's radar. She'd played in Europe and helped launch the ABL as a founding player. She'd worked for sponsors, done motivational speaking, and served as a global ambassador for the NBA. She had never even been an assistant coach. But the opening at USF intrigued her. It was 10 miles from her home in Marin County. She considered it going "back to her roots."

USF has a storied place in men's college basketball as the source of some of the game's legendary players—Bill Russell, Bill Cartwright, and K. C. Jones. The USF women's program did not have the same legacy. And when the job presented itself to Azzi, the Dons were in need of a significant rebuild; the team had won only one game the previous season. Azzi called VanDerveer for a reality check. In a sense, it reminded VanDerveer of her decision to come to Stanford. VanDerveer warned Azzi about how tough the job would be to build a winning program. But she also knew Azzi was what she called a "basketball lifer" and that her former player missed being part of a team structure. "Jennifer loves a challenge; she's fearless," VanDerveer said.

Azzi took the job, coaching at USF from 2010 to 2016 and leading the Dons to an NCAA tournament berth in 2016, the program's first appearance in the tournament since 1996–97. Their first-round opponent: Stanford. The Cardinal won that game 85–58. "It was all weird," Azzi said after the game. "I'm hugging Tara, and we're both saying how it's just strange. My mom and dad are up in the stands and they are in USF gear, not Stanford gear." Even VanDerveer's mother, Rita, had tears of disappointment for Azzi's team's loss. For VanDerveer, it reminded her of playing against one of her sister Heidi's teams. "You go back so long with somebody, over 20 years. There's a lot of different emotions."

Another of VanDerveer's players who eventually joined the Stanford coaching tree was Bobbie Kelsey, who started her playing career at Stanford in the fall of 1992, following the Cardinal's second NCAA title. She finished her career watching from the bench with a knee injury in 1996, the year VanDerveer left to coach the US Olympic team.

Amy Tucker found Kelsey at the high-profile Boo Williams Tournament in Virginia as she prepared to enter her junior season in high school. Tucker had gone to watch a guard named Michelle Marciniak, who would eventually end up at Tennessee with Pat Summitt and win a national championship. But Kelsey was suddenly intriguing because of her length, her quickness, and her rebounding. And she was having a very good day. Kelsey later joked, "I could have thrown it up behind my head with my eyes closed and it would have gone in. It was one of those days."

After the game, Kelsey got a note from Tucker that Stanford was interested. She knew about Stanford only because of its academic reputation. Her mother certainly knew Stanford. Kelsey was suddenly being recruited by a school on the other side of the country, and it was promising. "They came out to visit me twice," Kelsey said. "They made me feel like they really wanted me."

But in the summer before her senior year of high school, Kelsey tore her ACL. She had not yet signed her letter of intent. Stanford, and every other school that was recruiting her, could have walked away then and there. But Stanford kept calling. Kelsey's final five schools were Virginia, Stanford, Georgia, Clemson, and Auburn; Stanford was her first choice. Her grandmother thought she would never move across the country, away from her mother. But there was one more significant detail: she was still waiting to hear from the Stanford admissions office to see whether she had gotten in.

While she waited, Virginia head coach Debbie Ryan called Kelsey, asking her whether she was coming. Kelsey, still without a solid offer from Stanford in hand, said no. "Immediately in my head, I was thinking, *What did I do?*" Kelsey said. And then her call-waiting beeped. She ended her call with Ryan and switched over to hear VanDerveer and Tucker on the other end, yelling, "You got in!"

The start of Kelsey's college career was delayed by the recovery from her knee injury. When she did return, Kelsey felt tested by VanDerveer as she struggled to find a role on the floor. VanDerveer depended on her as a defensive stopper, a role that is difficult for many players to embrace, as it lacks the glamour and recognition that comes with being a scorer. She built a rapport with Tucker and assistant coach Julie Plank, but she was still trying to figure out the head coach. "Tara needed to trust you on the floor," Kelsey said. "If you didn't know that, you would take that the wrong way, and I took it the wrong way. When the game was on the line and somebody else was in, I didn't like it. I would get mad about it."

Kelsey went to VanDerveer directly after one particularly difficult game in which she was the only player not to get off the bench. She steeled herself for the conversation. "I didn't cry about it. I know she respects strength. I went to her and I asked her if I had done something wrong. She told me what she needed from me, and I understood more after that," Kelsey said.

Over the course of four years, Kelsey ultimately became a captain, and a player who was asked to help keep other players in line, to teach them the "Stanford way." She became a player VanDerveer trusted.

Another ACL injury as a senior cut Kelsey's college career short, and after college, she spent a decade bouncing around the coaching ranks—her first job, at Boise State, was under former Stanford forward Trisha Stevens. In 2007, she called VanDerveer in need of a job. "I was walking through a shopping center by myself. I had gotten fired from Virginia Tech. I didn't know what to do," Kelsey said. "And I believe this—God said, 'Call Tara.' I wasn't even sure I wanted to work for her, but I knew she had an opening. I called and she answered, and I started explaining everything that was going on, and she stopped me and said, 'Don't worry about it. Come out.' And I did."

In June 2007, Kelsey joined the staff at the same time as Kate Paye, her former teammate for two seasons. Stanford hadn't been to the Final Four in more than a decade. It was time to get back to doing things "the Stanford way." VanDerveer made room for the two coaches and former Cardinal players to come in and set a tone. "I think we felt like keepers of a legacy," Kelsey said, who left Stanford in 2011 to take the head coaching job at the University of Wisconsin in Madison. "We had *Stanford* across our chest, and in that moment, we needed to remember who we were."

"They made us tougher," Jeanette Pohlen said of Paye and Kelsey. "They brought a level of intensity that we needed at that time."

All of the coaches who have come through Stanford as players are indeed keepers of a legacy. They understand what it takes to win, to keep up with Stanford academics, to find your place both on the team and in the large student body of the highest achievers.

Another of VanDerveer's former players, All-American guard Molly Goodenbour, ended up as Azzi's successor at USF starting in 2016 and is still the head coach there now. Goodenbour admits she is a reflection of VanDerveer's meticulous preparation. She sees her old coach in the way she runs her practices—purposeful and precise. Goodenbour didn't lean in to her former coach's advice the way some others have. In a way, she didn't need to. What VanDerveer taught her is embedded. "I know that if I pick up the phone and call her, I can have a really good, honest conversation with her about whatever I need," Goodenbour said. "And I appreciate that I can do that. She's never wavered in her willingness to give me good advice."

One of VanDerveer's earliest players at Stanford, Charli Turner (now Charli Turner Thorne), became her biggest coaching rival in the Pac-12 for a quarter of a century, as the head coach at Arizona State from 1996 to 2022. Turner Thorne became the winningest coach in ASU program history.

Like Nygaard, Turner Thorne kept her Stanford notebooks from her playing days. She modeled the structure of film sessions and shootarounds after Stanford's, teaching offense and defense from what VanDerveer had taught her. "We are very different in a lot of ways in terms of how we coach, but I think the thing I really took from her was her ability to get the most out of people," Turner Thorne said. "It's a huge thing. And your players may not appreciate it while they are going through it, but years later, when they feel like there's nothing they can't do, they appreciate it."

VanDerveer put other former Stanford players on her staff too, allowing them to impart the Stanford experience to a next generation of players. In VanDerveer's final season, she brought on former forward Erica McCall, whose father was the longtime women's coach at Cal State Bakersfield, and whose sister is WNBA legend DeWanna Bonner. And Jeanette Pohlen, the All-American who led Stanford to back-to-back Final Fours in 2010 and 2011, joined as a coaching intern in 2022 and was promoted to assistant coach under Paye following VanDerveer's retirement announcement in 2024.

For Pohlen, the opportunity to surround herself with the familiarity of Stanford has had great personal significance. Late in 2012, while Jeanette was playing in the WNBA for the Indiana Fever, her father, John, passed away at the age of 54 after a three-year battle with pulmonary fibrosis. Eleven years later, as she was working at Stanford in a supporting staff role, her mother, Cindy Pohlen, died of cancer. "I was going through a lot, and Tara was completely supportive," Pohlen said. "Whenever I needed to travel to see my mom, she would tell me to just go. I didn't even need to tell her when I'd be gone."

Pohlen is among family at Stanford. And she is giving back to the program that gave her a chance to play professional basketball. "Seeing the other side of things—the things Tara had to deal with on a day-to-day basis, how she approached things, or put out different fires—it gives you a different perspective," Pohlen said. "When you come in as a player and you are playing for a Hall of Fame coach, you are trying not to make mistakes. But I've learned that she never asked players to do anything she didn't think they could do. And then there is her status in the women's game. You knew what she was saying and how we were doing things the right way."

VanDerveer's final staff at Stanford included four former players—Paye, Steding, McCall, and Pohlen—all with their own experiences under VanDerveer from their playing days, and all with a deep connection to what the head coach did at the school. "The coaches who went to Stanford understand our team, our culture, our program, our history. They love Stanford," Paye said. "They have played professionally, and all of the players in our program want to play professionally. Players connect with that."

The connections are personal and they are historical. Young players are receiving mentorship from women who have been where they are—from the toughest days at practice to road trip traditions to the thrill of pulling on a Stanford uniform. And they are *all* connected by the head coach who built the culture that has put them in a position to thrive and grow. VanDerveer's program has been a training ground and a common ground.

"As a player, I had the ultimate faith in what Tara said, because she taught us to do things, and they worked," Steding said. "Now as a coach on the sidelines . . . I've been with some great coaches, but I don't think there's anybody better than Tara in putting pieces together and preparing and helping people to be the best versions of themselves. It's all she's ever wanted."

## Chapter 16

# The Announcement

**THE STORY SHOOK THE WORLD** of women's college basketball—basketball in general—on April 9, 2024, at 7:00 PM Pacific Time, about 48 hours after the end of the groundbreaking NCAA Championship Game between Iowa and South Carolina at the Final Four in Cleveland, which drew more than 24 million television viewers. Dawn Staley's South Carolina Gamecocks, a team she rebuilt in one season after losing all five starters from the previous season, defeated the Iowa Hawkeyes and megastar Caitlin Clark 87–75.

But Tara VanDerveer didn't go to Cleveland to see it in person. She stayed home, preparing to go public with the news that was always going to come at some point but still felt stunning when it finally broke: at the age of 70, she was retiring. After 48 years as a basketball coach, 45 years as a head coach, and 38 years at Stanford, she was done.

She won 1,216 games in her career, shepherded the Cardinal to 14 Final Fours, and led three teams to the NCAA title. She won 26 regular-season conference championships and 15 conference tournament titles, and made 35 trips to the NCAA tournament. And she sent 33 players to the WNBA, a league she helped to launch by coaching the US women's basketball team to the gold medal in the Olympic Summer Games in Atlanta, Georgia, in 1996. Seven of those players have been WNBA champions. Among them, Nneka and Chiney Ogwumike were No. 1 WNBA draft picks, Nneka was the WNBA's MVP in 2016, and Chiney was WNBA Rookie of the Year in 2014.

VanDerveer's work in the game she changed for the better was done. It was time to hand the reins to associate head coach and heir-in-waiting Kate Paye, setting in motion a succession plan more than a decade in the making.

VanDerveer said that in her mind she had retired at the end of a lot of seasons before she always came back. Not this time. "You always think, *Can I do this again?*" VanDerveer said. "At the end of the season, you are exhausted."

The end of the 2022–23 season, which would turn out to be her second-to-last as a head coach, provided a different feeling. It had been a difficult season. Relationships within the program had been strained over a variety of issues, including the pressures placed on her frontline players by the demands of name, image, and likeness (NIL) deals, her decision to carry a large roster of players without enough minutes to go around, and a lack of cohesion among the staff. The season ended abruptly with a second-round loss at home to Mississippi. At the end of the season, three players—including Lauren Betts, who had been the nation's No. 1 recruit when she chose Stanford out of high school—transferred out of the program.

Betts transferred to UCLA, where she led the Bruins to their first-ever Final Four appearance in 2025 and was named an All-American. As the end of the 2025 season approached, by which time VanDerveer had already retired, Betts talked to national media about her struggles with mental health, including the difficult time she'd had at Stanford as a freshman. Betts told ESPN that Stanford was her dream school. Once she arrived, she said she felt as if she couldn't be the player the coaches wanted her to be, that she was afraid to make mistakes and that she was not happy. Her anxiety was building to a breaking point. "I was in constant fear of not being good enough," Betts said, also sharing that her anxieties in her first season at UCLA caused her to be hospitalized briefly.

VanDerveer said she was not aware that Betts was struggling so badly while at Stanford. "If something was ever bothering someone, if they ever brought it to me, I would address it," she said.

Still, Betts's decision to depart after one season was a blow. A dispiriting punctuation mark on a dispiriting season. VanDerveer wanted to turn the page quickly. "I didn't want it to end that way," VanDerveer said. "I just said, 'I'm going to be totally all in [for the 2023–24] season and see how it goes.' But I was preparing."

Back in 2014, VanDerveer was also preparing to retire. She had gone through the process of assessing the balance of her life—so much work and so little time to do the things she enjoyed—and she could feel her enthusiasm waning when she thought about starting again in a few months. She had dinner with Stanford donor and close friend John Arrillaga, who told her frankly, "Don't do it." Arrillaga told her to take the summer off, which was something VanDerveer had never truly considered. She headed home after dinner, and the phone rang immediately. It was Arrillaga. He had already called then–athletic director Bernard Muir and gotten Muir's buy-in on the summer vacation plan. VanDerveer took the summer off for the first time, and she returned reenergized and then coached for 10 more years and won another national title.

A decade later, her calculation was different. With the news that the Pac-12 was disbanding, VanDerveer began to ponder retirement again. Her mother, Rita, now in her mid-90s, was having health issues and had decided to move from Colorado back to the East Coast, where two of Tara's sisters, Beth and Marie, could help with her care.

VanDerveer decided during that summer that the theme for the season would be Best Year Ever, to stay focused on a positive experience, to put "everything" into 2023–24. VanDerveer talked to her leadership coach, Kirsten Moss, about transitions, and she confided in Kate Paye what she was considering. Paye joked that she would believe it when it actually happened. And then the Cardinal went about the start to their season.

Assistant coach Katy Steding, one of VanDerveer's first recruits when she took the Stanford job 38 years before, said that in hindsight, VanDerveer might have been dropping some breadcrumbs. "I feel like we had some inklings along the way, like, 'Oh, this could be . . . no, no never mind,'" Steding said. "There were things we all glossed over at the moment because we had the next game to play. But there were comments here or there. You just don't have the time to process it at that moment. I kind of hoped she would just keep going."

When it was announced that Stanford would move into the Atlantic Coast Conference after the breakup of the Pac-12, VanDerveer was intrigued. New teams, new coaches, new competition. Maybe it would be a reason to stay a little longer. Maybe.

Stanford's 2023–24 season had moments of brilliance thanks to the play of the All-American post tandem of Cameron Brink and Kiki Iriafen, but when it ended with a Sweet 16 loss in Portland, VanDerveer's intrigue eventually gave way to a sense of peace that it was time—a decision process that took about a week. "I did my end-of-season meeting with [former athletic director] Bernard [Muir] and [former Stanford women's administrator and player]

Heather Owen, and I didn't say anything to them," VanDerveer said. "I wanted to give it a week or so to sink in. But I knew I had to figure things out quickly to give Kate a chance to get into the transfer portal and be able to move the program forward."

Point guard Talana Lepolo said the players knew what was coming as soon as VanDerveer called a team meeting two weeks after the season ended. "Her motto for the whole year was 'Best Year Ever and some of us were thinking, *Do you mean the* last *best year?*" Lepolo said, recalling VanDerveer getting emotional during a team walk-through late in the season at Colorado. VanDerveer said she thought it would be one of the last games her mother, Rita, would get to watch in person. Rita was preparing for that move from Boulder, Colorado, back to New York at the time. In hindsight, that was another sign for VanDerveer.

By the time VanDerveer's announcement went public on the evening of April 9, 2024, she was emotionally spent. She had told her staff and players earlier that day, and then her mother. She was emotional in a way that not many people on the Stanford staff had seen before. And suddenly, as the news spread, her phone was blowing up with well-wishes and thank-yous.

The following afternoon there was a press conference for VanDerveer in Kissick Auditorium in the Arrillaga Family Sports Center that was closed to the public. With tributes pouring in from all corners of the sports world, VanDerveer walked into the auditorium with a broad smile on her face. The past, present, and future were all in the room to mark the last chapter of one of the most decorated coaching careers in the history of college sports.

As VanDerveer sat down at the table at the head of the room, in front of her were her coaching staff; members of her current team; fellow coaches and staff members from the Stanford Athletics Department; and members of the Bay Area press, including a phalanx of photographers with their cameras pointed directly at the legend.

VanDerveer pulled out a six-page letter, typed on both sides, exhaled, and began:

> *About 39 years ago, I called my father to tell him I was leaving Ohio State to take the Stanford coaching job. I wasn't completely honest, because I told him I was thinking about taking the Stanford job. He proceeded to tell me that it was impossible to win at Stanford and that the job was a graveyard job.*
>
> *After more about how crazy I was to consider Stanford, I interrupted him to tell him that I had taken the job. He hung up the phone and told my mother, 'She'll be unemployed, coming home, living with us in three months.'*
>
> *As a young and upcoming coach, I left a great job and team at Ohio State to prove something to myself. To win at Stanford with the strict academic requirements is the ultimate challenge. When I met assistant dean of admissions John Bonhomme, he told me straight up, 'Your recruits need to be able to jump through the same academic hoops as other admits.' I remember thinking,* John, I need recruits who can put it through the hoop.
>
> *My father was right about one thing: the Stanford job involved digging, but instead of a graveyard job, it has been a goldmine job. My 38 years as the head coach of the Stanford University women's basketball team have been nothing short of magical.*
>
> *Stanford is a beautiful place with incredible people. The strength of Stanford is unwavering commitment to excellence.*
>
> *At Stanford, the term 'student-athlete' isn't an oxymoron. What other basketball coach has Carolyn Bertozzi, a Nobel Prize–winning chemist, in their locker room for a game? Where*

*else would a star player, Chiney Ogwumike, have a former secretary of state, Condoleezza Rice, as an advisor? How fortunate are we to have Middle East correspondent Janine Zacharia to do directed reading with a player so they could represent their country in summer competition? Who else has world-renowned happiness professor Fred Luskin meet with their team weekly developing mindfulness training?*

*When our team and I needed help with leadership, I turned to the No. 1 business school in the country at Stanford and former dean of admissions Kirsten Moss. She did custom leadership sessions with our team, coaches, and me.*

*The S in* Stanford *is for* special. *Thank you to all our great faculty for your brilliance, dedication, and accessibility to our student-athletes. I am proud of the championships we have won and how we have built a great tradition. What brings me the most satisfaction, however, is to see the transformation of the young women on our team both on and off the court. . . .*

*Off the court, young, unsure women become steady, confident leaders. In the classroom they've excelled and gone on to become doctors, lawyers, professors, businesswomen, and leaders.*

*Just walking into Maples for practice and hearing the balls bouncing and the music playing has brought me great joy. Coaching has never felt like a j-o-b job. I've loved the game of basketball since the third grade, when we did three-player weave in gym class. From the beginning, the strategy of basketball intrigued me, but what really attracted me to the game is the importance of teamwork. It is thrilling to be connected in a successful team.*

*As a daughter of two educators, I've enjoyed teaching basketball fundamentals and skills. Basketball is so much more than dribbling, passing, and shooting. Great teams love playing with and for each other. Basketball is the ultimate team sport, and I'm part of a great team.*

*Thank you to my parents, Rita and Dunbar, for their love and support. My parents have always been my role models. My mom would always say to me, 'You sure move faster around the basketball court than you do around the kitchen.' That wasn't hard. My dad told me, 'Basketball will never take you anywhere.' I sent him postcards from all over the world.*

*As a young girl, I never played on a high school team or had camps or travel basketball. Our college schedule was only eight regular-season games. Coaching wasn't a profession for women.*

*I got into coaching by accident. I had taken a year off after graduating from Indiana as a sociology major and I was planning to go to law school. My sister Marie was on the newly formed high school team. Title IX had just passed. They had lost 99–11 the night before. My dad basically made me go help that team.*

*I learned two very important lessons in my first year. First, after games my parents would say, 'Why didn't you play Marie more?' Parents see things through a different lens than coaches. Second, I love my sister, and through my years as a coach, as upset as I might get with a player, I would always come back to [the idea that] she was someone's sister.*

*Thank you to Marie, my siblings Nick and Beth. I also want to give a big shout-out to my sister Heidi, the head coach at UC San Diego. We talk daily and help each other. I love you, Heidi, and you are the No. 1 coach in the family.*

*Coaching feels like it was my destiny. I watched hours of boys' practice from the seventh grade on. At Indiana I took Coach Bobby Knight's basketball coaching class. I got an A. And I watched his practice for three years. While at Ohio State I got to know the legendary Fred Taylor. Don Monson was my colleague at Idaho, and here at Stanford I've had the incredibly great fortune of becoming friends with the late Pete Newell.*

*Thank you to Andy Geiger for hiring me in 1985 and Bernard Muir for keeping me. One of my greatest supporters isn't here today in person, but he is with us in spirit, and we are in his building. Thank you, John Arrillaga. No one has cared more about Stanford and Stanford athletics than John. I'm so thankful for the love and support from the entire Arrillaga family. . . .*

*Coming to Stanford wasn't an easy decision for me. I initially said no to Andy Geiger. He asked me why, and I told him, 'I don't know enough about Stanford.' So he said, 'Come back.' I actually learned a lot about recruiting from Andy.*

*On my second recruiting trip to campus, I met the track coach, Brooks Johnson. Andy had instructed Brooks to keep walking me around campus until I said yes. We walked and walked, and not only did I say yes to Brooks, but we became best lifelong friends. He is my soul mate.*

*From the beginning, I've understood the importance of outstanding assistant coaches. I have always had incredible assistants. Thank you to Amy Tucker, who along with Julie Plank and the late June Daugherty, came with me from Ohio State back in 1985. Amy, I'm so grateful for your confidence in me. Thank you for the sacrifices you made to come to Stanford. . . .*

*When I took a year off to coach the Olympic team in 1996, Amy took over as the head coach. She coached the team for an undefeated Pac-12 championship and Final Four. She has the best winning percentage at Stanford.*

*Thank you to associate head coach Kate Paye. I love working with you. Kate is a phenomenal coach. She is knowledgeable, an excellent communicator, and totally invested in Stanford.*

*Thank you to Katy Steding. I'm so thankful for your loyalty and hard work. Katy was our first player to sign at Stanford. She was a key to our 1990 championship along with being a member of the 1996 Olympic team.*

*Thank you to Tempie Brown for coming back this season. I appreciate your calm, mature demeanor and how you always would check to make sure I was wearing matching shoes.*

*Thank you, Bird—Erica McCall—for joining our staff this season after a wonderful pro career. I have enjoyed working with you as much as I enjoyed coaching you. You are the quintessential coach.*

*Thank you to my sport administrator Heather Owen and our basketball staff: Eileen Roche, Jeanette Pohlen, Casey Spinetti, Brian Shank, Katelin Knox, John Cantalupi, and Erin Poindexter McHan. Working with our coaches and staff has been a highlight of my time at Stanford. I have thoroughly enjoyed the opportunity to plan, strategize, argue—lots of my ideas get shot down—and laugh with such great colleagues. Thank you for making work so much fun.*

*I would be remiss if I didn't recognize the women's basketball coaches' sorority and fraternity for their friendship and competition. Thank you to the giants of our game who I have admired: Pat Summitt, Jody Conradt, Geno Auriemma, Ceal Barry, Andy Landers, Muffet McGraw, Nancy Darsch, Kim Mulkey, Lisa Bluder, and Dawn Staley.*

*I also want to thank the other coaches at Stanford who I have learned from and cheered for. When I first came to Stanford, it was very intimidating to be in the company of people like Dick Gould, 17 NCAA championships, Bill Walsh, Skip Kenney, but in fact they were welcoming, helpful, and supportive.*

*Once I was walking into the Athletics Department following five-time NCAA champion Dante Dettamanti. I thought to myself,* If he can do it, I can do it. *We did win a couple of championships, and later in the same spot, I met Sadao Hamada, who had coached the gymnastics team. I said to Sadao, 'What got you coaching?' He said, 'Tara, I said to myself, "If you can do it, I can do it."'*

*Working and learning alongside great coaches and great people like Mike Montgomery, Trent Johnson, Johnny Dawkins, Tyrone Willingham, Jim "Who Has It Better Than Us?" Harbaugh, David Shaw, John Dunning, Mark Marquess, Greg Meehan, Anne Walker, John Tanner—just to name a few—has been inspiring. Thank you all for your support and encouragement.*

*Another joy of working at Stanford has been watching and getting to know the accomplished student-athletes in other sports. Once during a rainy winter week, a young man asked me if he could putt on the side of the court. You guessed it: Tiger Woods.*

*During the pandemic, I got to swim in a lane between Olympians Simone Manuel and Katie Ledecky. Talk about humbling. I've rebounded for Mark Madsen and led Andrew Luck and Christian McCaffrey onto the field as their guest coach.*

*Most importantly, I want to thank all, all of the women I have coached at Stanford. I admire and respect the dedication that our student-athletes have to excellence in the classroom and on the court. As their coach, I have aspired to help each player get to a place they couldn't get on their own. I've wanted to be a coach that I would want to play for—someone who works very hard to give our team the best chance of being successful, along with a person who demonstrates empathy and compassion. Through the game of basketball, I have taught the importance of teamwork, hard work, discipline, determination, unselfishness, and resilience. I've had many former players tell me the demands of playing basketball have helped them be successful in their careers. Most importantly, I've wanted our team to have fun and be great teammates.*

*Our players have been inspiring and motivating. When I asked the 1990 team members to write down on an index card what [was their] contribution to the team, walk-on Angela Taylor, who rarely got in the game, wrote, 'Spread sunshine.' We won the NCAA championship. When I asked Chris MacMurdo, an incoming freshman, as we drove onto campus on Campus Drive, 'What are you thinking about?' instead of the expected answer, she said, 'I want to make a difference in this world.' She's a doctor now.*

*When our US national team was in Ukraine in January, our bus was leaving for the airport at 3:30 AM. As we boarded the bus, 12 to 15 women shivering in thin coats were begging. Everyone, including me, walked right by, ignoring them. Not Jennifer Azzi. She reached in her pockets and gave them her money and then opened her suitcase and gave away her clothes. Everyone on the bus followed Jennifer.*

*After losing arguably the toughest game ever to Old Dominion in 1997, the players were inconsolable. Jamila Wideman commanded the room, [saying,] 'Pick your heads up. I would rather lose with you than win with anyone else.'*

*Later, after a very tough loss to UConn in the national title game, Jayne Appel emotionally told me she didn't want to take her uniform off because she knew she would never put it on again.*

*I have so many stories of how the people I have coached have motivated me, influenced [me], and inspired me. I have learned so much from each player. I'm eternally grateful for having them in my life.*

*I'm incredibly proud of the Stanford sisterhood. We've had real sisters. Karlie could find Bonnie open anywhere on the court. Nneka was another coach for Chiney, and Lexie and Lacie competed daily. In tough games, the sisterhood is a key to victory. It was very exciting this season to win three overtime games—I don't think we've ever had three before—and [to] see how hard everyone was playing for each other.*

*Yes, the championship years are on the wall in Maples, but what I see when I look up there is Kiki high-fiving Cam; Jennifer and Sonja leaving the court, arms around each other; Candice hugging me; and Nneka embracing Ros [Gold-Onwude]. It is the friendship that we have that makes it so special.*

*It has been an honor and a pleasure to be part of these women's lives. My goal has been to be a teacher, mentor, confidant, and eventually a lifetime friend for them.*

*I have grieved at funerals of parents and former players. I have celebrated at weddings. When children are born, I've been called within the hour, or I talk my way into the hospital to see the new mother and newborn.*

*As John Pohlen said to me when recruiting Jeanette, "Tara, we are family."*

*Thank you, fans, and the Stanford Fast Break Club. Our fans are fantastic. It's been thrilling to see the attendance at our games go from being able to count on my fingers and toes the number of people in the gym to sold-out Maples. I will be sitting up with you next season cheering for our team.*

*I'm very sad about losing the great Pac-12 Conference. Thank you to the outstanding coaches that I have competed against for close to 40 years.*

*Thank you to our conference administrators, conference game officials, and the Pac-12 Network. Thank you, media, for your coverage of our teams through the years. Thank you for telling the stories of our games and great players.*

*There is a young girl out there who will watch or read about Stanford women's basketball, and her dad will say to her, "Basketball will take you everywhere."*

It took VanDerveer more than a month to get in and clean out her office. The Pac-12 championship trophies—regular-season and tournament titles—wrapped around the room. There were a dozen or so unaccounted for.

The walls became white and bare very quickly as items moved to the conference table behind her desk, which quickly became strewn with memorabilia, including a copy of John Wooden's *Pyramid of Success,* which he had signed to VanDerveer. In the closet were nearly four decades of game tapes—from VHS to DVDs to Blu-ray discs.

Most of VanDerveer's collection of a lifetime's worth of success, accolades, and accomplishments moved down the hall to her new office, where she began her new job as an adviser to then-athletic director Bernard Muir, putting in four hours a day on development and coaching other coaches.

What she felt was "a tremendous lightness." After all, for VanDerveer, it was never about the stuff on the walls, on the table, and in the closet. It was about the players and the coaches and the successes and failures that led to more success. It was about impact and purpose, and work—her life's work.

## Chapter 17

# The Succession Plan

**ON NOVEMBER 10, 2024,** as the crowd at Maples Pavilion threw one last party for the now-retired Tara VanDerveer, celebrating the naming of Stanford's home court in her honor, VanDerveer waved Kate Paye over, grabbed her by the elbow, and literally pulled her into the spotlight. Paye demurred as best she could, wanting VanDerveer to have the moment to herself. But Paye ultimately gave in, and the two stood together on the floor—legend and successor.

Paye's own celebratory moment came over the next 40 minutes of basketball, in a nationally televised game for the Cardinal against Gonzaga. This new-era Stanford team, which opened the season outside of the national rankings for the first time in 25 years, handily defeated the Bulldogs 89–58, a strong start to a season that would end up being more transitional than anyone realized. "We are a new roster, and we are starting to build and find our own identity," Paye said after the game.

One of those new players on that new roster was transfer Mary Ashley Stevenson, who came to Palo Alto after spending one season at Purdue and being named the Big Ten Freshman of the Year in 2024. Stevenson was aware of the legacy that she joined, even if she never played a minute for VanDerveer, the person who built it. "Kate gave us a speech before the game, talking about how our team as it is now has grown off every single person that has put on this jersey or been a part of this program," Stevenson said. "It's incredible what Tara built, and we are building off that with Kate."

Point guard Talana Lepolo said she was moved to be part of a legendary program in transition, having played two seasons for VanDerveer and the next two for Paye. "It's an honor," Lepolo said.

Eileen Roche is Stanford's director of basketball operations, or the DOBO, as they are known in the college basketball business. Roche was an assistant coach at Stanford for two seasons before VanDerveer's arrival in the mid-1980s, and was lured back by VanDerveer 20 years ago to run the program's day-to-day operations—scheduling games, overseeing travel and game day management, and working with university staff in compliance and marketing. She said the early months of the transition were "seamless," thanks to the groundwork laid by both VanDerveer and Paye. Roche said, "We are still Stanford women's basketball as far as what we want to do, who we want to be, how hard we work, and how we want to achieve our goals."

Six days after VanDerveer's public retirement announcement, Kate Paye was introduced as the Cardinal's new head coach. Paye entered the same room in Kissick Auditorium where VanDerveer had made her farewell speech, and even sat in the same seat at the same table. Her introduction happened in front of many of the same people who were at VanDerveer's retirement announcement: current players; fellow coaches; family members; her wife, Raquel; and her children, Cass, Anne, and Lauren.

Stanford athletic director Bernard Muir stood at the podium and made a joke about the "exhaustive search" the university had engaged in to land on her as VanDerveer's successor. There was no search. The right person was sitting on the bench next to Tara VanDerveer for the past 17 years.

And then Muir held up a No. 3 jersey with the name *Paye* on the back—the exact one Paye had donned when she was a player at Stanford. On April 16, 2024, Paye was named the fifth head women's basketball coach in Stanford history. The circle of Paye's life was complete.

She had a mentor like no other. Which is why Paye turned to VanDerveer at the end of her own press conference; looked her coach, mentor, and dear friend in the eyes; and said, "Thank you for trusting me with your life's work."

Paye kept a seat warm on the Stanford bench for nearly two decades, including the last eight as the associate head coach after Amy Tucker's retirement. She passed up other offers—including several head coaching offers—to stay with the Cardinal program, to coach Cardinal guards into All-Americans and WNBA prospects, and to buy in to the succession plan to replace a legend that had been at least a decade in the making.

Through the years, people asked Paye how much longer VanDerveer would coach, when it would be her turn. They asked her if it was difficult to be patient and wait for her opportunity. "I've never felt like that," Paye said. "This is the only place I've ever wanted to be. These are the people that I love."

Muir, who came to Stanford in 2012, said the plan to install Paye as VanDerveer's successor predated his arrival. Muir said he realized quickly that in order to maintain continuity at a place as singular as Stanford—with its recruiting challenges and its campus culture—this was a plan that "made a lot of sense."

Muir and Paye began to build their relationship, knowing that Paye's day would eventually come. And with VanDerveer's retirement announcement on April 10, Paye became a head coach for the first time, a true believer in all things Stanford. "I assure you all, you could not have found anyone who feels a greater sense of honor, privilege, responsibility, enthusiasm, and passion to lead Stanford women's basketball into the next chapter of our storied legacy," Paye said.

Paye was born in Stanford Hospital, a quarter of a mile from where her office sits. She grew up 14 minutes away in Woodside. "I guess someone could say I haven't gotten very far in life," Paye cracked.

The Paye family is Stanford royalty. Her father, John, was a running back for Stanford in 1961–62 and a political science major like his daughter after him. "He challenged me, pushed me, and provided me every chance to pursue my love of sports," Paye said. "He believed basketball could take me places."

Paye's mother, Anne, got her degree in English literature at Stanford and was an English instructor at a local community college for more than 40 years before she passed away in 2013. Paye called her "the guiding light in my life and the strongest person I've ever known."

Paye's brother John was a two-sport athlete at Stanford, a quarterback for the football team from 1984 to 1987 and a guard on the men's basketball team. He played for the San Francisco 49ers, his younger sister's "childhood idol." "The biggest things I learned from watching my brother as an athlete and a coach was how hard he competed and how much he cared."

And Paye's sister Amy graduated from Stanford with a double major and serves on Stanford's Buck/Cardinal Club, which fundraises for the athletics department.

Paye's mother tried to talk Kate into going to an Ivy League school, to take a more "adventurous" path than anyone else in the family. That was a nonstarter for young Kate. She wasn't looking for the road less traveled. "Stanford is where I always wanted to be," Paye said.

She began attending Stanford basketball camps at 10 years old, before VanDerveer had even arrived on The Farm. At her second year of camp in the summer of 1985, Paye met VanDerveer at the new coach's first basketball camp. Every summer after that Paye would go to the first camp session of the season and then beg her father to go back the next week, and the week after that.

She idolized star players Jennifer Azzi and Sonja Henning and Katy Steding. She got scholarship offers to play elsewhere and a lot of advice about what she should do. She didn't want either. She remained focused on Stanford.

Despite not being recruited by Stanford, Paye joined VanDerveer's program as a walk-on. She was a reserve guard on the 1992 national championship team, and went on to earn a scholarship the following season, where she was the floor leader who led the Cardinal to the Final Four in 1995. She was a three-time Pac-10 All-Academic selection and two-time team captain. "I listened to my gut," Paye said. "I knew it was my dream to play on that team and on that Maples floor and for Tara."

Paye said being a walk-on is part of her identity to this day. It is what drives her in many ways. "Waking up every day and having to earn it," Paye said. "Nobody expected anything of me, but that experience of betting on myself, doing what worked for me—there have been other parts of my life where I've drawn on that."

Paye graduated from Stanford in 1995, spent seven seasons playing professionally in the ABL and WNBA, and went to law school in the off-season. The people in her life told her she was meant to be a coach. Paye stubbornly resisted at first.

She earned her law degree and her master's in business in 2003, but it turned out practicing corporate law was not the life and career she wanted. She discovered that very quickly. "I lasted six months," Paye said. "Actually, I rounded up. It was five and a quarter months."

At 30 years old, she was being pulled back to basketball—serving as an assistant coach at Pepperdine and San Diego State—and ultimately back to Stanford, where she joined VanDerveer's staff in 2007. She became a constant, coaching the guards, coordinating recruiting, and eventually serving as VanDerveer's right hand.

It's ironic that the decision to return to Stanford as a coach was tougher than it was when she was a young player, hell-bent on wearing the Cardinal and White. Paye wanted to know she could make an impact and wondered how difficult that would be sitting on the bench with one of the greatest coaches of all time, who had already experienced all the successes the sport had to offer.

"Kate's ready," said Heather Owen, the athletic director at Santa Clara University and Paye's former teammate at Stanford. "She's paid her dues."

Paye has national respect and admiration, named in 2024 as the Division I Assistant Coach of the Year for the second time in three years by the Women's Basketball Coaches Association.

Paye has always had a strong relationship with players, and keeping the coaching and support staff intact in her first season allowed for the smooth transition that it was always meant to be. "She is genuinely interested in them and what will help them learn to get better," Steding said. "She's got a good handle on each of our individual players."

Her charge as VanDerveer's successor is maintaining the program's place among the national elite. In her first season, that proved more challenging than perhaps anyone expected. Without Cameron Brink (graduation) or Kiki Iriafen (transferred to USC), the Cardinal leaned hard into young players. The team's most veteran players—seniors Elena Bosgana and Brooke Demetre—had been role players for much of their careers. The team's only returning starter, point guard Lepolo, missed most of the season with a knee injury.

A 6–1 start to the 2024–25 season began to crumble following an overtime road loss against No. 5 LSU in early December 2024. Stanford lost five of its next six games, including a historic 83–63 loss to rival Cal to open the Atlantic Coast Conference (ACC) schedule, the worst loss to the Bears in more than 40 years.

Paye guided the Cardinal's transition into the ACC, with all of its travel and scheduling challenges. No team in the country other than Cal traveled more miles than the Cardinal—who logged more than 23,000 miles—in the 2024–25 season. Stanford finished 8–10 in its ACC debut (tied for 10th) and fell in the first round of the ACC tournament despite winning five of six to close the regular-season schedule.

By Selection Sunday, there was no Cardinal in the NCAA brackets. Stanford missed the NCAA tournament for the first time since 1987—VanDerveer's second season at Stanford—ending a streak of 36 consecutive appearances. It was the second-longest streak in women's basketball history. The end of the streak earned national media coverage.

The Cardinal earned an invitation to the inaugural Women's Basketball Invitation Tournament, but even that didn't go as expected, with Stanford losing at home to Portland in the first round.

"It was a very challenging season," Paye said to the media after the final game, which gave Stanford a 16–15 record. "There was a lot of change, a lot of challenge. But no matter how much adversity we faced and things not going our way, our team stuck together. They did not come apart at the seams.

"But obviously we have high expectations here at Stanford, and this time next year, we hope to be in a very different position. But if we want something different, we are going to have to work."

Paye had good reason for optimism. She had already been leading recruiting efforts for the past eight years under VanDerveer, putting her stamp on the program. And in her first season as head coach, she reeled in the nation's No. 3–ranked recruiting class, a group of McDonald's All-Americans in point guard Hailee Swain, forward Lara Somfai, and forward Alexandra Eschmeyer, a trio that could quickly right the Stanford ship.

The quality of the recruiting class proved that the Stanford brand remains strong, even as the sport is changing both rapidly and dramatically. "There is change to navigate, but the standards and the expectations remain the same. Excellence in the classroom and on the court," Paye said. "We will continue to stand on our program values of hard work, unselfishness, toughness, and togetherness every day.

"In this highly competitive world, a Stanford education, the Stanford experience, the Stanford degree, and the Stanford network are more valuable than ever, especially for women. Quite simply, Stanford changes your life."

The week before her formal introduction as the new head coach in 2024, Paye sat in the front row of VanDerveer's farewell press conference, riding the waves of emotion with the rest of the room. And having some feelings of her own, knowing that she was the chosen person to step into the shoes of one of the most legendary figures in the history of college sports. "It's a little bit surreal," Paye said, when the VanDerveer press conference was over. "I've been with Tara for a long time, and I know how much she pours into what she does.

And most seasons, when the season is over, she says, 'That's it. I can't do it anymore.' I used to joke with her, 'I won't really believe you until I see the news conference.' I guess I believe her now."

The next day Paye walked into her staff meeting, and everyone looked at each other awkwardly as she sat in the head coach's chair.

The chair and the Stanford legacy belong to Paye now.

# Afterword

**FROM THE WRAPAROUND PORCH** at Tara VanDerveer's family home on Chautauqua Lake in western New York, she can see the water, and more importantly, she can assess it. Like a scouting report. The flag on the pole at the 144-year-old Athenaeum Hotel, right across the lawn, tells her what the wind looks like. Is it a day to sail? Can she get a ski run in at 7:00 AM?

The summer after announcing her retirement in 2024, VanDerveer retreated to the place that's been as much a home to her as much as any place she's ever lived. The family-named Lakeside Lodge on the property of the 2,000-acre Chautauqua Institution is the place where the VanDerveer family has spent their summers since Tara was 10 years old. The Chautauqua Institution is a not-for-profit educational center and summer resort that sits on the shores of Chautauqua Lake, a 90-minute drive from Buffalo, New York, and 45 minutes from Erie, Pennsylvania.

The property includes 900 private homes, an amphitheater, a post office, a library, and cafes and restaurants. Every summer, the Chautauqua Institution offers courses in art, music, theater, writing, and more, and public events such as concerts and speaker series, with more than 100,000 people attending annually.

For Tara VanDerveer, it was her childhood playground, the place where she found her passion to sail and ski, where she worked as a camp counselor, a swim instructor, a house cleaner, and a waitress at the Triangle Restaurant, where one patron told her, "You are the worst waitress I have ever had." It is the place where she saw Ella Fitzgerald, Robert Kennedy, Van Cliburn, Duke Ellington, the Beach Boys, Diana Ross, and the Mormon Tabernacle Choir perform.

For all of the times her family moved to new houses and new cities when she was a girl, following her father's academic career, this was the place they always landed when school got out, the family packing up the station wagon and leaving on the first day of summer vacation, not returning until the night before the first day of the new school year. Despite Rita VanDerveer imploring her husband, Dunbar, to head home a little early, to give her time to get her five kids their new shoes and some school supplies, they always stayed until the last possible moment. Which was how Tara wanted it.

Friends always came to the lake, giving the VanDerveer kids constant playmates, and they still come, with plenty of old stories to swap decades later. Tara's parents would rent out rooms in the two-story home to visitors. Her father ran a reading program as part of the Chautauqua Institution's programming connected to his work with Syracuse University. Her mother did her best to keep track of five busy kids.

There was the day when Tara crashed her bike hard on the hilly road that led back down from the main part of the resort to the house, and she was lying in the middle of one of its narrow streets, "a little out of it," she remembered. A neighbor told Rita that there was a little girl who had fallen off her bike and appeared to be "dead."

Rita replied, "It's probably one of mine." Tara eventually got up, dusted herself off, and rode home.

VanDerveer's parents owned the home in Chautauqua for nearly 30 years. When her mother decided to sell it following Dunbar's death in 1997, Tara bought it immediately and then spent nearly a year renovating it. The attic roof, sharply pitched, was built out to accommodate a couple of large bedrooms. The kitchen and bathrooms were more recently remodeled, as was the porch, and she installed an elevator. There is a sailboat in one slip in the marina, a ski boat in another. There are bikes on the porch and a workout space on the second floor.

The Chautauqua Institution property is part resort and part academic campus. Homes with manicured yards dating back to the early 20th century line narrow streets and sit only a couple of arm's lengths from the neighbors' houses next door. Residents and visitors park their cars in a lot outside the property's gates.

People walk past VanDerveer's house who have known her nearly all her life. She can show you all the places where she crashed her bike, and where she taught the younger kids how to sail. She can remember her father grabbing her out of bed in her pajamas to throw her in the lake on her 10th birthday, much to the delight of the group of younger kids she'd been bossing around most of the summer.

Following her retirement announcement in April 2024, VanDerveer came to Chautauqua to stay for a while for the first time since the COVID pandemic back in 2020. She arrived in early June and planned to be at the house for at least two months. She wanted to get in all the waterskiing and sailing she could before the hip replacement she had scheduled for the fall when she returned to California.

She did some work from New York, making phone calls to try and put together a webinar with three members of the Stanford business school faculty for the rest of the coaches in the Athletics

Department. And she worked on preparing a syllabus for a class she would teach online in the winter called A Basketball Master Class.

That class would become the most popular class in Stanford's extended education catalog, with nearly 400 people registered in person and online, hanging on every word once a week through the winter quarter.

And one way or another, every day she was going to hit the lake in a boat—either the ski boat at 7:00 AM or the sailboat in the afternoon as long as the water wasn't too choppy. By midafternoon, VanDerveer was playing an online bridge game with her mother, Rita; her sister Beth; and her longtime friend Vikki Howard, who played for VanDerveer in her first season as a head coach at Idaho, a frequent visitor to the house. A stack of books on the coffee table would be read in short order. "Have you read *A Gentleman in Moscow*?" she asked me during my five-day visit. "I loved it."

Chautauqua residents and visitors stopped by to congratulate her on her retirement. One afternoon, as she walked the dogs, a man came running from his rented home to tell her how much he had always admired her. His voice cracked a bit with nerves. Even the FedEx delivery driver, who has been delivering on the grounds for years, bounded off the truck with a package and well-wishes for "Coach."

Dinner on the porch—she's never been one for eating out if she can cook at home—was followed by whatever musical offering or lecture was being offered up at the amphitheater, part of the Chautauqua Institution's nine weeks of summer programming that lures visitors from all over the world. On the first night that the Chautauqua Symphony played, including professional musicians from across the country, VanDerveer sat in the audience cheering for the flutist she had endowed in her parents' names for the summer's performances.

When it was time again to walk the dogs, which happens several times a day, she would crisscross the property, pointing out the many, many homes of the families she knew who had lived in them through the years.

On the day before her 71st birthday in late June—the first time in a long time she wouldn't be spending her birthday at Stanford basketball camp with a few hundred kids—VanDerveer and Howard were up early. They were going skiing, and I was going to join them as the spotter that day. Her evenings are frequently spent texting friends to find a third person to ride in the boat the next morning. I would need to be ready to go at 6:50 AM sharp. Sharp, indeed.

Her ski boat is bright green and fast. She bought it from some competition skiers who had only used it for a year. By 7:00 AM, with an armload of life jackets and wetsuits, VanDerveer was prepping the boat with the precision of an in-bounds play. Load the boat with gear; lower the boat into the water; and guide it carefully out of its claustrophobic slip, through the marina, and onto the open lake. On this particular early summer morning, the lake was a little choppy, but VanDerveer knew a spot, a cove that is sheltered from the wind where the water would be perfect.

VanDerveer drove the boat to the spot she knows, a large cove off the main lake lined by lakeside homes, and as always, she was the first in the water. She pulled on a wetsuit and a snug purple life jacket, pulled her slalom ski off its rack, and double-checked that her towrope was the right length. In a few moments, she was strapped into her ski and in the water. Howard slowly pulled the boat out to the right length, and when VanDerveer gave her the thumbs-up, Howard accelerated and VanDerveer quickly popped up out of the water.

The next 10 minutes were clearly VanDerveer's bliss, as she flew out beyond the boat's wake on each side, kicking up her own wave, called a rooster tail. There was not a second of struggle or uncertainty about what she was doing on the water, not unlike most of the days she spent on the bench with Stanford.

Preparation. Confidence. Purpose. It was all there on a lake in the middle of western New York on a June morning. The childhood she tries to recreate when she's at this place is, as it turns out, an extension of who she has always been.

She dropped into the water after about 10 good minutes of gliding across the smooth water, energized and satisfied and ready to tackle whatever came next.

One very good run—that was enough for VanDerveer.

# Acknowledgments

**BASKETBALL WAS NOT MY SPORT.** I tried out for the junior varsity team as a freshman in high school and was absolutely baffled by the three-player weave. The coach kept trying to direct me to the right spot: "Pass the ball and run behind the player you just passed to." I would stop, confused about where to be, disrupting the drill.

When the roster was posted on the bulletin board in the girls' gym and my name wasn't on it, I was not surprised, wasn't even that sad. But a few of my best friends were on the team, so when the coach asked if I wanted to keep the scorebook and the stats, I said yes. The universe obviously knew something I didn't.

The first time I got assigned to cover a Stanford women's basketball game was the first game of the 1995–96 season. I grabbed my press pass at the back door (before we started calling them credentials), made my way up to the media seating area, and sat down. Maples Pavilion was full, the Cardinal coming off another Final Four appearance.

As the Stanford band began to play "All Right Now," the school's fight song, the crowd stood and cheered loudly while the players were introduced.

As a former athlete (softball was a sport that didn't challenge my spatial awareness), part of the second-generation of athletes after the passage of Title IX, I was hooked by the energy directed at these young women. I would be hooked for the next three decades.

I mark so many moments of my own life over the past 30 years in direct relation to Stanford women's basketball. Bringing my toddler daughter to practice and watching her climb the steps behind the Stanford bench while I talked with Tara VanDerveer; finding out I was expecting my second child on a game day and taking that news with me to Maples; making my first road trip after having that second baby to the 1997 Final Four; shopping for birthday gifts on NCAA road trips after missing another of my daughter's late-March birthdays because of the NCAA tournament; selling Girl Scout Cookies to the coaching staff; eating Tex-Mex in San Antonio, BBQ in Kansas City, and Cuban food in Tampa Bay.

For three years running, on the night before the Elite Eight game that Stanford was playing in, four traveling writers would head to the Stanford team hotel to listen to Tara VanDerveer play the piano. When the Cardinal lost each of those games, the writers made the decision that tradition needed to end.

Those of us who had the good fortune of covering VanDerveer over the years knew things about the legendary coach that other people didn't seem to understand: She would answer every question. Everything she said after a game had a purpose. She smiled when she was about to try out a new line she thought was funny. She was funny, even when she didn't try. And when she got emotional, it was for good reason.

Watching her glasses fog up when Stanford reached the Final Four for the first time in 11 years in Spokane in 2008 was something to see.

A group of writers insisted on taking her to dinner to celebrate the 2021 national championship, which had happened in the bubble in San Antonio. Thanks to COVID restrictions, none of us who had followed her team around the country for decades were in the building to see it happen. She snuck away before dessert and picked up the check.

To the assistant coaches, led by Amy Tucker and Kate Paye—you have always been fountains of both information and levity. To athletic directors Ted Leland, Bob Bowlsby, and Bernard Muir, thank you for taking my calls.

VanDerveer has always had impeccable staff, including Eileen Roche, the director of basketball operations, longtime athletic trainer Marcella Shorty, and the late and great DeeDee Zawaydeh, who ran the office like clockwork.

The Stanford sports information directors—my friends and traveling companions—Steve Raczynski, Beth Goode, Scott Leykam, Jessica Raber, Brian Risso, Aaron Juarez, and John Cantalupi. My road SIDs—Darcy Couch at USC and Steve Rodriguez at Arizona State, the lifers who always got me the player I needed and never got (too) annoyed when I called the coach without telling them.

The Stanford players themselves have unfailingly been some of the smartest, most thoughtful, and most poised young women I have ever encountered. They have shared their joy and their disappointment with me. They have shared some very personal stories with me. The relationships I still have with them, the hellos and the hugs, mean that I did my job right.

The end of the Pac-12 (as we knew it) will always be heartbreaking.

The coaches of the Pac-12 have been a huge part of my long hoops journey, going to bat for me so that I could keep writing—Cori Close, Lindsay Gottlieb, Charli Turner Thorne, Charmin

Smith, Lynne Roberts, J.R. Payne, Kelly Graves, Mark Trakh, Joan Bonvicini, Scott Rueck, Adia Barnes, and the late June Daugherty.

To my Pac-12 people—Julie Reuvers, Bri Niemi, Natalia Ciccone, Teresa Gould, Rhonda Lundin Bennett, Heather Vaughan, Chris Dawson, Lisa Peterson, Susan Reid, and Craig Heyamoto—and my sisters in broadcasting: Mary Murphy, Krista Blunk, Cindy Brunson, Anne Marie Anderson, Tammy Blackburn, Ann Schatz, Elise Woodward, and Ashley Adamson.

I have been lucky enough to share press row with some of the best ever to do this job: Ann Killion, Joan Ryan, Janie McCauley, Scott Ostler, Darren Sabedra, Elliott Almond, Tom Fitzgerald, Candace Murphy, Rick Eymer, and the late Gwen Knapp. A special shout-out to my dear friend with the camera Don Feria, who always saw things through his lens the same way I saw them in my notebook.

To my dear friend Shelley Fischer, who gave me her house key and a beautiful place in Lake Tahoe to get some work done.

To my ESPN partner in hoops, Michael Voepel, you are the standard for us all, and I'm so proud to be your colleague. To Joanne Gerstner for making my ESPN era possible, and thank you to ESPN editors Melanie Jackson and Heather Burns and Joy Russo for being such great editors. To Howard Megdal for keeping my career going at the Next.

To my forever sports editor, Glenn Schwarz, who always wanted to know what I ate when I was on the road and never let me use the word *suffering*, no matter how many ACL injuries I had to write about.

To the team at Triumph Books: Clarissa, Jesse, Noah and Katy. My bucket list project has been a pleasure because of all of you. It won't be my last.

And to Tara. I got to cover one of the most important figures in sports history. It's my honor.

My best comes last. To my parents, John and Rosemarie, who always indulged my dreams to be a writer, bragged about my stories to anyone who would listen, and took care of their grandchildren so I could do this. To my sister, Linda, who figured out the three-player weave and became the best basketball player in the family.

To Annie and Matthew. Stanford women's basketball is every bit as much of your childhood stories as your mom's adulthood storytelling. I missed a lot of baseball games, school plays, and more than a few birthdays. You always rolled with it. A special shout-out to Annie for her pro-level editing on this book. You really have missed your calling.

To Jerry. I married a sportswriter. For 34 years, you've always got it and you've always got me. I never feel more supported than when you are cheering for me. Love you, JMac.

Appendix A

# Program Accomplishments

**STANFORD HIGHLIGHTS FROM THE CAREER** of coach Tara VanDerveer, who coached from 1986 to 1995 and from 1996 through 2024:

**Overall Stanford Record:** 1,064–220 (VanDerveer's all-time record is 1,216–271)

### Year-by-Year Records Overall, Conference, and NCAA Tournament

**1985–86:** 13–15, 1–7 in Pac-West (7th)
**1986–87:** 14–14, 8–10 in Pac-10 (tie, 6th)
**1987–88:** 27–5, 14–4 in Pac-10 (3rd), Sweet 16
**1988–89:** 28–3, 18–0 in Pac-10 (1st), Elite Eight
**1989–90:** 32–1, 17–1 in Pac-10 (1st), NCAA Champions
**1990–91:** 26–6, 16–2 in Pac-10 (1st), Final Four
**1991–92:** 30–3, 15–3 in Pac-10 (1st), NCAA Champions
**1992–93:** 26–6, 15–3 in Pac-10 (1st), Sweet 16
**1993–94:** 25–6, 15–3 in Pac-10 (2nd), Elite Eight
**1994–95:** 30–3, 17–1 in Pac-10 (1st), Final Four

**1995–96:** Took year off to coach Olympic team
**1996–97:** 34–2, 18–0 in Pac-10 (1st), Final Four
**1997–98:** 21–6, 17–1 in Pac-10 (1st), first round
**1998–99:** 18–12, 14–4 in Pac-10 (3rd), first round
**1999–2000:** 21–9, 13–5 in Pac-10 (tie, 2nd) second round
**2000–01:** 19–11, 12–6 in Pac-10 (tie, 1st), second round
**2001–02:** 32–3, 18–0 in Pac-10 (1st), Sweet 16
**2002–03:** 27–5, 15–3 in Pac-10 (1st), second round
**2003–04:** 27–7, 14–4 in Pac-10 (tie, 1st), Elite Eight
**2004–05:** 32–3, 17–1 in Pac-10 (1st), Elite Eight
**2005–06:** 26–8, 15–3 in Pac-10 (1st), Elite Eight
**2006–07:** 29–5, 17–1 in Pac-10 (1st), second round
**2007–08:** 35–4, 16–2 in Pac-10 (1st), runner-up
**2008–09:** 33–5, 17–1 in Pac-10 (1st), Final Four
**2009–10:** 36–2, 18–0 in Pac-10 (1st), runner-up
**2010–11:** 33–3, 18–0 in Pac-10 (1st), Final Four
**2011–12:** 35–2, 18–0 in Pac-12 (1st), Final Four
**2012–13:** 33–3, 17–1 in Pac-12 (tie, 1st), Sweet 16
**2013–14:** 33–4, 17–1 in Pac-12 (tie, 1st), Sweet 16
**2014–15:** 26–10, 13–5 in Pac-12 (tie, 3rd), Sweet 16
**2015–16:** 27–8, 14–4 in Pac-12 (tie, 3rd), Elite Eight
**2016–17:** 32–6, 15–3 in Pac-12 (tie, 2nd), Final Four
**2017–18:** 24–11, 14–3 in Pac-12 (2nd), Sweet 16
**2018–19:** 31–5, 15–3 in Pac-12 (2nd), Elite Eight
**2019–20:** 27–6, 14–4 in Pac-12 (tie, 2nd), COVID-19
**2020–21:** 31–2, 19–2 in Pac-12 (1st), NCAA champions
**2021–22:** 32–4, 16–0 in Pac-12 (1st), Final Four
**2022–23:** 29–6, 15–3 in Pac-12 (tie, 1st), second round
**2023–24:** 30–6, 15–3 in Pac-12 (1st), Sweet 16
**Pac-10/12 Championships (26):** 1989, 1990 (co), 1991, 1992, 1993, 1995, 1997, 1998, 2001 (co), 2002, 2003, 2004 (co),

2005, 2006, 2007, 2008, 2009, 2010, 2011, 2012, 2013 (co), 2014, 2021, 2022, 2023 (co), 2024

**Pac-10/12 Tournament Championships (15):** 2003, 2004, 2005, 2007, 2008, 2009, 2010, 2011, 2012, 2013, 2015, 2017, 2019, 2021, 2022

**NCAA Tournament Appearances (35):** 1988, 1989, 1990, 1991, 1992, 1993, 1994, 1995, 1997, 1998, 1999, 2000, 2001, 2002, 2003, 2004, 2005, 2006, 2007, 2008, 2009, 2010, 2011, 2012, 2013, 2014, 2015, 2016, 2017, 2018, 2019, 2021, 2022, 2023, 2024

**NCAA Tournament Sweet 16 Appearances (28):** 1988, 1989, 1990, 1991, 1992, 1993, 1994, 1995, 1997, 2002, 2004, 2005, 2006, 2008, 2009, 2010, 2011, 2012, 2014, 2015, 2016, 2017, 2018, 2019, 2021, 2022, 2024

**NCAA Tournament Elite Eight Appearances (21):** 1989, 1990, 1991, 1992, 1994, 1995, 1996, 1997, 2004, 2005, 2006, 2008, 2009, 2010, 2011, 2012, 2014, 2016, 2017, 2019, 2021, 2022

**NCAA Final Four Appearances (14):** 1990, 1991, 1992, 1995, 1997, 2008, 2009, 2010, 2011, 2012, 2014, 2017, 2021, 2022

**NCAA Final Four Appearances (15):** 1990, 1991, 1992, 1995, 1996, 1997, 2008, 2009, 2010, 2011, 2012, 2014, 2017, 2021, 2022

**NCAA Championships (3):** 1990, 1992, 2021

**Tara VanDerveer Honors**

**WBCA National Coach of the Year:** 1988–89, 2010–11

**Associated Press Coach of the Year:** 2010–11 (shared with Katie Meyer, Miami, and Geno Auriemma, UConn)

**Converse Coach of the Year:** 1988–89

**US Basketball Writers Association Coach of the Year:** 1989–90, 2020–21

**Naismith College Coach of the Year:** 1989–90, 2010–11, 2020–21

**Pac-10/12 Coach of the Year (18):** 1988–89, 1989–90, 1994–95, 1996–97, 2001–02, 2002–03, 2004–05, 2007–08, 2008–09, 2010–11, 2011–12, 2012–13, 2013–14, 2017–18, 2020–21, 2021–22, 2023–24

## Associated Press All-Americans

**First Team:** Kate Starbird (1996–97), Nicole Powell (2003–04), Candice Wiggins (2007–08), Jeanette Pohlen (2010–11), Nneka Ogwumike (2011–12), Chiney Ogwumike (2012–13 and 2013–14), Haley Jones (2021–22), Cameron Brink (2023–24)

**Second Team:** Kate Starbird (1995–96), Kristin Folkl (1997–98), Nicole Powell (2002–03), Candice Wiggins (2004–05 and 2006–07), Jayne Appel (2007–08 and 2009–10), Nneka Ogwumike (2011–12), Chiney Ogwumike (2011–12), Alanna Smith (2018–19), Cameron Brink (2022–23)

**Third Team:** Kiana Williams (2020–21), Cameron Brink (2021–22), Haley Jones (2022–23)

**Honorable Mention:** Lindsey Yamasaki (2001–02), Brooke Smith (2005–06 and 2006–07), Jayne Appel (2007–08), Kayla Pedersen (2009–10), Amber Orrange (2014–15), Karlie Samuelson (2016–17), Erica McCall (2016–17), Brittany McPhee (2017–18), Kiana Williams (2019–20), Haley Jones (2020–21), Kiki Iriafen (2023–24)

## WBCA Coaches' All-Americans

Jennifer Azzi (1988–89, 1989–90), Sonja Henning (1990–91), Val Whiting (1991–92, 1992–93), Kate Starbird (1995–96, 1996–97), Kirstin Folkl (1997–98), Nicole Powell (2001–02, 2002–03, 2003–04), Candice Wiggins (2004–05, 2005–06, 2006–07, 2007–08), Jayne Appel (2008–09, 2009–10), Nneka Ogwumike (2009–10,

2010–11, 2011–12), Chiney Ogwumike (2011–12, 2012–13, 2013–14), Alanna Smith (2018–19), Kiana Williams (2020–21), Haley Jones (2021–22), Cameron Brink (2021–22, 2022–23, 2023–24)

### John R. Wooden Award All-Americans

Nicole Powell (2003–04), Candice Wiggins (2007–08), Jayne Appel (2009–10), Jeanette Pohlen (2010–11), Nneka Ogwumike (2009–10, 2010–11, 2011–12), Chiney Ogwumike (2012–13, 2013–14), Cameron Brink (2022–23, 2023–24)

### US Basketball Writers Association All-Americans

Jennifer Azzi (1989–90), Val Whiting (1991–92, 1992–93), Kate Starbird (1995–96, 1996–97), Kristin Folkl (1997–98), Nicole Powell (2001–02, 2003–04), Candice Wiggins (2005–06, 2006–07), Jayne Appel (2008–09), Jeanette Pohlen (2010–11), Nneka Ogwumike (2010–11, 2011–12), Chiney Ogwumike (2012–13, 2013–14), Alanna Smith (2018–19, third team), Kiana Williams (2020–21, second team), Haley Jones (2022–23, third team; 2021–22, second team; 2020–21, honorable mention), Cameron Brink (2021–22, third team; 2022–23, second team; 2023–24, first team)

### Pac-10/12 Players of the Year

Jennifer Azzi (1988–89, 1989–90), Sonja Henning (1990–91), Van Whiting (1991–92, 1992–93), Kate Starbird (1995–96, 1996–97), Nicole Powell (2001–02, 2003–04), Candice Wiggins (2004–05, 2005–06, 2007–08), Jayne Appel (2008–09), Jeanette Pohlen (2010–11), Nneka Ogwumike (2009–10, 2011–12), Chiney Ogwumike (2012–13, 2013–14), Haley Jones (2021–22), Cameron Brink (2023–24)

Appendix B

# Coaching Tree

**Stanford Players to Head Coaches**

- Kate Paye: player (1991–95), assistant coach (2007–16), associate head coach (2016–24), Stanford head coach (2024–present)
- Jennifer Azzi: player (1986–90), USF head coach (2010–16)
- Molly Goodenbour: player (1989–93), Cal State East Bay head coach (2016), USF head coach (2016–present)
- Lindy La Rocque: player (2009–12), assistant coach (2017–20), UNLV head coach (2020–present)
- Bobbie Kelsey: player (1992–96), assistant coach (2007–11), University of Wisconsin–Madison head coach (2011–16)
- Nicole Powell: player (2000–04), Grand Canyon head coach (2017–20), UC Riverside head coach (2020–23)
- Charmin Smith: player (1994–97), assistant coach (2004–07), Cal head coach (2019–present)
- Charli Turner Thorne: player (1985–88), Arizona State head coach (1996–2022)

- Vanessa Nygaard: player (1993–98), Phoenix Mercury head coach (2022–23)
- Trisha Stevens: player (1987–91), Boise State head coach (1996–2002)
- Katy Steding: player (1996–2001), Boston University head coach (2014–18)

**Assistant Coaches to Head Coaches**

- Amy Tucker: associate head coach (1985-2017), Stanford interim head coach (1996–97)
- June Daugherty: assistant coach (1985–89), Boise State head coach (1989–96), Washington head coach (1996–2007), Washington State head coach (2007–18)
- Karen Middleton: assistant coach (1997–2007), Western Carolina head coach (2009–15)
- Julie Rousseau: assistant coach (2000–04), Pepperdine head coach (2004–13)
- Tia Jackson: assistant coach (1999–2000), Washington head coach (2007–11)
- Marianne Stanley: Cal co–head coach (1996–2000)

**Stanford Players to Stanford Assistant Coaches**

- Ann Adkins Enthoven
- Bobbie Kelsey
- Lindy La Rocque
- Erica McCall
- Kate Paye
- Jeanette Pohlen
- Charmin Smith
- Katy Steding
- Angela Taylor

# Interviews Conducted for This Book

- Jayne Appel-Marinelli
- Fran Belibi
- Bob Bowlsby
- Cori Close
- Chris Gobrecht
- Beth Goode
- Molly Goodenbour
- Lacie Hull
- Lexie Hull
- Hannah Jump
- Bobbie Kelsey
- Lindy La Roque
- Ted Leland
- Talana Lepolo
- Erica McCall
- Bernard Muir
- Vanessa Nygaard
- Chiney Ogwumike
- Nneka Ogwumike
- Heather Owen
- Kate Paye
- Jeanette Pohlen
- Eileen Roche
- Olympia Scott
- Charmin Smith
- Marianne Stanley
- Kate Starbird
- Katy Steding
- Angela Taylor
- Amy Tucker
- Charlie Turner Thorne
- Heidi VanDerveer
- Rita VanDerveer
- Tara VanDerveer
- Willette White
- Val Whiting
- Kiana Williams

# Sources

**Prologue**

Stanford 125.edu, 2022, "The First Game."

Stanford Fast Break Club, 1998, "Escaping from Roble," Mariah Burton Nelson.

**Chapter 2**

ESPN.com, March 28, 2021, "Stanford coach Tara VanDerveer on her decades-long love affair with basketball and her fight for equality."

*Shooting from the Outside,* Tara VanDerveer and Joan Ryan, 1997, Avon Books.

*Sports Illustrated,* January 22, 2024, "Tara VanDerveer's First Win Looked Nothing Like the One That Made Her the Winningest Coach."

*Columbus Dispatch,* March 27, 2009, "Emotional Reunion."

**Chapter 3**

Foundation on the Farm, Sirius XM Radio, May 15, 2024, Krista Blunk (host).

*Shooting from the Outside,* Tara VanDerveer and Joan Ryan, 1997, Avon Books.

*Stanford* magazine, January/February 2010, "Game On," Mike Antonucci.

"In the Game," *Frontline,* PBS, Video, March 29, 1994.

**Chapter 4**

*San Francisco Chronicle,* March 25, 2021, "In Tara They Trusted: Stanford's 1990 NCAA Championship team began a Powerhouse," Ann Killion.

*San Jose Mercury News,* January 14, 2024, "On verge of tying Coach K's all-time wins record, how Tara VanDerveer changed college basketball," Danny Emmerman.

"In the Game," *Frontline,* PBS, Video, March 29, 1994.

Foundation on the Farm, Sirius XM Radio, July 4, 2024, Krista Blunk (host).

*Shooting from the Outside,* Tara VanDerveer and Joan Ryan, 1997, Avon Books.

*Los Angeles Times,* April 6, 1992, "Stanford Stands Tall."

**Chapter 5**

*Washington Post,* March 27, 1996, "Stanford's Lame Duck Takes Wing," Karl Hente.

*New York Times,* November 19, 1995, "An Odyssey of Championships and Hardships," Jane Gottesman.

*San Francisco Chronicle,* March 26, 1996, "Fending off Pressure with Whimsy," Gwen Knapp.

**Chapter 6**

Tacoma Sports Museum, December 2021.

*Sports Illustrated,* March 17, 1997, "Out of the Shadows," Gary Smith.

*Boosters Always Win,* Harriett Benson, 2003.

**Chapter 8**

*San Francisco Chronicle,* December 12, 1998, "Olympics were not a Golden Situation for Stanford," Jake Curtis.

*San Francisco Chronicle,* February 28, 2001, "Every Little Thing She Does is Magic," Michelle Smith.

Associated Press, March 17, 2004, "Carey Leading Longhorns After Leaving Troubles Behind," Jim Vertuno.

**Chapter 9**

*Eurostep* Podcast with Anthony Goods, November 14, 2024.

**Chapter 10**

*Geno: In Pursuit of Perfection,* 2006, Geno Auriemma and Jackie MacMullan, Grand Central Publishing.

**Chapter 11**

Sirius XM Radio, "Foundation on the Farm," June 17, 2024, Krista Blunk (host).

*Andscape,* January 24, 2018, "A Letter to My Family," Chiney Ogwumike.

AuProSports.com, January 31, 2023, "Lexie Hull Reflects on the Impact of Twin Lacie on her Basketball Career," Jade Thomas.

*USA Today,* March 23, 2022, "Hull twins hustle plays, floor burns lead defending national champ Stanford," Lindsay Schnell.

**Chapter 12**

ESPN story, February 5, "Inside Stanford Women's Basketball's Nine-Week Road Trip."

*PBS News Hour,* April 6, 2021.

**Chapter 13**

Associated Press, February 1, 2017, "Tara VanDerveer Chases More History," Janie McCauley.

**Chapter 15**

Sports Illustrated, May 10, 2010, "Jennifer Azzi in an unlikely spot—coaching USF", Ann Killion

**Chapter 16**

ESPN.com, March 20, 2025, "The Blessing and the Curse of Lauren Betts' 6-foot-7 height," Aishwarya Kumar.

**Chapter 17**

*San Francisco Chronicle,* November 3, 2024, "Stanford was my Dream," Ann Killion.